Successful
Nonverbal Communication

DALE G. LEATHERS

The University of Georgia

Successful Nonverbal Communication

Principles and Applications

Macmillan Publishing Company
New York

Collier Macmillan Publishers
London

Macmillan Publishing Company
866 Third Avenue, New York, New York 10022

Collier Macmillan Canada, Inc.

Library of Congress Cataloging in Publication Data

Leathers, Dale G.
  Successful nonverbal communication.

  Includes index.
  1. Nonverbal communication (Psychology)   I. Title.
BF637.C45L435 1986   153.6   84-29470
ISBN 0-02-369010-0

Printing: 5 6 7 8   Year: 9 0 1 2 3 4 5

ISBN   0-02-369010-0

To Nancy
who is the ultimate source
of inspiration and love

PREFACE

Successful Nonverbal Communication is written for the introductory course in nonverbal communication. To be more specific; this book is written for the students who take and instructors who teach the introductory course in nonverbal communication. This is a course that I have taught for a number of years. This experience has convinced me that there is a need for a book that is directly responsive to the concerns of this audience. As a result, I have asked many students and instructors of introduction to nonverbal communication to describe in detail the book that they would like to see written for this course. *Successful Nonverbal Communication* is the book that they described.

Serious students of nonverbal communication have long recognized that knowledge of nonverbal communication gives them the potential to be much more effective communicators. A source of frustration has remained, however. Most existing books on nonverbal communication focus exclusively on the nature of nonverbal communication. They describe and classify different kinds of nonverbal messages. They do not address the pressing need to *demonstrate how knowledge of the informational potential of nonverbal cues can be used to communicate successfully in the real world. Successful Nonverbal Communication* is designed specifically to meet that central need.

The title of the book reflects my conviction that knowledge about nonverbal communication is not enough. We must know *how* to use that knowledge to communicate successfully in applied settings of particular concern to us. Chapter 12, for example, serves to illustrate the applied emphasis of the book that is reflected in the title. This chapter not only provides concrete guidelines for communicating effectively in the job interview but also prioritizes the kinds of nonverbal cues associated with the successful interview.

Part I of this book identifies and describes the different classes of nonverbal cues, illustrates the desirable and undesirable functions they can serve, and provides original tests that can be used to measure and develop nonverbal communication skills. The seven chapters in Part I examine the research literature with the objective of identifying central principles of effective nonverbal communication.

Parts II and III demonstrate how these principles can be used by the individual communicator. Part II demonstrates how individuals can use the information in Part I to develop their communicative skills, and, more particularly, to project a desired image. Thus, separate chapters in this section are devoted to the subject of selling yourself nonverbally, detecting deception, communicating consistently, and impression formation and management.

Finally, Part III is designed to demonstrate how knowledge of nonverbal communication can be used by the reader to communicate more successfully in applied settings of particular importance. Separate chapters are devoted to nonverbal determinants of successful interviews, female-male interaction, successful intercultural communication, and to the communicative impact of microenvironmental variables in the classroom, conference room, and office.

The readers of this book learn how to *use* detailed knowledge of nonverbal cues and their communicative functions to communicate more successfully in a variety of real world contexts. Readers can assess the appropriateness of their own nonverbal communication by applying detailed sets of behavioral guidelines. These guidelines represent an operational definition of successful nonverbal communication.

The guidelines pinpoint the nonverbal communicative behaviors that are associated with success in detecting deception, formulating consistent messages, making favorable first impressions and more enduring impressions, interacting with members of the opposite sex, and communicating with members of another culture. In short, the guidelines specify how knowledge of nonverbal communication should be used.

To derive maximum value from this book, instructors and students can make use of the instructional aids provided in the *Instructor's Manual* (available upon request of instructors from Macmillan Publishing Company). This manual features a course syllabus for a semester and a quarter course, in-class and out-of-class exercises that can be used to explore the theoretical and practical implications of concepts discussed in the book, and detailed summaries of the content of each chapter with sets of key terms that can be used to review for examinations.

For purposes of preparing examinations on the book, detailed sets of true-false and multiple choice items on each chapter are included along with long and short-answer essay questions. Finally, the *Instructor's Manual* also includes an enumeration of films, videotapes, and outside readings that can be used to explore and demonstrate how knowledge of nonverbal cues should be used to communicate more successfully.

The book and the *Instructor's Manual* fully explore the central role that nonverbal cues frequently play in the development and deterioration of interpersonal relationships, in shaping interpersonal perceptions, in personal selling, and in the development of a positive self-concept. Because of this focus, I believe that *Successful Nonverbal Communication* can be particularly valuable as one of the required textbooks in introductory courses in subjects such as interpersonal communication, personal selling, and business communication.

A number of individuals made noteworthy contributions to this book. Chris Maxwell played a central role as research assistant and author of the *Instructor's Manual.* Derek Yaniger deserves full credit for the creative cartoons and line drawings that illustrate concepts in the book. Jim Morgenthaler, who did outstanding work on an earlier book of mine, did the photographs and photographic displays. He even risked life and limb by invading a local pasture to take the photograph of the cow that appears in Chapter 2. The five scholars who did the substantive reviews of the manuscript deserve special thanks for their shrewd and helpful criticism: Barbara A. Larson, University of Wisconsin, Milwaukee; Steven A. Rollman, James Madison University; H. Dan O'Hair, Texas Christian University; Dennis S. Gouran, Pennsylvania State University and Gail E. Myers, Trinity University. Finally, I would like to thank Lloyd Chilton at Macmillan, for his valuable insights and guidance. He is an extraordinarily fine editor and person.

On a very personal level, my wife Nancy was, once again, the source of much inspiration and love. Cat_2 is now much older and wiser than he was when I wrote my earlier book on nonverbal communication systems. This time he refused to inspect the manuscript on a daily basis or even to serve as paper weight on windy days. He did, however, agree to look at the page proofs of the manuscript.

Dale G. Leathers
University of Georgia
Athens, Georgia

CONTENTS

PART THREE
Successful Communication in Applied Settings   217

Nonverbal Communication

FORTLND
CAMPUS
CENTER

4:51P 09/19/91
030#0180 E 0001

#2-5022-00782526
3-02
CN SODA $0.70T
HOSTESS $0.65T
MDS ST $1.35
TAX1 $0.00
TAX2 $0.00

**TTL $1.35
 ;5 $1.35
NEWBAL $303.65
CHNG $0.00

CHAPTER ONE

The Nature of Nonverbal Communication

Human interaction is a quest for meaning. We look anxiously to others to determine whether we have communicated our intended meaning. We are concerned that we may have communicated unintended meanings that will negatively affect the image we wish to project. If we are skilled in the art of impression management, we may cultivate a certain look or sound that is designed to control the judgments that people make about us. Thus, General George Patton practiced his "war face" in front of a mirror so that he would be perceived as unusually determined, powerful, and brave. Richard Nixon made repeated attempts to eliminate the shifty eye behaviors and nonfluencies that helped reinforce the widespread public perception that he was "Tricky Dicky."

Those individuals with whom we communicate are also on guard. They look apprehensively at us, to judge whether they have accurately perceived our intentions. Do our communicative behaviors accurately reflect our inner feelings, or do they represent a carefully controlled presentation of self? The quest for meaning often produces, or results in, anxiety, apprehension, and uncertainty. This is so because interpersonal communication is so complex.

The ways we communicate meanings are varied. And the sources of error in interpersonal communication are multiple. A single error may make us uncomfortable in an important situation. Multiple errors may be catastrophic.

Consider the following situations. You and your partner are at a fraternity party, on your first date. As the evening progresses and the second keg of beer is tapped, you notice that your date's hand is resting lightly on your arm; a strong and rather rapid pulse is detectable. You make your judgments as to what your date is communicating to you. Later, you fidget on

the doorsteps of the sorority house. Suddenly, you lean forward to kiss your date, but she turns her face away from you, recoils, and walks briskly into the sorority house. You are left alone, to ponder the complexities of the evening's communication situation.

Four years later, you are about to be interviewed by the head of a major advertising firm. The job interview is vitally important to you. You realize that you must communicate very effectively if you are to get the job offer. As you enter the interview room, you introduce yourself to the advertising executive and she offers you a seat on the other side of a small table. You feel that it is important to sustain eye contact, and attempt to do so. The executive often looks away from you as she speaks, however. She frequently leans far back in her chair. You think you are doing well. As the interview concludes, you cannot help but notice that the advertising executive has her chin tilted up into the air and is looking down at you over her glasses. While looking at you, she remarks that she has found your dossier to be most unusual. You are then left alone to ponder the complexities of the afternoon's communication situation.

These two situations may be interpreted in a number of different ways. Your goal is to determine what meanings you communicated and what meanings were communicated to you. To achieve such a goal you must recognize at least two facts. First, great differences often exist between the meaning you think you communicated and the meaning that was actually perceived. Second, meanings may be communicated through a great variety of channels.

You may have interpreted your date's hand on your arm as an invitation to more intimate behavior later in the evening; the quickened pulse may have suggested a certain amount of arousal on her part. Her perception of the situation may have been quite different. The hand on your arm could have been a sympathetic response to your nervous mannerisms. The quickened pulse may have been triggered by her apprehension as to what actions you would take on the sorority steps. You need more information and more time before attempting a thorough analysis of this situation.

The job situation is also difficult to interpret. You have more facts at your disposal, however. You wisely focused on important factors in this situation. You should not be disturbed by the fact that the interviewer looked away from you as she spoke; this is characteristic eye behavior in an interview situation. You should be concerned about her tendency to lean far back in the chair. Body lean is the best indicator of an individual's involvement in this situation. Your biggest problem is the ambiguous message your interviewer conveyed to you (her chin was perceptibly tilted in the air as she said, "I find your dossier to be most unusual"). The verbal and nonverbal cues convey conflicting meanings. Unhappily for you, the nonverbal cue—the upraised chin, in this case—is apt to be a much more accurate indicator of your interviewer's true feelings than the verbal cue.

Both situations emphasize what society has been slow to recognize: human beings do not communicate by words alone. Individuals have many sensory mechanisms that play a vital role in interpersonal communication. Undeniably, we speak and hear, but we also move and touch and feel. As a communicator, we have a multidimensional capacity.

Some publications have drawn public attention to nonverbal communication. Books such as *Here Comes Everybody*, by William Schutz (1971), and *Body Language*, by Julius Fast (1970), have served a useful purpose. They may have had some undesirable side effects, however. They may have helped to create the misleading notion that knowledge of nonverbal communication is chiefly useful to investigate and invigorate a communicator's sex life. Schutz (1971) notes that "when a group gets advanced and comfortable and trusting with each other, even deeper body concerns can be dealt with. In groups for couples we will often ask them to use a speculum to examine the interior of the vagina" (p. 168). Similarly, Fast (1970) talks in some detail about the meaning transmitted nonverbally when a man's "hips are thrust forward slightly, as if they were cantilevered, and his legs are usually apart. There is something in this stance that spells sex" (p. 96).

The functional importance of nonverbal communication is hardly limited to the semantics of sex, however. LaFrance and Mayo (1978) document that nonverbal cues serve a wide variety of valuable functions in the development of social relationships. The determinants of successful communication in real-world contexts are frequently nonverbal. To disregard the functions served by nonverbal cues is to invite unflattering characterization as an insensitive and inept communicator.

Most of us spend a great deal of time attempting to persuade others, attempting to be liked or loved by others, attempting to control others, and trying to enhance our own self-image. Whatever our communicative goal, the nonverbal channels of communication frequently function very effectively to help us attain it. To persuade others, for example, you must usually convince them of your honesty, sincerity, and trustworthiness. Think back to the last congressional hearing you observed on television. Did you think the witness was honest, sincere, and trustworthy on the basis of what the person said, or on the basis of the nonverbal behavior of the witness?

Consider your attempts to develop an intimate relationship with another person. Did you assess the level of intimacy of the relationship primarily on the basis of the words that were spoken, or on the basis of the implicit messages communicated by nonverbal cues? Did you attempt to communicate your own feelings primarily by words or by nonverbal cues?

Consider also those instances of face-to-face interaction when you have tried to control the communicative behavior of another person. Among the primary means of control at your disposal were your gestures, your posture, and the way you used the small space that separated you.

Consider, finally, the great amount of time you spend trying to attain or to retain a positive self-image. To a very large degree your self-image and social identity are shaped by your personal appearance. This image is controlled to a striking extent by nonverbal factors unrelated to the content of your speech.

The Functional Importance of Nonverbal Communication

When we write of the functional significance of nonverbal communication, the obvious question is, what do we mean by *function?* The answer is complex. Most basically, the function of communication is the creation of meaning. The functional significance of nonverbal communication, therefore, is related to: (a) the *purposes* for which meanings are communicated (information, persuasion, and so on); (b) the *accuracy* with which meanings are communicated (facial communication has more potential than tactile communication, for example); and (c) the *efficiency* with which meanings are communicated (the time and effort required for the communication of meanings).

Viewed from any of these perspectives, nonverbal communication has great functional significance in our society. In a great variety of situations, communicators can much more easily achieve their communicative purpose by improving the accuracy and efficiency of their nonverbal communication.

More specifically, nonverbal communication has great functional significance, for six major reasons. First, nonverbal, not verbal, factors are the major determinants of meaning in the interpersonal context. Birdwhistell (1970) asserts that "probably no more than 30 to 35 percent of the social meaning of a conversation or an interaction is carried by the words" (p. 158). Mehrabian (1968) goes even further, estimating that 93 percent of the total impact of a message is the result of nonverbal factors.

Children, army recruits, and dating couples often find themselves in communication situations that are similar in one respect: They must quickly and accurately determine the meanings of messages being transmitted to them. They typically rely on tone of voice, facial expression, and bodily movement to accomplish this purpose. Children soon learn that the tone and intensity of a parent's voice are their best guide to action. Army recruits do not determine the priority of directives from their drill sergeant by analyzing the manifest verbal content of those directives. They focus on the sense of physical involvement the sergeant conveys to them nonverbally through the notoriously rough and tough voice. When your girlfriend or boyfriend says *no* to your most artful advances, you do not stop and apply the semantic differential to the verbal response in order to measure his or her meaning. You rely on facial and bodily expressions as the primary determinants of intent.

Second, feelings and emotions are more accurately revealed by nonverbal than verbal means. Davitz (1964) has conducted an impressively detailed set of studies on emotional expression. He concludes that "it is the nonverbal, of the formal characteristics of one's environment . . . that primarily determine the emotional meaning of one's world" (p. 201). Expressions like "keep your chin up," "down in the mouth," and "walking on air" are much more than empty figures of speech. They have emotional referents that are rich in meaning and communicative significance.

The rapid development of *t*-group training, encounter sessions, psychiatric services, and, more recently, sexual therapy clinics is eloquent testimony to society's need to understand what emotions are communicated, how they are communicated, and how they are received. Because intromission and ejaculation are the only emotion-laden behaviors that universally take the same form, our need to understand variability in emotional expression is evident.

Significantly, we now know not only that nonverbal communication is our richest source of knowledge about emotional states but also that nonverbal cues are reliable and stable indicators of the emotion that is being conveyed or received. Specifically, we now know that nonverbal communication can provide us with the following information about emotions: (a) how sensitive communicators are to emotional expressions, measured in terms of accuracy of identification; (b) the kinds of emotional expressions that can be correctly identified; (c) the specific nature of incorrect identification of emotions; and (d) the degree to which communicators attend to the emotional meaning of a total communication (Leathers & Emigh, 1980).

Third, the nonverbal portion of communication conveys meanings and intentions that are relatively free of deception and distortion. Nonverbal cues such as gestures are rarely under the sustained, conscious control of the communicator. For this reason communicators can rarely use nonverbal communication effectively for the purpose of dissembling. In contrast, the verbal dimension of communication seems to obfuscate the communicator's true intentions much more frequently.

In an age that places a very high priority on trust, honesty, and candor in interpersonal relationships, nonverbal communication takes on added importance. Interpersonal relationships are built by using the most effective kinds of communication at our disposal. These are primarily nonverbal. Not only do nonverbal cues usually convey a communicator's real meaning and intent, but they also suggest, rather precisely, what the communicator thinks of us.

Even such nonverbal cues as gesture, posture, and facial expression may of course be under the conscious control of the communicator. For all but the consummate actor—and possibly the notorious used-car salesperson—such conscious control is a temporary phenomenon. In most cases, nonverbal cues are not consciously controlled for so long a period of time as verbal cues, nor do they serve as frequently to transmit deception, distortion, and confusion. Although nonverbal cues may be used to deceive, they are more likely to reveal deception than to conceal it.

Fourth, nonverbal cues serve a metacommunicative function which is indispensable in attaining high-quality communication. Often the communicator provides additional cues that serve to clarify the intent and meaning of his or her message. Verbal expressions such as "now, seriously speaking" and "I'm only kidding" are metacommunicative. A comforting hand on the shoulder or a radiant smile may represent nonverbal ways of performing the same function. Although both verbal and nonverbal cues can function metacommunicatively, nonverbal cues seem to take precedence in the mind of the receiver of the message.

But what does this mean? How do we know that nonverbal cues are so important metacommunicatively? I designed an experiment to answer those specific questions. One hundred subjects were exposed to a set of messages in which the words conveyed one meaning and the facial expressions of the "planted" communicators conveyed a conflicting meaning.

Imagine yourself in a small group and faced with the following situation: One of the discussants responds to a remark you have just made. As he responds, he scratches his head vigorously and gets a very confused expression on his face. While looking utterly confused, he says to you, "Yes, I understand. What you just said seems completely clear to me."

You are faced with a clear-cut decision. To resolve the seeming contradiction in meaning, you must rely on either the verbal cues (words) or the nonverbal cues (facial expression). In the laboratory situation, the subject almost invariably relied on the facial expression as the true indicator of the communicator's meaning (Leathers, 1979a).

When the verbal and nonverbal portions of a message reinforce each other by conveying the same basic meaning, the metacommunicative value of the two types of cues is relatively unimportant. In contrast, when the verbal and nonverbal cues in a message convey conflicting meanings, the metacommunicative value of these cues becomes of primary importance. At that point the communicator, much like the subjects in the experiment, is faced with a serious problem. Should verbal or nonverbal cues be used to determine the meaning and intent of the message? In effect, the communicator must decide which type of cue has greatest metacommunicative value. Typically, people who face such a decision rely on nonverbal rather than verbal cues.

Mehrabian (1971) indicates that individuals employ a systematic and consistent approach to determine the meaning of conflicting cues. The impact of facial expression is of primary importance, tone of voice (or vocal expression) is the next in importance, and words are the least important. In short, facial expressions have the greatest metacommunicative value. Words have the least value.

We can safely conclude, therefore, that nonverbal cues serve the primary metacommunicative function in interpersonal communication. Because the metacommunicative function is a crucial determinant of high-quality communication, the proper decoding of nonverbal cues is one of the most important factors in attaining high-quality communication (Leathers, 1972).

Fifth, nonverbal cues represent a much more efficient means of communicating than verbal cues. Time is a vital commodity in many communication situations. Corporations willingly pay communication consultants handsome fees to improve the communicative efficiency of their executives. These executives want to know how to communicate more—in less time.

This goal is not easily achieved in our highly verbal culture. Verbal discourse is by its very nature a highly inefficient means of communication. Redundancy, repetition, ambiguity, and abstraction have become standard qualities of verbal discourse in America. Although their use is sometimes necessary, these qualities help to make communication inefficient.

Do qualities such as repetition and ambiguity represent inherent liabilities of verbal discourse, or do they simply reflect the ineptitude of the individual communicator? That question is probably debatable, but there is solid evidence to indicate that verbal communication is intrinsically more inefficient than nonverbal communication.

Reusch and Kees (1956) write that

in practice, nonverbal communication must necessarily be dealt with analogically and this without delay. Although verbal communication permits a long interval between statements, certain action sequences and gestures necessitate an immediate reply. Then the reaction must be quick and reflexlike, with no time to ponder or to talk. And whenever such a situation occurs, the slower and exhaustive verbal codifications are out of the question for practical reasons and are clearly more time-consuming and inefficient than nonverbal reactions. (p. 14).

These authors go on to point out that the nature of our language is such that words typically deal with the time dimension in a very inefficient manner. In a limited time frame there are few, if any, sequences of events that cannot be described more quickly with gestures than with words.

The old axiom that a picture is worth a thousand words may lack precision, universal applicability, and empirical verification. The axiom suggests an idea of great importance in interpersonal communication, however.

Sixth, nonverbal cues represent the most suitable vehicle for suggestion. The nature of a communication situation often dictates that ideas and emotions can be more effectively expressed indirectly than directly. Suggestion is an important means of indirect expression in our society. When it is employed, either the verbal or nonverbal channels may be used. For tangible reasons, however, suggestion is more closely associated with nonverbal than verbal communication.

In spite of the immense personal satisfaction and control potential associated with interpersonal communication, it is a high-risk endeavor. One's ego, self-image, and even psychological equilibrium are intimately bound up in the communicative interaction with other people. Most of us are so acutely sensitive about our own image that we devote a significant proportion of our efforts to preserving or enhancing that image. Hence, the integrative function of communication is becoming increasingly important.

Because many of us are so concerned about our own image, we prefer to use communication that has a maximum potential for enhancing our image with a minimum risk of deflating it. Nonverbal suggestion is a particularly suitable vehicle for attaining these ends.

One can always deny the seeming intent of nonverbal cues. Therefore, one can probably avoid many of the negative psychological consequences that may result from nonverbal suggestions. After all, the man across the room can never be sure that a woman's sustained and seemingly suggestive eye contact is not an idiosyncrasy rather than an open invitation to sexual intimacy. In contrast, as any frustrated lover knows, the most subtle suggestions couched in verbal terms do not provide the same psychological safeguards.

Hence, although nonverbal suggestion does not entail the same risks as verbal suggestion, it may be used for the same purpose. For this reason, nonverbal communication is increasingly associated with suggestion.

In review, the intent of this part of this chapter has not been to establish that verbal communication and nonverbal communication are separate, or completely separable, entities. Indeed, the enlightened student of communication would be well advised not to study one to the exclusion of the other. The foregoing has been included in order to emphasize the compelling need to examine and expand our knowledge of nonverbal communication. To satisfy this need, we must understand the specific functions served by nonverbal communication.

The Functions of Nonverbal Cues

Nonverbal cues serve a number of communicatively significant functions (Harper, Wiens, & Matarazzo, 1978). They not only function as powerful determinants of interpersonal perception but they have a major impact on interpersonal relationships. Although nonverbal cues frequently reinforce or supplement information provided by the spoken word, they also provide specific kinds of information that cannot be obtained from speech communication.

A moment of reflection may help to confirm the central role nonverbal cues play in shaping interpersonal perceptions and behaviors. For example, the airplane passenger who conforms in appearance and mannerism to the highjacker profile is apt to be interrogated, at minimum; the highjacker profile is essentially nonverbal in nature. A prospective juror may be stricken if he or she does not conform to the profile the defense attorney or prosecutor wants or needs on the jury. The strike usually is based on information provided by nonverbal rather than verbal cues. Telephone callers seeking a first date run a high risk of rejection if their vocal cues suggest an undesirable personality profile.

To be more specific, what communicative functions are most directly associated with nonverbal cues? Authorities provide somewhat different answers to this question. Burgoon (1979) identifies the six functions as symbolic representation, expressive communication, structuring interaction, impression formation and management, metacommunication, and social influence. In her distinctive treatment of the symbolic functions of nonverbal cues, Burgoon notes that the predisposition to attack, to escape, and to form affiliative bonds may be communicated in the most socially acceptable ways by nonverbal means. In addition, she emphasizes the symbolic importance of such nonverbal cues as flags, black arm bands, picketing, marching, and music.

The most detailed classification of the functions of nonverbal cues, which is grounded in numerous empirical studies of those functions, has been developed by Patterson (1982). He concludes that the major functions of nonverbal cues are providing information, regulating interaction, ex-

pressing intimacy, exercising social control, and facilitating service or task goals. Our own classification of the functions of nonverbal cues is based upon this model, with two modifications. Although the expression of intimacy focuses upon the communication of emotions, the communication of emotions does not necessarily involve the expression of intimacy. In addition, nonverbal cues clearly serve one other important function not identified by Patterson—metacommunication.

Nonverbal cues can, therefore, be used to serve six major communicative functions: (a) *provide information;* (b) *regulate interaction;* (c) *express emotions;* (d) *metacommunication;* (e) *exercise social control;* and (f) *facilitate service or task goals.* These communicative functions of nonverbal cues are not mutually exclusive because any single attempt to communicate nonverbally may serve a number of functions.

The informative function of nonverbal cues is the most basic because all nonverbal cues in any communicative situation are potentially informative to both the encoder and the decoder. Nonverbal cues are a potentially rich source of information because encoders frequently are unaware of their own nonverbal cues. When this is the case, they may inadvertently communicate a constellation of meanings that reveal much about their self-image, social identity, attitudes, and behavioral propensities.

In fact, I (Leathers, 1979b) suggest that nonverbal cues can provide certain distinctive kinds of information that cannot usually be obtained from the spoken word. The nonverbal behaviors of individuals reveal not only how they feel about themselves but how they feel about the individual with whom they are communicating. More specifically, nonverbal cues can be used to determine both an individual's level of *self-assurance* and *responsiveness*. The ability to determine an individual's level of confidence and interest at different points in time is indispensable to successful communication.

When the encoder's nonverbal cues are not consciously controlled and monitored by the encoder, the decoder derives from such cues the most valuable information. When the encoders nonverbal cues are consciously controlled and monitored, the informational value of such cues is minimized for the decoder. This is so because the conscious control and monitoring of nonverbal cues frequently takes the form of impression formation and management. In this case, impression managers strive to provide only those kinds of information that will help them attain their own objectives.

The second function of nonverbal cues, *regulating interaction*, is an important one. Although they are frequently nonreflective, nonverbal cues represent the most efficient and least offensive means of regulating interaction in interpersonal situations. To say "shut up, John" may trigger a hostile and defensive reaction; to communicate the same message by eye behavior or hand movement is a more socially acceptable way of achieving one's objective. The sensitive communicator will recognize that the turn-taking rules of a given culture are usually communicated nonverbally, and the cultural expectation is that such rules will not be violated.

The third function of nonverbal cues is to express emotions. As indicated previously, nonverbal communication represents the primary medium for the expression of emotions. If we believe that successful communication requires a sensitive reading of, and response to, the feelings, moods, and emotions of those with whom we communicate, the expressive potential of nonverbal communication becomes particularly important. In subsequent chapters, we will demonstrate that more detailed and precise information about the emotions of communicators can be obtained from their nonverbal cues than from any other source. We will also caution that some of that information may be counterfeit, because certain kinds of nonverbal cues can be consciously controlled for purposes of deception.

The fourth function of nonverbal cues, metacommunication, is a particularly distinctive one. In effect, metamessages, in the form of nonverbal cues, aid the communicator in both assessing the intent and motivation of the message sender and in determining the precise meaning(s) of verbal messages. Burgoon (1979) defines metacommunication as the use of nonverbal messages to qualify, complement, contradict, or expand verbal or other nonverbal messages. The importance of the metacommunicative function of nonverbal cues is particularly apparent when an individual is confronted with the task of decoding a multichannel message that seems to be communicating inconsistent meanings.

Social control is the fifth function of nonverbal cues. It is perhaps the most important function, in view of its relevance to a wide variety of socially significant communication contexts in the real world. *Social control* means that one individual attempts to influence or change the behavior of another individual.

Efforts to exercise social control frequently take the form of persuasion. Edinger and Patterson (1983) have convincingly demonstrated that the social-control function of nonverbal communication is also centrally involved in carefully calculated efforts to enhance one's status, power, and dominance; to provide selective feedback and reinforcement; and to deceive. They maintain that impression management is a social-control function so broad in scope as to embrace the more specific control functions. They write that, in a way, "all of the topics considered so far involve impression management. That is, in attempting to exert power, persuade others, provide feedback, or deceive, individuals are at least indirectly managing impressions" (p. 43).

The last on our list of nonverbal communication functions, the service-task function, is like the social-control function in one respect. Communicators who exercise this function are continuously aware of the nonverbal cues they use, and the cues are used with the conscious intent of achieving specific goals. The nature of the communication is impersonal but task-oriented. Touch is closely associated with this function. Examples of relationships where touch is used to treat, teach, or otherwise serve the needs of concerned individuals include physician–patient, golf professional–student, fireman–fire victim, and barber– or hairdresser–customer (Patterson, 1982).

In short, nonverbal cues serve a number of communicative functions that are vitally important to successful outcomes in the real world. The time is past when nonverbal communication can be treated as a support system of secondary importance, whose chief use is to help clarify the meaning of the spoken word.

Communicating Nonverbally in Specific Contexts

The different kinds of nonverbal communication have been treated in detailed and enlightening ways by authors such as Knapp (1978) and Malandro and Barker (1983), among others. These textbooks, like their predecessors, are designed to tell us *about* nonverbal communication. For example, they define, identify, and describe different classes of visual cues, such as facial expressions, gestures, and posture. What these books do not do, however, is demonstrate *how* we can successfully communicate in a nonverbal way.

This book, *Successful Nonverbal Communication*, is designed to *demonstrate* how knowledge of nonverbal cues can be used to communicate more successfully in contexts of particular importance to the reader. As this chapter suggests, *detailed knowledge of nonverbal cues and their communicative functions can be used to communicate more successfully in a variety of real-world contexts.* Succeeding chapters provide concrete guidelines which indicate how knowledge of nonverbal cues should be used if we are to communicate successfully.

From a conceptual perspective, this book is a successor to my earlier book, *Nonverbal Communication Systems* (Leathers, 1976). In Part One, the emphasis is on describing the different classes of nonverbal cues, illustrating the various kinds of information they can provide, and comparing and contrasting their communicative functions. Particular attention is given to the specific kinds of nonverbal cues that are desirable and undesirable in different communicative contexts.

This book departs most sharply from conventional practice, in the content of Parts Two and Three. These sections are designed to demonstrate how the knowledge presented in Part One can be used by individuals to project a desired image, and to communicate more successfully in particular settings. The value of this emphasis on application should be apparent to any person who has contemplated the communicative intricacies of an upcoming job interview, considered the formidable barriers to effective intercultural communication, or pondered the complexities of communicating in a sensitive way with a member of the opposite sex.

Do you create a favorable first impression? Do others judge you to be less credible in certain situations than you would like to be? Are you easily manipulated and deceived? Are you usually seen as an insincere and untrustworthy individual? If your answers to these questions give you cause for concern, the contents of Part Two should prove to be valuable. You may not know how to sell yourself nonverbally, to detect deception, to communicate consistently, or to manage the impressions you make on others. Each of these subjects is addressed in separate chapters in Part Two.

Chapters in Part Three of this book focus on specific guidelines for using nonverbal cues to communicate successfully in applied contexts. The contexts range from the selection interview to the classroom to the conference room to the office. Special attention is given to the distinctive contextual features of female–male interaction and to intercultural communication, as well as to the distinctive requirements for successful nonverbal communication in each of these contexts.

These particular contexts are emphasized because of their social significance and because of the importance of nonverbal cues in these contexts. The job interview is a good case in point. Existing knowledge suggests that the interviewee's verbal communication may contribute less to the relative success or failure of a job interview than nonverbal communication. To undertake a job interview with no knowledge of the potentially powerful communicative effects of one's nonverbal cues may be ill-advised, at best, and masochistic, at worst.

In short, this book is designed for the reader who wishes to use knowledge of nonverbal cues to communicate more successfully. Such knowledge is neither simple nor easy to apply. The judicious use of nonverbal cues should help to communicate more successfully, but it does not guarantee success.

Summary

Nonverbal communication functions in vitally important ways in our society. Frequently, communicators can achieve their purpose by using accurate and efficient nonverbal communication.

The functional importance of nonverbal communication is obvious when we realize that (a) nonverbal communication is usually the dominant force in the exchange of meaning in the interpersonal context; (b) feelings and emotions are exchanged more accurately by nonverbal than by verbal means; (c) meanings exchanged nonverbally are relatively free of deception and distortion; (d) nonverbal cues serve a metacommunicative function which is indispensable in attaining high-quality communication; (e) nonverbal cues represent a much more efficient means of communicating than verbal cues; and (f) nonverbal communication is a particularly suitable vehicle for using suggestion.

Major functions served by nonverbal cues include providing information, regulating interaction, expressing emotions, metacommunication, exercising social control, and facilitating service or task goals. Of these six functions, the social-control function is perhaps the most important, in views of its relevance to a wide variety of socially significant communicative contexts in the real world.

This book is designed for the reader who wishes to use knowledge of nonverbal cues to communicate more successfully in real-world contexts. This knowledge can be particularly valuable because the determinants of successful communication are frequently nonverbal.

References

Birdwhistell, R. L. (1970). *Kinesics and context.* Philadelphia: University of Pennsylvania Press.

Burgoon, J. (1980). Nonverbal communication research in the 1970's: An overview. D. Nimmo (Ed.). *ICA Communication Yearbook 4.* New Brunswick: Transaction Books.

Davitz, J. R. (1969). *The communication of emotional meaning.* New York: McGraw-Hill.

Edinger, J. A., & Patterson, M. L. (1983). Nonverbal involvement and social control. *Psychological Bulletin, 93,* 30–56.

Fast, J. (1970). *Body language.* New York: Evans.

Harper, R. G., Wiens, A. N., & Matarazzo, J. D. (1978). *Nonverbal communication: The state of the art.* New York: Wiley.

Knapp, M. L. (1978). *Nonverbal communication in human interaction,* 2nd ed. New York: Holt.

LaFrance, M., & Mayo, C. (1978). *Moving bodies: Nonverbal communication in social relationships.* Monterey, CA: Brooks/Cole.

Leathers, D. G. (1972). Quality of group communication as a determinant of group product. *Speech Monographs, 39,* 166–173.

Leathers, D. G. (1976). *Nonverbal communication systems.* Newton, MA: Allyn.

Leathers, D. G. (1979a). The impact of multichannel message inconsistency on verbal and nonverbal decoding behaviors. *Communication Monographs, 46,* 88–100.

Leathers, D. G. (1979b). The informational potential of the nonverbal and verbal components of feedback responses. *Southern Speech Communication Journal, 44,* 331–354.

Leathers, D. G., & Emigh, T. H. (1980). Decoding facial expressions: A new test with decoding norms. *Quarterly Journal of Speech, 66,* 418–436.

Malandro, L. A., & Barker, L. (1983). *Nonverbal communication.* Reading, MA: Addison-Wesley.

Mehrabian, A. (1968). Communication without words. *Psychology Today, 2,* 51–52.

Mehrabian, A. (1971). *Silent messages.* Belmont, CA: Wadsworth.

Patterson, M. L. (1982). A sequential functional model of nonverbal exchange. *Psychological Bulletin, 89,* 231–249.

Reusch, J., & Kees, W. (1956). *Nonverbal communication.* Berkeley: University of California Press.

Schutz, W. C. (1971). *Here comes everybody.* New York: Harper.

Facial Expressions and Eye Behaviors

"**T**he human face—in repose and in movement, at the moment of death as in life, in silence and in speech, when alone and with others, when seen or sensed from within, in actuality or as represented in art or recorded by the camera—is a commanding, complicated, and at times confusing source of information. The face is commanding because of its very visibility and omnipresence" (Ekman, Friesen, & Ellsworth, 1972, p. 1).

The face has long been a primary source of information in interpersonal communication. It is an instrument of great importance in the transmission of meaning. Within a matter of seconds, facial expressions can move us to the heights of ecstasy or the depths of despair. We study the faces of friends and associates for subtle changes and nuances in meaning, and they in turn study our faces.

In a very real sense, our quest for meaning in this world begins and ends with facial expression. We study the faces of infants to determine their immediate needs, and they reciprocate by communicating many of their needs and emotional states through facial expressions. The elderly hospital patient studies the face of the surgeon to determine the chances of surviving the next operation, and the surgeon's facial expression often provides the definitive answer.

We know that the face may be used to complement or qualify the meaning of spoken messages and to replace spoken messages. We may also speculate that such facial features as a low forehead, thick lips, and jumbo ears are all associated with undesirable personality characteristics, but such conclusions are speculative (Knapp, 1978). This speculation may of course be somewhat amusing for individuals who do *not* have low foreheads, thick lips, and jumbo ears. Even if a connection between specific facial features and personality traits were firmly established, however, such a finding would tend to divert attention from the primary communicative function of the human face. The primary function of the human face is to provide information about the emotions experienced by the communicator.

The Face as the Most Important Source of Emotional Information

Successful communication places a premium on the ability to not only identify general emotional states of individuals with whom we communicate but on the ability to differentiate among the more subtle kinds of emotional meaning, which are constituents of the more general emotional states. The ability to identify fear is undeniably useful. However, the ability to distinguish accurately specialized kinds of fear, such as terror, anxiety, and apprehension, is much more useful.

To obtain both general and specific kinds of emotional information, the communicator must develop the ability to decode facial expressions accurately. This is so because the human face is now widely recognized as the most important source of emotional information. The face is the primary site for the communication of emotional states (Knapp, 1978) and, as such, is the primary signal system for communicating emotions (Ekman & Friesen, 1975). One prominent researcher has gone so far as to assert that facial expressions not only accurately communicate an individual's emotional states but that facial expressions *are* emotions (Tomkins, 1962).

The human face has great communicative potential. This is so in large part because the complex and flexible set of muscles in the human face may be used to communicate a great variety of facial meanings. The Facial Action Coding System (FACS), for example, was developed for the purpose of classifying the units of facial expression that are anatomically separate and visually distinguishable. FACS distinguishes 44 *action units* (Ekman & Friesen, 1978). (The reader who is offended by jargon may be amused to discover that in this system the human smile is identified not as a smile but as Action Unit 12.)

Consider, in contrast, the limited repertoire of facial expressions of an animal, such as a cow. When was the last time you saw your cat smile? Our cat has not smiled in the last ten years. Our dog's face seems to be equally unexpressive; this dog has never exhibited facial surprise, contempt, or disgust. Study the facial expressions of the cat and the dog in the photographs, and try to determine what facial emotions they are displaying. (see p. 21).

Even if these particular animals had incredibly high IQs, they could communicate little emotional information via their facial expressions. This is true in large part because their facial muscles are not sufficiently complex and flexible to reveal very much about how they may be feeling at the moment.

There is disagreement among theorists and researchers as to how the human face functions communicatively. Two major approaches have been used by researchers in an attempt to describe or identify with some degree of precision the meanings communicated by facial expressions—the categoric and dimensional perspectives.

The Categoric Perspective

Proponents of the categoric perspective maintain that the human face, at any given moment, transmits one dominant type of meaning, often associated with such affective states as happiness or anger. The meaning transmitted facially is believed to have a single referent that will stand out in the mind of the decoder. Although any given facial expression may combine two or more classes of meaning in the form of a facial blend (Ekman et al., 1972), the decoder will use a single categoric label to describe the *dominant* facial meaning that is displayed.

Classes of Facial Meaning.   Not surprisingly, researchers who believe that the face functions denotatively have attempted to identify and label all classes of meaning that they believe can be communicated accurately by facial expressions. Some of the earliest and most insightful research on the denotative functions of facial expression was conducted by J. Frois-Wittmann (1930). Using himself as the photographic subject, Frois-Wittmann made a series of 72 facial photographs. These photographs were designed to represent all the classes and subclasses of facial meaning that human beings were believed capable of communicating.

This early study suggested that facial expressions are most accurately described by means of classification. Pain, pleasure, superiority, determination, surprise, attention, and bewilderment were among the facial meanings most consistently and accurately classified by the subjects. At the same time, it became apparent that the denotative meaning of some facial expressions was unclear. For example, subjects often had difficulty in distinguishing between hate and anger, disappointment and sadness, disgust and contempt, and horror and fear.

Frois-Wittmann may be faulted for failure to standardize the labels used to describe facial expressions, but he was ahead of his time in a number of ways. His detailed description of the facial muscles used to communicate certain emotions bears a striking resemblance to more recent efforts to develop "facial blueprints." Furthermore, his use of a large number of descriptive labels suggests that he recognized that the face communicates not only broad classes of facial meaning but also subtle kinds of facial meaning that are constituents of the broader classes.

More recent attempts to describe the denotative meanings of facial expressions have focused on the attempt to use a limited number of descriptive labels that identify *only* the broader classes of meaning that are communicated by facial expression. Thus, Woodworth (1938) concluded that the six basic classes of meaning communicated facially are happiness, suffering, surprise, determination, disgust, and contempt. Of 390 subjects using 6 categoric labels, 366 correctly identified happiness. Accuracy of identification for the other expressions was suffering, 325; determination, 310; surprise, 304; disgust, 294; and contempt, 190.

Tomkins (1962) attempted to increase the precision with which facial expressions may be classified. He uses the following *sets* of labels to identify the eight classes of affective information that he contends can be communicated by facial expressions: (a) Interest–Excitement; (b) Enjoyment–Joy; (c) Surprise–Startle; (d) Distress–Anguish; (e) Fear–Terror; (f) Shame–Humiliation; (g) Contempt–Disgust; and (h) Anger–Rage. The first label in each pair represents a low-intensity manifestation of the given class of facial meaning, and the second represents a high-intensity counterpart.

In his influential book, *The Face of Emotion* (1971), Izard used the same set of labels to develop a decoding test that measured the ability of nine different national-cultural groups to identify facial expressions. Surprisingly, decoders were not forced to differentiate between facial interest and excitement or facial distress and anguish. They were simply asked to determine the meaning of a given facial expression by placing it in one of the eight categories.

Ekman et al. (*Emotion in the Human Face,* 1972) have done an exhaustive review, summary, and analysis of many of the major studies that treat the face as if it functions denotatively. They conclude that the face is capable of communicating eight basic classes of meaning: (a) happiness; (b) surprise; (c) fear; (d) anger; (e) sadness; (f) disgust; (g) contempt; and (h) interest.

Areas of the Face: Meaning Cues.   The categoric perspective is particularly useful for individuals who wish to determine how accurately they can distinguish among the basic classes of emotion that can be communicated by facial expressions. In fact, there is now evidence to indicate that certain areas of the face provide meaning cues that are particularly useful in identifying specific kinds of emotions.

The Facial Affect Scoring Technique (FAST) breaks down the face into three areas: the brows and forehead; the eyes, lids, and bridge of the nose; and the lower face (Ekman, Friesen, & Tomkins, 1971). The upper portion of the face is apt to provide more useful cues for identifying anger than the lower part of the face, for example. Thus, when anger is displayed facially the brows are lowered and drawn together, vertical lines appear between the brows, and both the upper and lower lids exhibit tension.

The Dimensional Perspective

Few would deny that the face is capable of functioning denotatively in a given context or situation. Many students of facial communication believe, however, that the face usually functions *connotatively.* That is, at any particular time, the face conveys not one dominant meaning but a number of dimensions of meaning. Those who see the face as functioning connotatively have generally accepted the conceptual model developed by Osgood (1966) in their attempt to identify and measure the dimensions of meaning that are conveyed by verbal means.

Dimensions of Facial Meaning.   Until fairly recently, the multidimensional framework and the concept of semantic space had not been applied to the study of meanings transmitted by nonverbal means. In the 1950s, Schlosberg began research to determine *how* and *how many* meanings are communicated by facial expression. He concluded that facial communication is multidimensional and connotative because the face typically communicates not a single meaning but some combination of meanings. Specifically, Schlosberg (1954) found that meanings communicated by the face are adequately represented by three dimensions: (a) pleasant–unpleasant; (b) attention–rejection; and (c) sleep–tension.

Since, then, Engen, Levy, and Schlosberg (1957) have done follow-up studies that tend to confirm the presence and stability of the same three dimensions in facial communication. The findings of Levy, Orr, and Rosenzweig (1960) and of Abelson and Sermat (1962) also support the existence of the same three dimensions of facial expression. Using "pictomorphs" (schematic faces), consisting of head shape and eyebrow, eyes, and mouth in various positions, rather than photographs as his data base, Harrison (1967) also found that facial communication is represented by three dimensions: (a) approval; (b) social potency; and (c) interest. Similarly, in an impressively detailed study, Williams and Tolch (1965) found that facial expression includes the two dimensions of *general evaluation* and *dynamism* (they did not find the usual third factor).

Recently, Charles Osgood (1966) turned his attention from the study of verbal to nonverbal meaning. Both his objective and his conceptual framework were as praiseworthy as they were in his earlier research on verbal meaning, which led to the development of the *semantic differential*. He wanted to determine how many dimensions of meaning accurately and adequately characterize facial communication. In pursuit of this objective, he treated facial communication as if it took place in "semantic space," a multidimensional space composed of an unknown number of dimensions of meaning. Osgood's factor-analytic research suggests that facial communication includes the following factors: (a) pleasantness; (b) control (represented by such specific expressions as annoyance and disgust versus amazement and excitement); and (c) intensity (rage, scorn, and loathing versus boredom, quiet, and complacency). A fourth, though weaker, factor is labeled *interest*.

Osgood's research is supported by Mehrabian, who has adopted Osgood's concept of "semantic space" as well as his multidimensional approach to facial communication. As with Osgood, Mehrabian (1970) contends that facial communication consists of three dimensions of meaning, which he labels: (a) evaluation; (b) potency or status; and (c) responsiveness.

Because so many researchers have found three dimensions of facial meaning, one might conclude that they have all found the same dimensions. Such a conclusion is not necessarily warranted. Often investigators apply their own, idiosyncratic labels to dimensions of meaning making direct comparisons very difficult. Also, there has probably been a natural tendency to conclude that facial meaning is comprised of the same three dimensions as verbal meaning.

Indeed, some of our most impressive and recent research suggests that facial communication includes not three but at least six dimensions of meaning. In an early study, Frijda and Philipszoon (1963) found four dimensions of facial meaning, which they identified as: (a) pleasant/unpleasant; (b) naturalness/submission; (c) intensity of expression/control of expression; and (d) attention/disinterest. The second expression, naturalness/submission, was considered to be new, not previously found by the "three dimensional" students of facial communication. In a follow-up study, Frijda (1969) conducted a more detailed study, which once again identified four dimensions as well as two additional dimensions. Dimension 5 is now labeled *understanding/amazed*, and dimension 6 is *simple/complicated*. Frijda concludes that "the two studies both suggest the importance of not less than five dependent aspects of dimension, at least two or three more than in the usual analysis" (pp. 178–179).

There is still controversy as to how many dimensions of meaning can be communicated by facial means. From a review of research to date, we can, however, reach the following conclusions: (a) the face communicates evaluative judgments through either pleasant or unpleasant expressions that indicate whether the communicator sees the current object of his or her attentions as good or bad; (b) the face communicates interest or disinterest in other people or in the surrounding environment; (c) the face communicates intensity and, hence, the degree of involvement in a situation; (d) the face communicates the amount of control individuals have over their own expressions; and (e) the face probably communicates the intellectual factor of understanding, or lack of it.

Each of the foregoing five dimensions of facial meaning has both positive and negative qualities. For example, although the face may communicate pleasantness in one situation, it may communicate unpleasantness in the next. Similarly, the face may communicate interest or disinterest, involvement or uninvolvement, control of emotions or lack of control. (Whether the quality of facial meaning is considered positive or negative will probably depend on the situation and numerous other factors.)

Clearly, the face has the potential to produce communication of very high quality, where the meanings transmitted and received are virtually identical. The preceding dimensional analysis of meaning in facial expressions establishes that the face is capable of conveying positive reinforcement, interest, involvement, a sense of control over one's self and the immediate environment, and an image of a thoughtful person deliberating on the facts. All of these meanings are of great importance in interpersonal communication, and are necessary—singly and in various combinations—to produce high-quality communication.

At the same time, it is now obvious that the face is capable of communicating negative reinforcement, disinterest, withdrawal, lack of control, and a visceral rather than a thoughtful reaction to various messages. The potentially disruptive effects of such meanings are often dependent upon matters such as context.

Sides of the Face: Meaning Cues. If you subscribe to the *denotative* approach to facial expression, you will study the human face to try to determine which basic class of emotion is being communicated. You may be able to make more accurate judgments by concentrating on certain areas of the face. If you believe that the face functions *connotatively*, you will be particularly concerned with determining the *intensity* of the emotion being communicated facially. You may be able to *more accurately* assess intensity of emotion by concentrating on the left side of the communicator's face.

One study (Sackeim, Gur, & Saucy, 1978) found that emotions are expressed more intensely on the left side of the face. Although the evidence is far from conclusive at present, this study does suggest that the *left side of the face may provide more accurate intensity cues than the right side.*

If true, this finding may be attributed to the fact that *facial displays of emotion, as well as other kinds of nonverbal cues, are controlled by the right side of the brain.*

As you look at the two photographs of the right and left side of the face, can you determine what emotion is being communicated and with what degree of intensity? Consider the face on the left side of the page first. Does the left side of the face communicate disgust and the right side happiness? Now consider the face on the right side of the page. Does the left side of the face communicate happiness and the right side disgust? Did the right or left side of the faces provide the most useful intensity cues?

The categoric and dimensional perspectives that are used to describe facial expressions should not be thought of as mutually exclusive, however. There is some evidence that the meaning communicated by a given facial expression can be determined most accurately by first placing that facial expression in a descriptive category, and then rate it for intensity. Ekman, perhaps the foremost proponent of the categoric perspective, recently conducted research (Ekman, Friesen, & Ancoli, 1980) designed to determine whether facial expressions provide reliable information both with regard to the *kind* of emotion the encoder is experiencing and the *intensity* with which the emotion is experienced. The study seemed to confirm that *facial expressions are most accurately described by first classifying them and then rating them.*

These two perspectives help stimulate thought about how the face functions communicatively, but *neither perspective has produced an instrument that* provides a precise and detailed measure of an individual's ability to decode the meanings of facial expressions. Such measurement must be undertaken before an individual can determine whether he or she needs exposure to a training program designed to develop the ability to decode expressions accurately.

The Deceptive Face: How to Recognize It and Guard Against It

Facial expressions are usually a reliable source of meaning, but in some situations they may be unreliable. In those situations, the enlightened communicator must know for which signs of facial deception to watch. It is when facial expressions are consciously controlled that they are most apt to be deceptive; the individual will make his or her facial expression conform to certain norms or *display rules.*

Facial display rules may be classified as *personal, situational,* and *cultural.* Personal display rules may dictate that we inhibit the harshest display of facial expression when communicating with children or physically handicapped individuals, for example. Situational display rules may dictate that in certain business situations, for example, we modify or modulate genuine expressions of facial emotions, such as disgust, so as not to offend a client or colleague. Finally, cultural display rules may vary because cultural groups differ, not only in the intensity of their facial expressions but in the specific kinds of facial expressions they are likely to exhibit in public. We do know that Anglo-Saxons are more likely than Latins to consciously control their facial expressions. We also know that the Oriental's repertoire of publicly displayed emotions is quite limited; and that certain kinds of specialized facial expressions are confined to certain parts of the world, and even to certain regions of a given country.

The impact of display rules and/or the desire to deceive may mean that facial expressions are misleaading sources of information, in some cases. Thus, LaFrance and Mayo (1978) make the distinction between facial expressions that might be classified as *representational* and those that might be classified as *presentational.* Representational expression is associated with genuine facial expressions that accurately reflect the actual emotion that the communicator is experiencing. Presentation, in contrast, refers to the consciously controlled use of the face for purposes of public consumption. One type of facial presentation is the "emotional put-on," where there may be a marked disparity between the facial emotion displayed and the emotion actually experienced. LaFrance and Mayo (1978) capture the difference between truthful and deceptive facial communication when they write that the "distinction has been characterized as one between *presentation* and *representation.* The presentation is a performance, an arrangement and appearance designed to be seen. Its connection is less to inner feelings than to outer effect. In contrast, the representation refers to the expression of inner feelings" (p. 32).

Whatever the reason for controlling facial expression, or, in some cases, "putting on a false face," the receiver should recognize that the sender is apt to use one of three techniques (Ekman & Friesen, 1975): (a) *qualifying;* (b) *modulating;* or (c) *falsifying.* The basic classes of facial meaning that might be communicated are qualified when you add another facial expression to the original, in order to modify the impact. For example, the boss who gives the subordinate a look of anger, immediately followed by a look of bewilderment, may be trying to communicate to the subordinate that he or she is very upset by what the subordinate did, but doesn't want to believe that the subordinate really did it. Facial meaning is modulated when the intensity of the facial expression is changed to communicate stronger or weaker feelings than those actually being experienced. For example, you may communicate slight sadness, facially, when you feel abject grief.

Finally, facial falsification may take one of three forms. A person may: (a) *simulate,* by showing facial emotion when no emotion is felt; (b) may *neutralize,* by showing no facial emotion although some emotion is felt; or (c) may *mask,* by covering a felt emotion while displaying a facial emotion that is not really felt.

Whether facial deception is intentional or involuntary, deception complicates the task of the decoder and reduces the potential value of the face as a reliable source of emotional information. When facial deception is used, the question becomes, how can the receiver guard against being deceived by such facial expressions? The best method of guarding against such deception is to be trained to develop one's decoding skills. If the facial expression seems to lack spontaneity, to be poorly synchronized with the content of the words being uttered, or to involve seemingly calculated movement in the lower part of the face, beware. Finally, the receiver should be alert for involuntary micromomentary facial expressions. These facial expressions usually last for only a fraction of a second. When these fleeting facial expressions contradict the meaning of more sustained facial expressions, facial deception may be occurring.

Measuring Sensitivity to Facial Expressions

The face may be used to deceive; nevertheless it has unsurpassed potential for the communication of emotional information. We know now that individuals vary markedly in their ability to use the informational potential of the human face. Until quite recently, however, attempts to measure an individual's ability to decode meanings from facial expressions lacked specificity and precision. This was so because decoding tests did not require that decoders make fine distinctions between facial expressions that were closely related in meaning (Leathers & Emigh, 1980). Decoders were usually asked to view facial expressions and place them in one of seven or eight categories; each category represented one of the primary emotions.

The Facial Meaning Sensitivity Test

The Facial Meaning Sensitivity Test represents the most detailed and precise measure of the ability to decode facial expressions, which has been developed to date. Through application of this test to a national sample of decoders, the accuracy of meaning of the facial photographs in the FMST has been validated. The validation procedure established not only that decoders using the FMST accurately distinguish among ten basic classes of

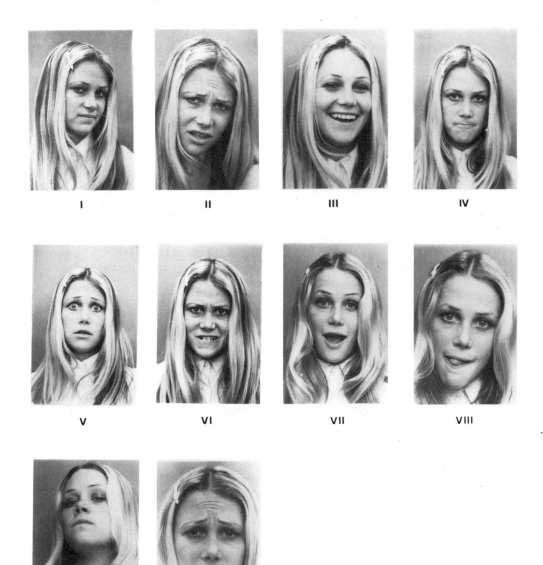

FIGURE 2.1 FACIAL MEANING SENSITIVITY TEST
Part I

emotion communicated by facial expressions, but that they can accurately label the subtle and closely related facial meanings which are constituents of each of the ten broad classes of facial meaning.

The Facial Meaning Sensitivity Test (hereafter referred to as the FMST) is composed of a set of photographs of different facial expressions; it is a three-part test. The photographs in the test are all of the same person, Loren Lewis. Loren was chosen because she has an expressive and photogenic face. In recognition of her dedication, determination, and sensitivity, this series of photographs is known as the *Loren Lewis Series.* The facial photographs that make up the FMST were chosen from over 700 photographs of Loren Lewis from the many sessions held in developing the Loren Lewis Series.

Part I of the FMST (see Figure 2.1) contains ten photographs that represent the ten basic classes of facial meaning. Study the ten photographs, and place the photograph numbers in the appropriate blanks of the chart in Step 1.

The correct answers for Step 1 of the FMST are: disgust = 1; happiness = III; interest = VIII; sadness = X; bewilderment = II; contempt = IX; surprise = VII; anger = VI; determination = IV; and fear = V.

On the following pages you will see thirty more photographs of facial expressions (Figure 2.2). Your task in Step II of the FMST is to group these facial expressions by class of meaning. Three of the photographs, for example, are intended to convey meanings that express a specific kind of disgust and, hence, should be perceived as part of that class of facial meaning. Among the thirty pictures are three expressions that may be classified as specific kinds of happiness. Your task, then, is to select the three photographs that you most closely associate with each of the ten classes of facial meaning, using each photograph only once, and to place the photograph numbers in the appropriate blanks of the chart in Step 2.

The correct choices for Step 2 of the FMST are: disgust = 8, 12, 30;

STEP 1.   Facial Meaning Sensitivity Test

Class of Facial Meaning	Number of Expression (from Figure 2.1)
Disgust	_____
Happiness	_____
Interest	_____
Sadness	_____
Bewilderment	_____
Contempt	_____
Surprise	_____
Anger	_____
Determination	_____
Fear	_____

STEP 2. Facial Meaning Sensitivity Test

Class of Facial Meaning	Expressions That Are Part of Each Class (Number of Expression, from Figure 2.2)		
Disgust	____	____	____
Happiness	____	____	____
Interest	____	____	____
Sadness	____	____	____
Bewilderment	____	____	____
Contempt	____	____	____
Surprise	____	____	____
Anger	____	____	____
Determination	____	____	____
Fear	____	____	____

happiness = 2, 9, 26; interest = 6, 15, 23; sadness = 5, 7, 14; bewilderment = 4, 17, 18; contempt = 13, 24, 29; surprise = 3, 16, 19; anger = 1, 20, 28; determination = 11, 22, 25; and fear = 10, 21, 27.

In Step 3 of the FMST you have a very specific discriminatory task. You must correctly identify very specific kinds of meaning. Consider the preceding thirty photographs three at a time, and place the photograph number in the blank provided in the chart in Step 3. For example, you must decide whether picture 8, 12, or 30 communicates aversion. You must also identify repugnance and distaste in this series of three photographs.

The correct choices for Step 3 of the FMST are: 30, 12, 8; 16, 19, 3; 28, 1, 20; 18, 4, 17; 10, 21, 27; 24, 13, 29; 9, 26, 2; 14, 5, 7; 23, 6, 15; and 11, 22, 25.

STEP 3. Facial Meaning Sensitivity Test

Specific Kind of Facial Meaning						Picture Number Choose from among the following expressions
Aversion	____	Repugnance	____	Distaste	____	8, 12, 30
Amazement	____	Flabbergasted	____	Astonished	____	3, 16, 19
Rage	____	Hate	____	Annoyance	____	1, 20, 28
Confusion	____	Doubt	____	Stupidity	____	4, 17, 18
Terror	____	Anxiety	____	Apprehension	____	10, 21, 27
Disdain	____	Arrogance	____	Superiority	____	13, 24, 29
Laughter	____	Love	____	Amusement	____	2, 9, 26
Disappointment	____	Distress	____	Pensiveness	____	5, 7, 14
Attention	____	Anticipation	____	Excitement	____	6, 15, 23
Stubborn	____	Resolute	____	Belligerent	____	11, 22, 25

FIGURE 2.2   FACIAL MEANING SENSITIVITY TEST
Part II

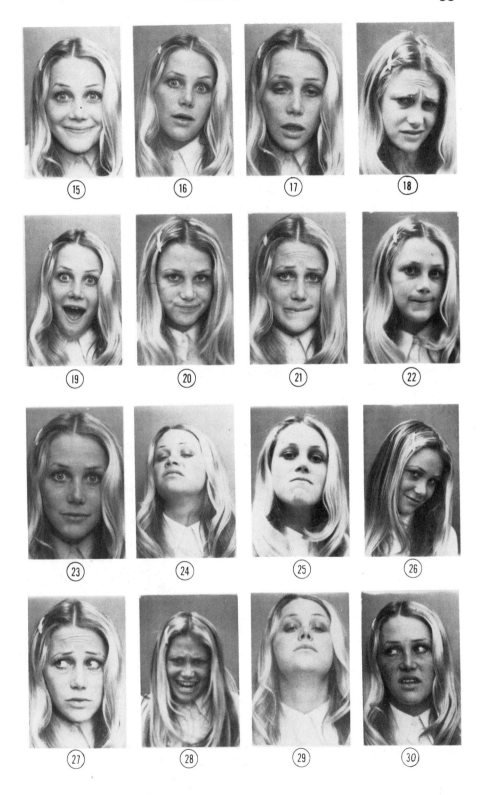

National Decoding Norms.   Results in Tables 2.1–2.3 provide decoding norms for each step of the FMST. The sample of decoders who produced these decoding norms were 118 engineers and corporate executives, 82 university students, and 68 members of fraternal and civic organizations; 201 decoders were males and 67 were females. To determine whether the level of skill reflected in your own attempts to decode the facial expressions contained in the FMST was good, average, or poor, you need to follow a simple procedure.

Results for each step of the FMST are scored separately because a weighted scoring system is used, with greater weight assigned to those decoding decisions or answers where the sample group of decoders exhibited their highest degree of consensus. For Step 1, each correct answer (see Table 2.1) is worth 10 points, with a possible total of 100 points. The average score for the sample of decoders ($n = 268$) for Step 1 was 90.9, with a standard deviation of 13.13.

Scoring weights for Step 2 are given in Table 2.4. Thus, an individual classifying photographs 2, 9, and 15 as kinds of facial *happiness* is given 4 points for each choice, for a total of 12 points. If the individual placed only photograph 9 in the *happiness* category, the point total for that class of

TABLE 2.1.   Accuracy of Identification for Basic Classes of Meaning Communicated by Facial Expression: Step 1 of the FMST

Class of Meaning	Photograph Number	Percentage of Correct Identification by Decoders	Type of Decoding Error	z-value
Happiness	III	98.88	Surprise (.75%) Interest (.37%)	42.84
Sadness	X	96.64	Bewilderment (2.24%) Interest (.37%)	48.47
Surprise	VII	95.90	Fear (2.99%) Interest (.37%)	48.08
Anger	VI	92.91	Determination (6.34%) Disgust (.37%)	45.91
Fear	V	91.41	Bewilderment (5.22%) Interest (1.40%)	37.83
Contempt	IX	89.18	Disgust (5.60%) Determination (2.61%)	43.93
Disgust	I	88.01	Contempt (4.49%)	42.84
Interest	VIII	87.31	Bewilderment (4.85%) Surprise (2.24%)	42.95
Determination	IV	86.94	Anger (5.97%) Contempt (4.48%)	43.54
Bewilderment	II	82.46	Fear (7.37%) Interest (3.86%)	39.29

All z-values are significant beyond the .0001 level. The two types of decoding errors that occurred most frequently for each class of meaning are reported in the Type of Decoding Error column.

TABLE 2.2. Accuracy of Classification of Facial Photographs into Classes of Meaning: Step 2 of the FMST

Class of Meaning	Photograph Number	Percentage of Decoders Correctly Classifying Each Photograph	Type of Decoding Error
Happiness	9	97.22	
	2	91.54	Interest (5.93)
	26	34.00	Interest (53.06)
	15	65.59	Happiness
Sadness	5	82.28	Fear (10.55)
	7	79.57	Bewilderment (7.18)
	14	70.17	Bewilderment (22.27)
Surprise	19	91.96	
	3	86.12	
	16	66.25	Fear (11.58); Interest (12.36)
Anger	28	85.59	Fear (11.52)
	1	65.56	Determination (25.31); Contempt (5.39)
	20	20.67	Disgust (48.56); Contempt (11.54) Determination (12.02)
Fear	10	87.87	
	21	56.17	Bewilderment (21.70); Sadness (16.60)
	27	62.98	Bewilderment (27.23); Sadness (7.80)
Contempt	13	73.30	Determination (21.26)
	24	85.20	Disgust (5.00)
	29	75.57	Determination (14.47)
Disgust	8	72.93	Bewilderment (7.42); Anger (6.11); Contempt (5.68)
	30	56.67	Bewilderment (12.86); Contempt (10.95); Fear (10.00); Anger (5.71)
Interest	6	91.95	
	23	81.86	Surprise (5.30)
	15	26.72	Happiness (65.59); Surprise (6.48)
	26	53.06	Interest
Determination	11	71.49	Anger (27.00)
	25	69.70	Anger (17.31); Contempt (8.66)
	22	51.91	Anger (29.36); Interest (6.80); Fear (5.10)
Bewilderment	18	77.12	Fear (6.78); Sadness (6.36); Disgust (5.93)
	17	56.52	Sadness (28.50); Fear (5.80);
	4	18.69	Disgust (40.19); Contempt (14.02); Anger (8.88); Determination (7.94); Interest (5.60)

TABLE 2.3. Accuracy of Identification of Specific Facial Expressions Within Each Class of Meaning

Class of Meaning	Photograph Number	Percentage of Correct Identification	Type of Decoding Error	Percentage of Decoders Correctly Identifying All Facial Expressions Within a Class
Anger	28	Rage (95.74)	Hate (3.49) Annoyance (0)	94.53
	1	Hate (94.92)	Rage (3.49) Annoyance (1.94)	
	20	Annoyance (98.96)	Rage (0.39) Hate (1.16)	
Happiness	9	Laughter (98.45)	Amusement (1.66) Love (0)	90.27
	26	Love (91.09)	Amusement (8.53) Laughter (0)	
	2	Amusement (90.31)	Love (8.14) Laughter (1.16)	
Bewilderment	18	Confusion (86.38)	Doubt (7.39) Stupidity (5.84)	85.66
	4	Doubt (88.72)	Confusion (10.51) Stupidity (0.39)	
	17	Stupidity (93.39)	Doubt (3.50) Confusion (2.72)	
Fear	10	Terror (98.44)	Anxiety (9.78) Apprehension (0.30)	76.74
	21	Anxiety (77.43)	Apprehension (21.40) Terror (0.78)	
	27	Apprehension (77.82)	Anxiety (21.40) Terror (0.39)	

Emotion	No.	Primary	Secondary 1	Secondary 2	Value
Interest	23	Attention (89.92)	Anticipation (6.98)	Excitement (2.33)	
	6	Anticipation (67.05)	Excitement (25.97)	Attention (6.20)	66.15
	15	Excitement (71.32)	Anticipation (25.97)	Attention (2.33)	
Sadness	14	Disappointment (56.59)	Pensiveness (25.19)	Distress (17.44)	
	5	Distress (72.48)	Disappointment (21.71)	Pensiveness (5.04)	53.91
	7	Pensiveness (86.61)	Disappointment (21.32)	Distress (8.92)	
Contempt	24	Disdain (55.25)	Arrogance (33.07)	Superiority (11.28)	
	13	Arrogance (47.47)	Disdain (35.41)	Superiority (11.28)	43.80
	29	Superiority (71.98)	Arrogance (19.07)	Disdain (8.56)	
Disgust	30	Aversion (78.68)	Repugnance (9.69)	Distaste (11.24)	
	12	Repugnance (49.61)	Distaste (43.02)	Aversion (7.36)	42.25
	8	Distaste (45.35)	Repugnance (40.70)	Aversion (13.95)	
Determination	11	Stubborn (51.55)	Belligerent (32.95)	Resolute (14.73)	
	22	Resolute (67.05)	Belligerent (22.09)	Stubborn (10.47)	37.98
	25	Belligerent (44.19)	Stubborn (37.60)	Resolute (17.83)	
Surprise	16	Amazement (45.74)	Astonishment (32.95)	Flabbergasted (20.93)	
	19	Flabbergasted (35.66)	Astonishment (34.11)	Amazement (29.35)	20.62
	3	Astonishment (32.17)	Flabbergasted (42.25)	Amazement (24.03)	

TABLE 2.4. Weighted Scores for Step 2 of FMST

Class of Meaning	1	2	3	4	5	6	7	8	9	10	11	12	13	14	15	16	17	18	19	20	21	22	23	24	25	26	27	28	29	30	
Happiness	4								4						4																Happiness
Sadness					4								4																		Sadness
Surprise			4														4		4												Surprise
Anger	4																		4												Anger
Fear									3												3						4				Fear
Contempt													4										4						4		Contempt
Disgust							3				3																			3	Disgust
Interest					4																4				4						Interest
Determination											3												3								Determination
Bewilderment																	3		3												Bewilderment

1 2 3 4 5 6 7 8 9 10 11 12 13 14 15 16 17 18 19 20 21 22 23 24 25 26 27 28 29 30

facial meaning is, of course, only 4. The possible scores for Step 2 range from 0 to 100. The average score was 72.4, with a standard deviation of 11.0. The same principle is used to compute your score for Step 3 of the FMST (see Table 2.5). For example, an individual who identified photographs 28, 1, and 20, respectively, as rage, hate, and annoyance is given 15 points. For Step 3, the possible range of scores is 0 to 101, the average score is 80.0, and the standard deviation is 9.8.

Compute your decoding scores for each step of the FMST and compare your decoding performance with the *decoding norms* of the sample of decoders. For Step 1, scores of 100–91 constitute good decoding, scores from 90–71 are average, and 70 and below are poor performance. For Step 2, good, average, and poor decoding is determined by the following range of scores: 100–83, 82–61, and 60 or below. For Step 3, 100–90 is good, 98–70 is average, and 60 and below is poor.

So far, you have tested your ability to decode meaning communicated by facial expression. Now you should test your encoding ability. The procedure is simple. Assemble a group of people you know and give them the answer forms for the FMST. Do not give them the Loren Lewis photographs, however. You will assume Loren's role and attempt to communicate each of the forty facial meanings in the FMST to the assembled group via your own facial expressions. Using the weighted scoring system just identified, compute the scores for the decoders for each step of the FMST, to see how much skill you exhibited as an encoder.

If your decoding scores for the FMST were average or low, you may want to consider the development of your decoding skills through exposure to a training program. In the following section some of the basic components of such a training program are identified.

Developing Sensitivity to Facial Expressions: Training Program

There can be little doubt that the ability to decode accurately the facial expressions of interactants in a variety of real-world situations is a vitally important communicative competency. *Such a competency, when fully developed, not only provides the interpreter of facial messages with a reliable means of detecting facial deceit but also provides a sound basis for identifying the emotions, moods, and feelings actually being experienced by the interactants.* That such information may be used to help achieve individual and/or organizational goals in given situations seems clear.

In particular, the training programs that are developed should be designed for the express purpose of developing skill in decoding facial expressions. A detailed description of such a training program is the subject of another book. However, the following are some of the essential features and components of the training programs I have used for business groups.

One of the most useful training tools is videotape. Wherever possible, the facial expressions of interactants in communication situations should

TABLE 2.5. Weighted Scores for Step 3 of FMST

Individual Facial Expressions Identified By Number of Photographs

Anger	1	20	28
Rage			5
Hate	5		
Annoyance		5	

Happiness	2	9	26
Laughter			5
Love		5	
Amusement	5		

Bewilderment	4	17	18
Confusion			5
Doubt	5		
Stupidity		5	

Fear	10	21	27
Terror	4		
Anxiety		4	
Apprehension			4

Interest	6	15	23
Attention	4		
Anticipation		4	
Excitement			4

Sadness	5	7	14
Disappointment			3
Distress	3		
Pensiveness		3	

Contempt	13	24	29
Disdain	2		
Arrogance		2	
Superiority			2

Disgust	8	12	30
Aversion			2
Repugnance	2		
Distaste		2	

Determination	11	22	25
Stubborn			2
Resolute	2		
Belligerent		2	

Surprise	3	16	19
Amazement			1
Flabbergasted	1		
Astonishment	*1		

be videotaped and subjected to subsequent analysis. With the aid of the trainer, the interactants should study these videotaped facial expressions in order to identify the use of display rules and the use of techniques of facial management; to identify inconsistency in meaning between facial expression and words; and to identify the subtle nuances of emotional meaning that are being communicated by facial expression.

In addition to the use of videotape, a training program should feature the use of *muscle-profile charts* and *facial blueprints.* We now know which facial muscles are used to communicate such emotions as contempt and disgust, although this is a difficult distinction to make. The individual who is fully familiar with the various facial muscles used to communicate facial disgust and contempt is not likely to make a decoding error when he or she observes such facial expressions.

Finally, sets of facial blueprints should be used, in combination with model photographs of specialized kinds of facial emotion. The facial blueprints developed by Ekman and Friesen (1975) are particularly useful because they break down the face into three areas. The trainee would learn that different emotions are more easily recognized by concentrating on certain areas of the face. For example, in facial sadness, the inner corners of the eyeborws are raised, the inner corners of the upper eyelids are drawn up, and the corners of the lips are drawn down.

In short, measuring and developing the ability to use facial expressions as a reliable source of emotional information should be a central concern to any individual who wishes to be a socially sensitive communicator. One hopes that this concern would be reflected in widespread efforts to use the full communicative potential of the human face.

The Functions of Eye Behaviors

The eyes have been the object of fascination for centuries. In fact, the adjectives we use to describe the eyes suggest that we believe that human eyes serve an almost endless number of communicative functions and provide many different kinds of information. Have you ever encountered an individual whose eyes were hard, beady, sly, shifty, radiant, shining, dull, and/or sparkling? If so, you will probably admit that such eyes not only affected your perception of the person and your desire to interact with that person, but also affected your own behavior.

There can be little doubt that people have well-developed stereotypic beliefs about the functions of the eyes. The Evil Eye is perhaps the best example, because people have believed in the Evil Eye since at least the seventh century B.C. Argyle and Cook (1976) write that belief in the Evil Eye

> is still held in Morocco, and to a lesser extent in remote country areas of European countries. The belief was connected with the idea that vision was due to rays emanating from the eye, together with the belief that most deaths and

accidents are caused by witches; it was supposed that a witch looking in a mirror would actually leave a thin poisonous film on it. If a person possessed the evil eye, it was believed that he placed a curse on anyone he looked at. (p. 30)

A well-developed eye-behavior stereotype continues to exist today. This stereotype suggests that honest and trustworthy individuals exhibit one type of eye behavior and devious and untrustworthy individuals exhibit another type of eye behavior. In the last several years, a colleague and I (Leathers & Hocking, 1982) have done in-depth examinations of police interviewers' beliefs as to which nonverbal cues are the most useful indicators of the deception of a lying criminal suspect. The police interviewers are convinced that eye behaviors are the most reliable indicators of deception. In fact, one police interviewer for the Georgia Bureau of Investigation told me that he had never observed a lying criminal suspect whose pupils did not dilate at the time of deception.

Clearly, people believe that the eyes serve vitally important communicative functions, but the sceptical reader may wonder whether such beliefs have a factual basis. To begin with, we can say that the eyes are important because they are the primary center of visual attention. Research by Janik, Wellens, Goldberg, and DeLosse (1978) established that more visual inspection time is spent looking in the region of the eyes than at any other part of the body. Attention is focused on the eyes 43.4 percent of the time; the second most important area of visual attention is the mouth, where attention is focused 12.6 percent of the time.

Because people do concentrate their attention on the eye region, it seems reasonable to ask: Why do the eyes receive so much attention? The answer seems to be that people attend to the eyes because the eyes do indeed serve a variety of important communicative functions. The eyes: (a) *indicate degrees of attentiveness, interest, and arousal;* (b) *influence attitude change and persuasion;* (c) *regulate interaction;* (d) *communicate emotions;* (e) *define power and status relationships;* and (f) *assume a central role in impression management.*

The Attention Function

Eyes play an important role in the initiation of interpersonal communication because they signal a readiness to communicate. Argyle and Cook (1976) emphasize that mutual gaze "has the special meaning that two people are attending to each other. This is usually necessary for social interaction to begin or be sustained" (p. 170). Eye behaviors do not only signal whether two people are attending to each other, they reflect the *degree of mutual interest.*

Length, direction, and kind of gaze, as well as pupil size, serve as accurate indicators of an individual's level of interest and/or arousal. In fact Hess (1975) discovered, in his fascinating research on pupil size, that the *size of the pupil is a reliable measure of an individual's interest level.* Our pupils enlarge when we find a stimulus to be interesting, and they contract when we fnd it less interesting. And pupil size increases as we become emotionally aroused.

The Persuasive Function

Eye behavior can also serve an important function in the modification of attitudes that are changed by persuasive communication (Harper, Wiens, & Matarazzo, 1978). The persuader who wishes to be perceived as credible must sustain eye contact while speaking and being spoken to by the persuadee. To avoid a marked decline in their credibility, persuasive communicators must not be shifty-eyed, look down or away from the persuadee frequently, blink excessively, or exhibit eye-flutter.

There can be little doubt that eye behaviors are important determinants of credibility. Burgoon and Saine (1978) provide convincing documentation for their claim that direct eye contact in our society is interpreted as a sign of credibility. Direct eye contact is apt to have a beneficial impact on the communicator's perceived competence and trustworthiness. We generally assume that individuals who look directly at us know what they are talking about, and are being honest with us. Conversely, when people avert their eyes before speaking to us or before answering a question, we are likely to make inferences that will limit their ability to be effective persuaders. The averted eyes may be interpreted as an effort to keep something from us, in which case we find them less trustworthy; or we may infer that the individual is having difficulty formulating a coherent message, in which case we find the individual less credible in terms of competence.

The Regulatory Function

Although the eyes can play a central role in persuasive communication, their regulatory function is especially important. In particular, eye behaviors serve the regulatory function by alerting the decoder that encoding is occurring and continuing, by signaling the encoder whether listening and decoding are occurring, and by indicating when the listener is to speak (Ellsworth & Ludwig, 1971).

Kendon (1967) helped illuminate the regulatory functions of eye behaviors through the extensive film recording of two-person conversations. The person attempting to communicate a message was identified as p, and the person to whom the message was directed was identified as q. The time p spent looking at q varied from 28 to 70 percent, depending on the individuals who were communicating. When p began addressing q, 70 percent of the time p began by looking away from q. Usually, p looked away from q when p began talking; p typically looked at q when p finished talking. In short, individuals usually look away from you when they begin to talk, and while they are talking; and they are apt to look at you and pause if they wish you to respond.

The Affective Function

As we have already indicated, the eyes combine with the face to function as a powerful medium of emotional communication. As Schlenker puts it so graphically (1980), "The eyes universally symbolize affect. The look in another's eyes can signal the start of a romance or the end of one. As the poet's mirror to the soul, the eyes express and intensify the affect present in a relationship" (p. 258). In short, the eyes can be used not only to monitor the state of an interpersonal relationship but to exert a measurable impact on the emotional component of the relationship. This is particularly true when the initiation, development, and termination of intimate relationships is concerned.

When one individual wishes to determine whether a person is experiencing a *positive* or *negative emotion*, and to determine the *intensity* of the *felt emotion*, the pupils of the eyes take on added importance. Pupils enlarge when individuals experience positive emotions such as happiness or joy, and contract when negative emotions, such as sadness or sorrow, are being experienced (Hess, 1975).

In short, the eyes can accurately reflect whether a person is experiencing a positive or negative emotion, and can reveal the *intensity* of the emotion. Thus, the individual who wishes to make an accurate judgment about the moods and emotions of another individual should rely on the information revealed in both the face and eyes. *We display the kind of emotion we are experiencing in our face, and the intensity of the emotion in our eyes.*

The Power Function

Eye behaviors also function as an effective and reliable index of the amount of power and status one individual possesses vis-à-vis another individual. People perceived as powerful usually *look* powerful. The license to stare at others for the purpose of domination is the exclusive prerogative of powerful people. In contrast, the averted and downward glance is universally recognized as a sign of weakness and submission. Individuals who are presumed to be afraid to look at others are judged to have minimal leadership capacity and are usually relegated to the perceptual category of low status.

Power, status, and personal dominance are all related to visual dominance behavior (Henley, 1977). A fascinating study of the eye behaviors of ROTC cadet officers (Exline, Ellyson, & Long, 1975) illuminated the nature of this relationship. The study confirmed not only that low-power cadets were much more visually attentive than high-power cadets, but that the low-power cadets who were most visually attentive were given the lowest leadership ratings by their commanding officers.

The Impression Management Function

We now know that eye behaviors frequently assume a central role in the formation of impressions and in impression management. Communicators who wish to exercise conscious control over their communicative behaviors, in order to project a winning image, would be well advised to begin by monitoring their eye behavior. Consider the people you know, those whom you feel lack self-esteem, assertiveness, and an ability to communicate in a straightforward manner. To what extent do their eye behaviors contribute to the negative image they project?

Public figures, such as General George Patton and Richard Nixon, have been very concerned about the impact of their eye behaviors on their public image. Although Patton was notably successful, and Nixon notably unsuccessful, in trying to cultivate the "look" of the powerful leader, both men recognized that impression management begins with the eyes.

Using the Communicative Potential of Eye Behaviors

Communicators should be aware of the potential value of eye behaviors as an aid in attaining rather specific communicative objectives. Successful communication requires a maximum amount of information about the perceptions of others, about their feelings, and their expectations. We must recognize that eye behaviors have the potential to provide us with precisely these kinds of information.

Message senders should be sensitive to the fact *that much of the information communicated by their own eyes operates out of their own level of awareness.* Because of this fact, our eyes may reveal much highly personal *information about us, that we would not choose to reveal if we could consciously control all of our eye behaviors.* Our eyes may show that we are uninterested in the message of a superior, while other consciously controlled nonverbal cues are calculated to suggest interest. Our eyes may reveal that our level of self-esteem and self-confidence is dissipating rapidly, even though we exude confidence through our verbal communication. Our eyes may reflect an attitude of indifference to an intimate while we are whispering words of love in the intimate's ear.

To avoid the constant transmission of inconsistent and/or unintended meaning via our eyes, we may wish to consciously control those eye behaviors that will help us project a winning image. Such an effort is called *impression management.* For example, we may eliminate the downcast and shifty eye movements that are associated with ineffective persuasion. We may carefully monitor the eye behaviors of those with whom we communicate, in order to be sensitive to their turn-signaling prerogatives. We may seek to enhance our perceived power, status, and leadership potential by avoiding sustained visual attentiveness to individuals who compete with us for leadership. We recognize the paradox of sustained visual attention: the prize for sustained visual attention is often unflattering characterization as a low-power and low-status individual.

Message receivers should exhibit some of the same information-seeking concerns as message senders but, in addition, they must be concerned with the role of their own eye behaviors in providing visual feedback to the message sender. They should recognize that the eyes may reveal more about their affective reaction to the message sender than to the message. If perception is, literally and figuratively, in the eye of the beholder, individuals should recognize that their perceptual responses may be most accurately reflected in their own eyes. Their eyes may not mirror their soul, but they will probably mirror the depths and intensity of their innermost feelings.

Summary

To enhance their potential to communicate successfully, individuals should fully develop their ability to differentiate among the subtle kinds of emotional meaning that are communicated by facial expressions. This is so because the human face is now recognized as the most important source of emotional information.

The two major approaches used to explain how the face functions communicatively are the *categoric* and the *dimensional* perspectives. Researchers who embrace the categoric perspective believe that the face functions *denotatively*. Results from categoric research have established that the face is capable of communicating at least eight basic classes of meaning: happiness, surprise, fear, anger, sadness, disgust, contempt, and interest. By concentrating on the facial muscles used in different areas of the face, decoders can increase their ability to differentiate accurately among these eight general classes of facial meaning.

The dimensional perspective is based on the assumption that facial expressions are *connotative*, and that they are best described by the dimensions of meaning that define them. Most dimensional researchers have found that facial expressions vary with regard to how pleasant and interested the communicator seems to be, and there is some evidence to suggest that facial expressions reflect the communicator's degree of understanding. Recent research also suggests that emotions are displayed more intensely on the left as opposed to the right side of the face.

Although facial expressions are often an accurate reflection of the communicator's feelings, they may also be used to deceive. Genuine facial expressions are identified as *representational*, and deceptive facial expressions are known as *presentational*. In putting on a false face, communicators may use the techniques of qualifying, modulating, or falsifying.

Previous attempts to measure an individual's ability to decode meanings from facial expressions lacked specificity and precision. Most decoding tests lack precision because they do not require that decoders make the difficult discriminations between facial expressions that are closely related in meaning. The Facial Meaning Sensitivity Test can be used by decoders to measure their ability to make such difficult discriminations and compare their decoding accuracy against a set of decoding norms that have been developed for the FMST. If readers find their decoding skill to be deficient, they may wish to consider use of a training program designed to develop this important communicative skill.

The eyes have been a source of fascination for many centuries. Throughout the ages many cultures have retained a belief in the insidious power(s) of the Evil Eye. Even in the age in which we live, stereotypical beliefs about the human eyes remain strong and well developed. These stereotypical beliefs have supported the development of eye behavior profiles which some individuals use to separate the straightforward, honest individual from the devious, lying individual. Central to the eye behavior stereotype is the notion that eye behaviors are reliable indicators of deception.

Because the eyes are the center of visual attention for the decoder, their importance as a source of information is enhanced. Empirical research has established that eye behaviors serve six communicative functions: the eyes (a) indicate degrees of attentiveness, interest, and arousal; (b) influence attitude change and persuasion; (c) regulate interaction; (d) communicate emotions; (e) define power and status relationships; and (f) assume a central role in impression management.

References

Abelson, R. P., & Sermat, V. (1962). Multidimensional scaling of facial expressions. *Journal of Experimental Psychology, 63,* 546–554.

Argyle, M., & Cook, M. (1967). *Gaze and mutual gaze.* Cambridge, MA: Cambridge University Press.

Burgoon, J. K., & Saine, T. (1978). *The unspoken dialogue: An introduction to nonverbal communication.* Boston: Houghton.

Ekman, P., & Friesen, W. V. (1975). *Unmasking the face: A guide to recognizing emotions from facial expressions.* Englewood Cliffs, NJ: Prentice-Hall.

Ekman, P., & Friesen, W. V. (1978). *Manual for the facial action coding system.* Palo Alto, CA: Consulting Psychologists Press.

Ekman, P., Friesen, W. V., & Ancoli, S. (1980). Facial signs of emotional experience. *Journal of Personality and Social Psychology, 39,* 1125–1134.

Ekman, P., Friesen, W. V., & Ellsworth, P. (1972). *Emotion in the human face: Guidelines for research and an integration of findings.* New York: Pergamon.

Ekman, P., Friesen, W. V., & Tomkins, S. S. (1971). Facial affect scoring technique: A first validity study. *Semiotica, 3,* 37–58.

Ellsworth, P. C., & Ludwig, L. M. (1971). Visual behavior in social interaction. *Journal of Communication, 22,* 375–403.

Engen, T., Levy, N., & Schlosberg, H. (1957). A new series of facial expressions. *American Psychologist, 12,* 264–266.

Exline, R. V., Ellyson, S. L., & Long, B. (1975). Visual behavior as an aspect of power role relationships. In P. Pliner, L. Krames, & T. Alloway (Eds.), *Nonverbal communication of aggression.*

Frijda, N. H., & Philipszoon, E. (1963). Dimensions of recognition of expression. *Journal of Abnormal and Social Psychology, 66,* 46.

Frijda, N. H. (1969). Recognition of emotions. In L. Berkowitz (Ed.), *Advances in experimental and social psychology.* New York: Academic.

Frois-Wittmann, J. (1930). The judgment of facial expression. *Journal of Experimental Psychology, 13,* 113–151.

Harper, R. G., Wiens, A. N., & Matarazzo, J. D. (1978). *Nonverbal communication: The state of the art.* New York: Wiley.

Harrison, R. P. (1967). Picture analysis: Toward a vocabulary and syntax for the pictorial code: With research on facial communication. Unpublished paper.

Henley, N. M. (1977). *Body politics: Power, sex, and nonverbal communication.* Englewood Cliffs, NJ: Prentice-Hall.

Hess, E. H. (1975). *The tell-tale eye: How your eyes reveal hidden thoughts and emotions.* New York: Van Nostrand Reinhold.

Izard, C. E. (1971). *The face of emotion.* New York: Appleton.

Janik, S. W., Wellens, A. R., Goldberg, M. L., & DeLosse, L. F. (1978). Eyes as the center of focus in the visual examination of faces. *Perceptual and motor skills, 47,* 857–858.

Kendon, A. (1967). Some functions of gaze direction in social interaction. *Acta Psychologica, 26,* 34–35.

Knapp, M. L. (1978). *Nonverbal communication in human interaction*, 2nd ed. New York: Holt.

Leathers, D. G., & Emigh, T. H. (1980). Decoding facial expressions: A new test with decoding norms. *Quarterly Journal of Speech, 66*, 418–436.

Leathers, D. G., & Hocking, J. E. (1982, November). An examination of police interviewer's beliefs about the utility and nature of nonverbal indicators of deception. Paper presented at convention of the Speech Communication Association, Louisville, KY.

LaFrance, M., & Mayo, C. (1978). *Moving bodies: Nonverbal communication in social relationships*. Monterey, CA: Brooks/Cole.

Levy, L. H., Orr, T. B., & Rosenzweig, S. (1960). Judgments of emotion from facial expression by college students, mental retardates, and mental hospital patients. *Journal of Personality, 28*, 341–349.

Mehrabian, A. (1970). A semantic space for nonverbal behavior. *Journal of Consulting and Clinical Psychology, 35*, 248–249.

Osgood, C. E. (1966). Dimensionality of the semantic space for communication via facial expressions. *Scandinavian Journal of Psychology, 7*, 1–30.

Sackeim, H. A., Gur, R. C., & Saucy, M. C. (1978). Emotions are expressed more intensely on the left side of the face. *Science, 202*, 434–436.

Schlenker, B. R. (1980). *Impression management*. Monterey, CA: Brooks/Cole.

Schlosberg, H. (1954). Three dimensions of emotion. *Psychology Review, 61*, 81–88.

Tomkins, S. S. (1962). *Affect, imagery, consciousness, I*. New York: Springer.

Williams, F., & Tolch, J. (1965). Communication by facial expression. *Journal of Communication, 15*, 20.

Woodworth, R. S. (1938). *Experimental psychology*. New York: Holt.

CHAPTER THREE

Bodily Communication

Movement communicates meaning. Human beings have accepted this fact, through the ages. Although they have accepted the general proposition, they have rarely examined its implications in detail. If movement communicates meaning, it follows that different movements serve different kinds of communicative functions by communicating different kinds of meanings. Some of the meanings communicated by bodily cues help us attain specific communicative objectives, and other movements communicate highly dysfunctional meanings.

Certain bodily movements create lasting impressions. Think of the number of friends or acquaintances you remember because of the way they move or use movement to communicate. My own memories are filled with individuals who moved in distinctive ways. Two stand out in particular: Old swivel-hips Becker, the local elevator man, is probably still shuffling down the streets of my hometown, and moving with the awkward but fluid grace which suggested that his hip-joints had not been greased recently. One college professor stands out because his incredibly deliberate gestures drew attention to pauses of remarkable length in his speech. The students were convinced by the gestures and pauses that he was terribly profound.

We know that bodily movements assume important roles in successful interpersonal communication. Nonetheless most research efforts have been designed to identify bodily movements that are normative rather than specifying which kinds of bodily cues can be used to attain specific communicative objectives. *This chapter deviates from conventional practice. We shall specify not only how various bodily cues are typically used, but how they should be used.* In the past, little effort has been devoted to sensitizing individuals to the functional and dysfunctional uses of bodily cues.

The contrast between nonverbal communication and written communication is striking. Students in writing classes spend many hours trying to improve their ability to transmit their meanings clearly. Similarly, law students spend hours trying to determine the exact meaning of laws or court decisions on pornography, integration, or pollution. Their aim is to increase their capacity to encode and decode written messages.

This example should help make the point. We have studied communication by oral and written discourse intensively, and we assume that we will improve these communication skills by practice. In contrast, comparable energy has not been expended to contrast the functional and dysfunctional uses of bodily cues, or to develop our sensitivity to bodily cues. Consequently, this chapter focuses on useful perspectives for conceptualizing different kinds of bodily cues, on functional and dysfunctional uses of bodily cues, and on concrete means to increase skill in encoding and decoding them.

The need to know more about the meanings of bodily movements has resulted in a body of research called *kinesics.* Kinesics is the study of observable, isolable, and meaningful movement in interpersonal communications. Birdwhistell (1970) writes that "kinesics is concerned with abstracting from the continuous muscular shifts which are characteristic of living physiological systems those groupings of movements which are of significance to the communication process and thus to the interactional systems of particular social groups" (p. 192).

Kinesic research begins with the *kine,* the smallest identifiable unit of motion, and emphasizes the *kinemorph,* that combination of kines in any part of the body which convey a given meaning. Thus, "droopy-lidded" eyelids combined with "bilaterally raised median" brows have an evident differential meaning from "droopy-lidded" combined with a "Low unilateral brow lift," (Birdwhistell, 1960). The combination of very specific movement of the eyelids and brow into one larger unit, the kinemorph, conveys a meaning that is consistently recognized in our culture.

Movements that convey meaning are hardly limited to the brows. Many parts of the body convey meanings singly and in combination. In the strictest anatomical sense, the sources of movement in the human body are almost unlimited. From a more practical perspective, Birdwhistell (1952) identifies eight sources of potentially significant bodily movement: (a) total head; (b) face; (c) neck; (d) trunk; (e) shoulder-arm-wrist; (f) hand; (g) hip-joint-leg-ankle; and (h) foot. As we shall see, some areas have greater functional significance than others. Hand movements are more important than foot movements, for example, in part because of their visibility. At the same time, we should recognize that hand movements may be a less reliable source of information than foot movements because they are more frequently subject to conscious control, for purposes of deception.

In our society, the communicative significance of the hands is not confined to the ways we use them. "Handedness" is also very important because assumptions commonly made about right-handers and left-handers are quite different. This is a subject of more than passing interest to me because my six-year-old son Gregory eats, writes, and bats left-handed but throws, kicks balls, and fishes right-handed. Is he right-handed or left-handed?

Lee and Charlton (1980) have developed an instructive but amusing test to determine what type of handedness is dominant for a given individual. Among the tasks they use to determine handedness are the following: (a) draw the profile of a dog or a horse; (b) imagine that you are locked in a room, tied to a chair and with your hands tied behind you—which foot will you use to try to pull the phone closer?; (c) on which side do you chew your food?; and (d) when you applaud a performer, which hand is on top?

Left-handers will draw the profile of a dog or a horse with the head facing to the right; left-handers will reach out for the phone with their left foot; they will chew on the left side of their mouth; left-handers will clap with their dominant left hand on top, into the palm of their right hand. Everything is reversed, for right-handers.

If the handedness test established that your left hand is the dominant one, you will have to cope with the unfortunate connotations of the "left-hander stereotype." We know, of course, the left-handed baseball pitchers have been characterized as wild, spaced-out flakes. Indeed, one former major league pitcher, who is left-handed, is known as "the space man." The left-hander stereotype may be more than a bad joke, however. Lee and Charlton (1980) note that at least some serious students of handedness maintain that a disproportionate number of left-handers have been alcoholics, bed-wetters, poor achievers, slow learners, or chronic misfits.

The Nature of Bodily Cues

Much like facial expressions, bodily cues have been conceptualized as both denotative and connotative in nature. The denotative perspective is based on the assumption that bodily cues are best understood by classifying them with regard to: (a) the *level of awareness* and *intentionality* with which they are used; (b) the type of *coding* employed; and (c) the *communicative function* served. By contrast, the connotative perspective is based on the assumption that bodily cues are best described by rating them on scales that represent the dimensions of meaning communicated by the bodily cues. The theory and research of Paul Ekman and associates best illustrate the denotative approach, and the connotative approach is most closely associated with the works of Albert Mehrabian.

Communicative Functions of Bodily Cues

Ekman and Friesen (1969) have developed what is probably the most frequently cited conceptual framework for classifying bodily cues and the meaning they communicate. They emphasize that bodily cues vary not only with regard to their *usage* and the *code* employed but with regard to the *functions* they serve.

The way a bodily cue is used is important because it involves two questions of particular importance: (a) Was the communicator aware of exhibiting a specific kind of bodily cue? and (b) Was the bodily cue used with conscious intent to communicate a particular kind of information? Communicators who are aware that they are exhibiting certain bodily cues have the capacity to exert conscious control over those types of cues.

This capacity is a necessary, but not a sufficient, condition for individuals who wish to be successful as impression managers. For example, the individual who does not wish to be perceived as deceiving and untrustworthy must take pains to eliminate or minimize the shifty eye behaviors, hand-to-face gestures, and nonfluences that are part of the cultural stereotype for the deceiver. Determining whether bodily cues of the sender are used without awareness and intentionality is extremely important for message receivers. This is so because bodily cues of this type are apt to reveal much about the sender's attitudes, feelings, and level of self-esteem that he or she may not wish to reveal.

The coding of bodily cues is also extremely important because the type of code used determines the relationships between the bodily cue and that which it signifies (Ekman & Friesen, 1969). Nonverbal messages in the form of bodily cues may use *arbitrary, iconic,* or *intrinsic* codes. Although arbitrary coding is much more frequently used in verbal than in nonverbal communication, some bodily messages use an arbitrary code. The hand raised in greetings and departures is an example of arbitrary coding because the raised hand is not directly related to that which it signifies.

Bodily cues that are iconically coded carry some clue to their meaning because of their appearance. A person running a finger under his or her throat is using iconic coding, because the figurative and literal act of throat cutting bear a resemblance to each other. Finally, acts that are intrinsically coded are visually related to that which they signify. Angry individuals who tremble, turn red in the face, and shake their fist use intrinsic coding because the symbolic meaning and physical manifestations of anger are inseparable.

Individuals who wish to refine their skill in decoding bodily cues must be sensitive to the type of code employed. Certain kinds of bodily cues frequently combine more than one type of coding. For example, confident individuals who are receptive to the ideas of those with whom they communicate frequently exhibit "open" gestures and postures, by way of uncrossed arms and legs. Such bodily cues combine elements of both arbitrary and iconic coding, which makes it easier to determine their meaning. Even those bodily cues that are coded exclusively via the arbitrary code are susceptible to accurate decoding when a *set* of bodily cues (such as downcast eyes, hand-to-face gestures) and an indirect bodily orientation is consistently associated with an inferred psychological state, such as a decreasing level of self-confidence.

Bodily cues are perhaps most clearly defined and differentiated by the functions they serve. The five categories of nonverbal behavior identified by Ekman and Friesen (1969) are particularly useful in describing the different kinds of bodily cues that provide different kinds of information and communicate different kinds of meanings: *emblems, illustrators, affect displays, regulators,* and *adaptors.*

Emblems.   Emblems are bodily cues that have a direct verbal translation consisting of a word or two, and that have a precise meaning which is known by most of the members of a given culture. They are used with the conscious intention of communicating a particular message; the receiver recognizes that the message was deliberately encoded; and the message sender takes direct responsibility for the message (Ekman & Friesen, 1972).

Most middle-class Americans have command of about a hundred gestural emblems. Gestural emblems are used to communicate interpersonal directions or commands: ("Come here"); information about one's own physical state ("I've got a toothache"); insults ("Shame on you"); replies ("OK"); and greetings and departures ("Good-bye" and "Hello"), among other things (Johnson, Ekman, & Friesen, 1975).

Emblems are used most frequently where speech communication is not possible because of noise or distance barriers encountered by individuals. Because of this, emblems serve as a substitute for words. Emblems by their very nature are the most easily understood class of nonverbal cues. *Perhaps because emblems are used so much more intentionally than other nonverbal behaviors, they are apt to provide little personal information about the person who uses them.*

As we shall see when we discuss the cross-cultural aspects of nonverbal communication, many emblems carry culture-specific meaning. For example, the "chin flick" is a gestural emblem used in Italy, France, and other parts of Europe to indicate annoyance and a desire for the offending person to "bug off," but it has no generally recognized meaning in England and America (Lee & Charlton, 1980).

Illustrators.   Illustrators are like emblems in that they are used with awareness and intentionality. Illustrator gestures may be used to augment what is being said and to reinforce the perceived strength of emotion being experienced by the communicator. Illustrators include *batons, diectic movements, rhythmic movements,* and *pictographs.* Batons are movements that accent or emphasize a particular word or phrase, and diectic movements involve pointing to an object, place, or event. Rhythmic movements suggest the rhythm of an event being described, and pictographs draw a picture in the air of the shape of the referent.

Illustrators are typically used with the intent of increasing the clarity of verbal expression. The desire for clarity seems to be greatest in face-to-face interaction. Thus, Cohen (1977) found that subjects giving directions on how to get from one place to another used significantly more hand illustrators in a face-to-face situation than when giving directions over an intercom.

Although illustrators are used with a fairly high level of awareness and intentionality, they can provide valuable information about a communicator's mood, self-confidence, and power in a given situation. They also accurately reflect the difficulty the communicator is experiencing in communicating clearly by verbal means. Ekman and Friesen (1972) write that

> *Changes in the frequency of illustrator activity in any given individual depend upon mood and problems in verbal communication. When a person is demoralized, discouraged, tired, unenthusiastic, concerned about the other person's impression, or in a nondominant position in a formal interaction and setting, the rate of illustrators is less than is usual for that person. . . . When difficulty is experienced in finding the right words, or when feedback from the listeners suggests he is not comprehending what is being said, illustrators increase. (p. 359)*

Clearly, general illustrators serve useful communicative functions. Their chief function is probably to aid the listener in the comprehension of the spoken word. Rogers (1978) found that gestural illustrators can result in a significant increase in comprehension of the spoken word, even in the absence of facial cues. Gestural illustrators are increasingly useful as noise is introduced, and their value as aids to comprehending the meaning of the spoken word increases as the ideational content of the spoken message becomes more complex.

Affect Displays. The communication of affect displays or emotions is much more closely linked with facial expressions than with bodily cues. As we have already indicated, the face is the primary site for the display of emotions. The communication receiver would be well advised, therefore, to *look to the face to determine the kind of emotion the communicator is experiencing, and to rely on bodily cues to determine the intensity of the emotion being experienced.*

Affect displays are used with less awareness and intentionality than either emblems or illustrators. As a result, they are apt to provide some personal information about the communicator that the individual would be reluctant to disclose voluntarily. Anyone who observed John Dean testifying during the Watergate Hearings will agree that a relative absence of bodily movement and facial expressions makes it very difficult to determine what emotions the communicator is experiencing.

Regulators. Regulators are bodily cues used by interactants to exercise a mutual influence over the initiation, length, and termination of spoken messages. Regulators usually seem to be used with a low level of awareness and intentionality. But it is vitally important that interactants be sensitive to each other's turn-taking prerogatives. A lack of sensitivity in the use of regulators is likely to be attributed to rudeness or unmannerliness (Ekman & Friesen, 1969).

Knapp (1978) has developed a particularly useful classification of turn-taking behaviors. He notes that speakers use *turn-yielding* and *turn-main-*

taining cues and listeners use *turn-requesting* and *turn-denying* cues. Examples of turn-yielding cues are the cessation of illustrator gestures and a relaxed bodily posture. Turn-maintaining cues are manifested when we sustain our illustrator activity or touch the other person to indicate we wish to continue. For the listener, an upraised index finger and rapid head nodding represent particularly effective turn-requesting cues. Finally, when we do not wish to make a comment, we may use such turn-denying cues as a relaxed listening pose, or we may stare at something in the surrounding environment.

Regulators assume more importance when we greet other individuals and bid them farewell. This is so because greetings and farewells are such important determinants of successful interpersonal relationships. The individual who is successful in initiating and developing interpersonal interaction with others must rely heavily on the proper use of nonverbal cues.

A study by Krivonos and Knapp (1975) suggests that acknowledging the other person's presence with a *head gesture*, indicating a desire to initiate communication with *mutual glances*, and suggesting with a *smile* that you anticipate a pleasurable experience are the most important nonverbal cues used in successful greetings. In contrast, *eye-brow flashes*, sweeping hand gestures, in the form of *a salute*; an *open mouth*; and *winking* are nonverbal behaviors which should be avoided. These nonverbal cues are not used in the successful greeting; they deviate markedly from what has been found to be normative behavior in this kind of communicative situation.

An insightful study by Knapp, Hart, and Friedrich (1973) established leave-taking norms which formed the basis for identifying nonverbal behaviors that were both "proper" and "improper" for guiding, controlling, or regulating departures in communication situations that were rather task oriented. The study suggested that : (a) *breaking eye contract*; (b) *left-positioning* (pointing one's legs and/or feet away from the person with whom you are communicating, and toward the door); (c) *forward leaning*; and (d) *nodding behavior* all represent socially acceptable means of initiating the leave-taking that is a central part of farewells. In contrast, the fofllowing were found to be inappropriate nonverbal means of initiating a farewell: (a) *leveraging* (placing hands on knees or legs in such a manner as to suggest a desire to rise from one's chair); (b) *major truck movements* (postural shifts in one's chair, straightening up, and standing up); (c) *explosive hand contact* with some part of one's body; and (d) a *handshake*.

Reflection upon the nonverbal behaviors associated with successful, as opposed to unsuccessful, greetings and farewells suggests that subtlety and restraint in movement are particularly desirable. Sweeping hand gestures, winking, and gross postural shifts, for example, are such explicit and manipulative forms of behavior that they are apt to be associated with social insensitivity. To consistently use such nonverbal behaviors in greetings and farewells is to invite the inference that you are rude and tactless.

Adaptors. As a potential source of information about an individual's attitudes, level of anxiety, and self-confidence, bodily cues in the form of adaptors are apt to be more useful than emblems, illustrators, affect displays, or regulators. Communicators who exhibit adaptors do not use them with the intent to communicate, and they are usually aware that they are being exhibited. As a result, *adaptors are a potentially rich source of involuntary information about the psychological states of individuals who exhibit them.*

In their original form, adaptors were learned as adaptive actions that were used to satisfy bodily needs. The itch was scratched, the unruly hair was groomed, or the tears were wiped away from the eyes (Ekman & Friesen, 1969). Through socialization, the form of many adaptors has been changed, and they have become more important. Currently, their importance is based upon what they may reveal about communicators' psychological rather than physiological needs.

The two most important kinds of adaptors are *self-adaptors* and *object-adaptors.* Self-adaptors that involve hand-to-face movements are the easiest to decode, because of the symbolic significance of the face. For people in the Unitied States, the face symbolizes the self. As a result, hand-to-face gestures are apt to provide reliable information about a person's current level of self-esteem and self-confidence. Ekman and Friesen (1969) write that when "a person touches his face, the action can be conceived in terms of what the person has had done to him, what he wants done to him, or what he is doing to himself. Activities such as picking or scratching may be forms of attacking the self; holding may be giving nurture or support; rubbing or massaging may be caress or reassurance" (p. 87). When one covers the eyes with the hand, decoders will usually conclude that the communicator finds the content of the communication unpleasant and wishes to prevent further sensory input of the same sort.

Object-adaptors, as the term implies, refer to the use of the hands to touch or hold objects in one's immediate environment. One study (Sousa-Poza & Rohrberg, 1977) suggests that object-adaptors are used less frequently to reflect uncertainty on the part of the encoder than are self-adaptors. As we shall see in our treatment of the use of nonverbal cues to detect deception, however, police interviewers report that, at the moment of deception, lying criminal suspects frequently play with objects in the interview room.

Dimensions of Meaning

The denotative approach to bodily cues assumes that the meanings they communicate, and the information they convey, is best understood by classifying bodily cues as to usage, coding used, and functions served. In contrast, the connotative approach to bodily cues assumes that bodily cues can best be described by three independent dimensions of meaning, labeled by Mehrabian (1981) as *pleasure–displeasure, arousal–non-*

arousal, and *dominance–submissiveness*. Any bodily cue or nonverbal act can be measured by separate sets of scales, which reflect the degree of pleasure, arousal, and dominance that was communicated by the nonverbal cue. Thus, pleasure is measured by scales labeled with bipolar adjectives, such as pleasant–unpleasant and satisfied–unsatisfied. Similarly, scales used to measure degree of arousal and dominance, respectively, would be excited–calm and aroused–unaroused; and controlling–controlled and dominant–submissive. The attitudes, the emotional tone of nonverbal messages, and the preferences of the communicator are thought to be accurately reflected by ratings on scales representing each of these three independent dimensions of meaning.

In nonverbal or implicit communication, three metaphors are used to describe the distinct types of meaning represented by the dimensions of pleasure, arousal, and dominance: (a) *the approach metaphor;* (b) *the arousal-activity* metaphor; and (c) *the power metaphor*. Proponents of the connotative perspective believe that these metaphors suggest the full range of meanings that can be communicated by nonverbal means.

The approach metaphor is based on the generally accepted notion that people approach, and get more involved with, individuals they like, and that they avoid individuals they dislike. Thus, individuals translate their likes and dislikes, their positive and negative emotions, and their predispositions to respond in positive and negative ways directly through their nonverbal behaviors. This metaphor is represented by the pleasure dimension of meaning. Because there are a limited number of socially acceptable ways to express, verbally, strong feelings of pleasure and displeasure, nonverbal communication becomes the primary medium for the expression of this dimension of meaning.

The arousal–activity metaphor refers to those bodily cues that reflect an individual's level of attention and interest. As one's level of interest in another individual increases, the number and intensity of selected bodily cues also increase. In some cases, of course, an abnormal amount of bodily activity may imply that a person is experiencing an unacceptable level of anxiety. Anxiety cues, in turn, frequently serve as accurate indicators of an individual's current level of self-confidence, simply because they are difficult to consciously monitor and control. Not surprisingly, superiors can often be differentiated from subordinates on the basis of their more relaxed bodily gestures and postures (Henley, 1977).

Finally, the power metaphor has been associated with a set of nonverbal cues that communicate relative degrees of dominance and submissiveness. Dominance and power are associated with large size, height, open and relaxed body posture, and the prerogative to approach individuals with whom we communicate, among other things (Mehrabian, 1981).

The dominance–submissiveness dimension of nonverbal meaning is vitally important for individuals who wish to be perceived as leaders, or at least perceived as persons with substantial leadership potential. It was instructive to watch the first Ford-Carter debate on television, for example, because of Ford's carefully calculated efforts to gain dominance over Carter. A person who is unconcerned about shaping perceptions of dominance does not usually stand, as Ford did, with feet spread wide apart; and one does not use karate-type gestures, or fix one's debating opponent with an unremitting stare.

Gestures Versus Postures

In discussing the two perspectives used to describe nonverbal behaviors we have not differentiated between gestures and postures. There are a number of definitional benchmarks that can be used in differentiating between the two basic types of bodily cues. We may, of course, communicate with our entire body or only with some part of it. Thus, Lamb (1965) defines a gesture as an action confined to a part or parts of the body, and posture is an action involving a continuous adjustment of every part of the body, with consistency, in the process of variation.

The amount of bodily involvement in communication is not the only basis for distinguishing between gestures and posture, however. The amount of time used in communicating is also an important factor. Usually, an individual moves quickly from one gesture to another but maintains a given posture for a much longer period of time. The second or split second is the unit of time for gestures. In contrast, individuals often assume a given posture for a matter of several seconds and sometimes several minutes.

Scheflen's penetrating research on bodily communication (1964) helps clarify the relationship between gesture and posture. He maintains that the three basic units of bodily movement are the *point*, the *position*, and the *presentation*. The *point* is the nonverbal equivalent of an individual trying to make a point in discussion. While trying to make his point, "an American speaker uses a series of distinctive sentences in a conversation, he changes the position of his head and eyes every few sentences. He may turn his head right or left, tilt it, cock it to one side or the other, or flex or extend his neck so as to look toward the floor or ceiling" (p 321). Because one part of the body is usually involved for a short time, the *point* may be seen as a gesture.

In contrast, when several points or gestures are combined, we have the *position*. The position is marked by a gross postural shift involving at least half the body. A typical position is assumed by the discussant who leans toward the person on the opposite side of the conference table.

Finally, the *presentation* "consists of the totality of one person's positions in a given interaction. Presentations have a duration from several minutes to several hours, and the terminals are a complete change of location" (Scheflen, 1964, p. 323).

Rather than three units of bodily communication, Ekman and Friesen (1967) identify two—*body acts* and *body positions.* Body acts are readily observable movements with a definite beginning and end, which could occur in any part of the body or across multiple body parts simultaneously.

Body positions are identified by a lack of movement for a discernible period of time—two seconds or more—with any body part. Scheflen, and Ekman and Friesen define the position as a fixed configuration of the parts of the body, therefore the position might be properly identified as postural communication. Gestural communication is more properly associated with the *point* (Scheflen's term) and the *body act* (Ekman and Friesen's term), because both concepts involve movement of one or more parts of the body, with rapid changes to other movements.

Postures by definition represent a more limited medium of communication than gestures. Because they are more limited in number than gestures, they are probably most effectively used to communicate such general attitudes as one's desire to increase, limit, or avoid interaction with another individual; one's positive or negative reaction to someone; one's current level of self-confidence; and one's general presentation of one's self. In addition to their impact on perceptions of presumed status and power, the number and kinds of postures one assumes accurately reflect a person's degree of *responsiveness* to another person, as well as the strength of one's desire to establish *a closer or more immediate relationship* with another person.

The film *An Officer and a Gentleman* provides instructive examples of the communicative functions of postures. To watch drill sergeant Lou Gossett, Jr., is to realize that his "command presence" and "command look" were communicated forcefully by his postures. His words served merely to reinforce the emotional intensity of his commands, which were communicated by his postures.

Scheflen has provided a particularly satisfying answer to the most basic question that might be asked about postures. What meanings can be communciated by variation in posture, when communicators can choose freely from their postural repertoire? Scheflen (1964) maintains that there are three basic types of postures, which convey distinctive meanings. In the Type 1 postural orientation, an individual may communicate inclusiveness or noninclusiveness. When your body is placed in such a way as to exclude another person, you are clearly communicating your intent to limit or avoid interaction with that individual. In the Type 2 postural orientation, the individual may assume the vis-à-vis or parallel bodily orientation. The vis-à-vis orientation is associated with the exchange of rather intimate feelings, and the parallel bodily orientation conveys a desire to communicate with the entire group rather than with any individual in it. Finally, with the Type 3 postural orientation the individual may assume a congruent or incongruent posture. When you assume a posture similar to that of the person with whom you are communicating, you are probably suggesting that you agree with the individual and that the person is your equal in status. Hence, through postural orientation the individual may communicate involvement or withdrawal, feeling or unresponsiveness, and agreement or disagreement.

In the next section, we will identify both functional and dysfunctional kinds of gestures and postures. The difficulty of this task is highlighted by

Lee and Charlton's (1980) tongue-in-cheek guidelines that specify those kinds of nonverbal behaviors that should not be exhibited in public. Among other things, they warn against sticking a finger or a hand into an orifice—especially someone else's. They stress that one should not diddle, fiddle, or twiddle in public. Teeth-flossing, the pecking forefinger applied to someone's shoulder, playing a drum solo on your teeth, with a pencil, grooming your fingernails, or knuckle-cracking are also viewed as equally egregious types of nonverbal behavior that should not be displayed in public.

Functional and Dysfunctional Uses of Bodily Cues

Bodily cues can be used to communicate meanings and information that are both functional and dysfunctional from the perspective of the communicator. Such cues frequently play a central role in determining how confident, likable, assertive, and powerful an individual is perceived to be. Although it is difficult to generalize about bodily cues, certain types of cues generally have a much more positive impact than other cues on the perceptions, attitudes, and behaviors of those with whom we communicate. In this section, we hve identified bodily cues that have been found to be desirable in a variety of communicative situations, as well as those cues that are undesirable.

When considered from the perspective of the denotative approach to bodily communication, bodily cues that communicate a sense of *openness* and *confidence* have been found to be highly desirable. Communicating a sense of openness in interpersonal communication is very important. It signals the other person(s) that you are making a sincere effort to convey your feelings honestly. *Gestures of openness frequently trigger reciprocal gestures of openness in others* (Nierenberg & Calero, 1973). In one sense, gestures that communicate openness are the nonverbal equivalent of words that are self-disclosing. Both forms of communication have the effect of eliminating or diminishing behavior that is calculated to withhold or distort personal information.

Openness gestures stimulate interaction. Openness gestures seem to be a necessary condition in order for individuals to reach agreement. Thus, Nierenberg and Calero (1973) write that openness gestures are exhibited when "individuals unbutton their coats, uncross their legs, and move up toward the edge of the chair and closer to the desk or table that separates them from their opposer. This gesture-cluster is in most instances accompanied by verbal language that communicates a possible agreement, solution, or generally a positive expression of working together . . ." (p. 46).

Open hands, the unbuttoning of coats or loosening of ties, and the general relaxation of limb discipline often communicate openness. In contrast, crossed arms, crossed legs, and related gestures often communicate inaccessibility and defensiveness.

Confidence gestures are also important for the individual who wishes to be perceived as poised and in control of the communicative situation. Confidence gestures may be identified in two ways. First, a person who does not exhibit gestures that would tend to contradict a feeling of confidence is presumed to be confident. Hand-to-face gestures like covering the mouth, and nose-and head-scratching are strong signals that the communicator lacks confidence. Among the most representative of confidence gestures are: (a) steepling (the individual joins fingerprints on both hands to form a "church steeple"); (b) hands joined together at the back, with chin thrust upward; (c) feet on the table; and (d) leaning back, with both hands supporting the head (Nierenberg & Calero, 1973).

Openness and confidence gestures are generally desirable, but defensiveness and nervousness gestures are not. Defensiveness gestures take many forms but often they suggest a literal attempt to block out unpleasant ideas and/or individuals. If you have seen a baseball umpire retreat from an infuriated manager, you will recognize that crossed arms are a traditional gesture of defensiveness. Downcast eyes, indirect bodily orientation, and closed bodily postures are among the most notable of defensiveness gestures.

Finally, nervousness gestures take many forms but usually are exhibited unintentionally. Nervousness gestures are usually manifested in the form of adaptors which are associated with an increasing level of anxiety. Twiddling, fiddling, and fidgeting all suggest that a person is becoming more nervous. In fact, any extraneous movement that serves no instrumental purpose will probably be interpreted as a sign of nervousness. Tugging at clothing and ears, as well as playing with objects in the room (object adaptors) are among the many bodily movements that quite clearly suggest "I am nervous."

When considered from the connotative perspective, three types of nonverbal cues can be used to communicate varying *degrees* of pleasantness, arousal, and power: liking–disliking, assertiveness–nonassertiveness, and power–powerlessness cues. We will concentrate on those kinds of bodily cues that are associated with particularly strong manifestations of the distinctive types of meaning associated with pleasantness, arousal, and power. Other kinds of nonverbal cues associated with these dimensions of nonverbal meaning will be considered, as well.

Nonverbal Indicators of Liking Versus Disliking

Liking is not the only label used to identify those types of nonverbal cues that communicate pleasantness. *Attraction, immediacy, intimacy,* and *pleasantness* are all terms that have been used to describe clusters of nonverbal cues that communicate similar, but not precisely the same, kinds of information. To simplify matters, we have decided to use the inclusive terminology of liking–disliking cues.

Certainly, the desire to be liked is almost universal. To communicate your desire to be liked is not of course to assure that you will be. Nor is an expression of liking for another person certain to produce a reciprocal response. Nonetheless, these desires are closely related because we tend to like those who like us.

To establish that you like another person you must express your desire for *high immediacy* by exhibiting your interest in that person. *Positive indicators of liking* include, but are not limited to, the following nonverbal cues: (a) forward-lean during encounters; (b) body and head orientations that directly face the other individual; (c) open-body positions; (d) affirmative head nods; (e) moderate amounts of gesturing and animation; (f) close interpersonal distances; (g) moderate body relaxation; (h) touching; (i) initiating and maintaining eye contact; (j) smiling; and (k) assuming similar postures (Mehrabian, 1981; Schlenker, 1980).

Nonverbal indicators of disliking are of course associated with a relative absence of positive indicators of liking, or they may take the reverse form. *Nonverbal indicators of disliking include:* (a) indirect bodily orientations; (b) eye contact of short duration; (c) averted eyes; (d) unpleasant facial expressions; (e) a relative absence of gestures; (f) bodily rigidity; (g) visual inattentativeness; (h) closed bodily posture; (i) incongruent postures; and (j) bodily tension.

As we have already indicated, dislike—or its weaker manifestation, disinterest—may result when individuals violate social norms in their overzealous efforts to be liked. Individuals who use sweeping gestures, nod too much, smile too much, sit too close, stare, and use gross postural shifts may think that they are communicating liking cues. Actually, such unsubtle, manipulative efforts may have the unintended effect of promoting dislike.

Nonverbal Indicators of Assertiveness and Nonassertiveness

Social sensitivity is absolutely necessary for the development of satisfying interpersonal relationships. If individuals are to be perceived as socially sensitive, they must take pains to communicate that they are standing up for their rights, but without violating the rights of others. To communicate in a socially sensitive way, a person must be assertive without being nonassertive or aggressive.

Individuals who wish to be perceived as assertive must take special care to monitor their nonverbal cues. *Positive nonverbal indicators of assertiveness* include the following cues: (a) nonverbal and verbal components of the message are consistent; (b) gestures and postures are relaxed, with a forward-lean preferred; (c) gestures are firm but not expansive; (d) eye contact is maintained but staring is avoided; (e) key words and phrases are emphasized with illustrator gestures and vocal inflection; (f) the voice is appropriately loud; and (g) touching is used when appropriate.

Nonverbal indicators of nonassertiveness are more numerous, although some are simply the opposite of the indicators of assertiveness. To avoid the inference that you are nonassertive, you should seek to eliminate those nonverbal cues that are *indicators of nonassertiveness:* (a) nervous gestures such as hand-wringing and lip-licking; (b) clutching the other person as the assertive remark is made; (c) out-of-context smiling; (d) hunching the shoulders; (e) covering the mouth with the hand; (f) wooden posture (bodily rigidity); (g) frequent throat clearing; (h) an eyebrow raised deferentially; (i) evasive eye contact; and (j) pauses that are filled with nonfluencies (Lange & Jakubowski, 1976).

Nonverbal Indicators of Power and Powerlessness

The desire to be perceived as powerful may not be as universal as the desire to be liked, but for many people it is a compelling desire. Some people let their desire get out of control, of course. Nelson Rockefeller's persisting quest for greater power was not confined to repeated attempts to be elected president. In his office, Rockefeller had a special desk that contained pull-out steps. When he wanted to address a group of visitors in his office, he would simply ascend the pull-out steps and stand on top of the desk.

Schlenker (1980) illustrates that efforts to obtain power can reach the point of absurdity. He recalls that in Charlie Chaplin's famous movie, *The Great Dictator*, Hitler and Mussolini are trying to gain dominance over each other by finding some way to assert their superiority. In one scene, dictators are seated in chairs in a barber shop while getting shaves. Because they are seated, the only way they can think of to elevate their status is to elevate their chairs. Predictably, both begin pumping furiously to jack up their chairs. Their wild efforts to enhance their power stop only after they reach the ceiling and crash to the floor.

Nonverbal indicators of power, status, and dominance are not always clearly differentiated in the research literature, so we will identify them

"AS YOU KNOW, I HAVE NEVER BEEN CONCERNED WITH ELEVATING MY OWN STATUS."

under the single label of *power cues.* The following nonverbal cues have proven to be *positive indicators of perceived power:* (a) relaxed posture; (b) erect rather than slumped posture; (c) dynamic and purposeful gestures; (d) a steady and direct gaze; (e) variation in speaking rate and inflection; (f) variation in postures; (g) relative expansiveness in postures; (h) the option to touch; (i) the option to stare; (j) the option to interrupt; and (k) the option to approach another person closely (Archer, 1980; Schlenker, 1980).

As Schlenker (1980) points out, cues that communicate a sense of powerlessness or submissiveness are not always dysfunctional. In many instances, we encounter individuals with superior power and status whose self-presentation of relative submissiveness is expected. Everyone is accountable to someone else. For example, the general who takes pride in cultivating the "command look" and the "command voice" is apt to think twice about asserting such prerogatives of power when in the presence of a higher-ranking general. The use of nonverbal cues that communicate power in the presence of a more powerful person is to risk confrontation and even reprimand.

In general, however, the desire to be perceived as powerless is not a strong one. A relative lack of power is associated with the following *indicators of powerlessness*; (a) body tension; (b) excessive smiling; (c) continuous visual attentiveness while others are speaking; (d) not looking directly at others; (e) looking down frequently; (f) arriving early for parties; (g) sitting in the eleven o'clock position at conference tables (power moves clockwise—from twelve o'clock around to eleven o'clock); (h) exhibiting distracting foot movement; (i) not exposing the soles of your shoes; (j) assuming closed postures; (k) elevating your eyebrows frequently; and (l) never touching another individual (Archer, 1980; Korda, 1975; Schlenker, 1980).

Developing Sensitivity to Nonverbal Cues

The ability to encode and decode nonverbal cues accurately is vitally important to success in interpersonal communication. As Rosenthal (1979) writes, "There are increasing indications that the outcomes of interpersonal interactions may be affected in important ways by the interactants' ability to decode and to encode nonverbal cues. In such relatively formal relationships as therapist–patient, physician–patient, attorney–client, teacher–student, experimenter–subject, and employer–employee, the extent to which the goals of the dyad members are met may depend to an important degree on the member's skill in sending and receiving nonverbal cues" (p. 16).

This chapter has been designed to help you develop these nonverbal skills. In pursuit of this objective, considerable emphasis has been placed on the kinds of positive and negative information we communicate through the use of *emblems, illustrators, affect displays, regulators,* and *adaptors.* Even more emphasis has been placed on the nonverbal cues that should and should not be used to enhance perceptions of liking, assertiveness, and power. The detailed nonverbal indicators of liking–disliking, assertiveness–nonassertiveness, and power–powerlessness should provide the readers with concrete means for improving their encoding skills.

The development of skills in decoding nonverbal cues is perhaps even more important than encoding, because the refinement of such skills is linked directly to the development of our "social intelligence." Archer (1980) maintains that social intelligence consists of the ability to form accurate opinions about people—their experiences, their individual characteristics, their relationships, their concerns, and their emotions. Not surprisingly, our social intelligence is determined to a large extent by our ability to decode nonverbal cues.

To develop these skills, we suggest that the reader take tests that have been specifically designed both to measure and develop sensitivity to meanings communicated by nonverbal cues. Archer (1980), for example, has developed a fascinating test consisting of posed photographs. On the basis of their ability to detect important intimacy and power cues, decoders must determine whether pairs of individuals are close relatives or strangers, intimates or friends, superior or subordinate, or have some other kind of relationship.

A second decoding test that should be useful in the development of non-verbal decoding skills is a test I developed (Gulley & Leathers, 1977). The Visual Test of Nonverbal Cues in the Small Group consists of a set of ten photographs of discussants seated around a conference table. The tasks are to identify the specific kinds of meanings that are being communicated; to indicate what functions the cues will probably serve; and to explain how you would make use of the cues if you were a member of the group.

Summary

This chapter concentrates not only on how bodily cues are typically used but on how they should be used. In pursuit of this objective, the two major perspectives for conceputalizing bodily cues have been discussed, functional and dysfunctional uses of specific kinds of bodily cues have been illustrated, and concrete guidelines have been presented for developing skills in the use and interpretation of bodily cues.

Bodily cues have conceptualized from both the *denotative* and *connotative* perspectives. The denotative perspective is based on the assumption that the informational potential of bodily cues is best understood by classifying them with regard to the level of awareness and intentionality, the code used, and the functions served by the cues. The five types of non-verbal behavior identified by proponents of the denotative approach are *emblems*, *illustrators*, *affect displays*, *regulators*, and *adaptors*. Because communicators frequently use adaptors without awareness and intentionality, they are a particularly valuable source of information about the communicator's attitudes, feelings, and self-confidence.

The connotative perspective is based on the assumption that the meanings communicated by nonverbal cues are best described by three independent dimensions: *pleasantness*, *arousal*, and *dominance*. These dimensions of meaning are best understood by considering the communicative implications of the *approach*, *arousal*, and *power* metaphors.

To enhance communicative effectiveness, individuals should cultivate the use of gestures and postures of openness and confidence. On the other hand, bodily cues that communicate defensiveness and nervousness are dysfunctional. In order to gain more effective control over the meanings they communicate by bodily cues, individiauls should carefully consider the nature of the *nonverbal indicators of liking–disliking, assertiveness–nonassertiveness*, and *power–powerlessness*.

Finally, skill in decoding bodily cues is closely associated with the development of *social intelligence.* Social intelligence is defined as the ability to make accurate judgments about people with regard to their concerns, feelings, experiences, and relationships with other people. The decoding tests described in this chapter can be used to develop skill in decoding bodily cues, and, ultimately, develop one's social intelligence.

References

Archer, D. (1980). *How to expand your social intelligence quotient.* New York: Evans.

Birdwhistell, R.L. (1952). *Introduction to kinesics.* Louisville, KY: University of Kentucky.

Birdwhistell, R.L. (1960). Kinesics and communication. In E. Carpenter & M. McLuhan (Eds.), *Explorations in communication.* Boston: Beacon.

Birdwhistell, R.L. (1970). *Kinesics and context.* Philadelphia, PA: University of Pennsylvania Press.

Cohen, A.A. (1977). The communication functions of hand illustrators. *Journal of Communication, 27,* 54–63.

Ekman, P., & Friesen, W.V. (1967). Head and body cues in the judgment of emotion: A reformulation. *Perceptual and Motor Skills, 24,* 713–716.

Ekman, P., & Friesen, W.V. (1969). The repertoire of nonverbal behavior: Categories, origins, usage, and coding. *Semiotica, 69,* 49–97.

Ekman, P., & Friesen, W.V. (1972). Hand movements. *Journal of Communication, 22,* 353–374.

Gulley, H.E., & Leathers, D.G. (1977). *Communication and group process,* 3rd ed. New York: Holt.

Henley, H. (1977). *Body politics.* Englewood Cliffs, NJ: Prentice-Hall.

Johnson, H.G., Ekman, P., & Friesen, W.V. (1975). Communicative body movements: American emblems. *Semiotica, 15,* 335–353.

Knapp, M.L. (1978). *Nonverbal communication in human interaction,* 2nd ed. New York: Holt.

Knapp, M.L., Hart, R.P. & Friedrich, G.W. (1973). Verbal and nonverbal correlates of human leave-taking. *Communication Monographs, 40,* 182–198.

Korda, M. (1975). *Power! : How to get it and how to use it.* New York: Random.

Krivonos, P.D., & Knapp, M.L. (1975). Initiating communication: What do you say when you say hello. *Central States Speech Journal, 26,* 115–125.

Lamb, W. (1965). *Posture and gesture.* London: Duckworth.

Lange, A.J., & Jakubowski, P. (1976). *Responsible assertive behavior.* Champaigne, IL: Research Press.

Lee, L., & Charlton, J. (1980). *The hand book: Interpreting handshakes, gestures, power signals, and sexual signs.* Englewood Cliffs, NJ: Prentice-Hall.

Mehrabian, A. (1981). *Silent messages,* 2nd ed. Belmont, CA: Wadsworth.

Nierenberg, G., & Calero, H.H. (1973). *How to read a person like a book.* New York: Pocket Books.

Rogers, W.T. (1978). The contribution of kinesic illustrators toward the comprehension of verbal behavior within utterances. *Communication Research, 5,* 54–62.

Rosenthal, R. (1979). *Skill in nonverbal communciation.* Cambridge, MA: Oelgeschlage.

Scheflen, A.E. (1964). The significance of posture in communication systems. *Psychiatry, 27,* 320–323.

Schlenker, B.R. (1980). *Impression management.* Monterey, CA: Brooks/Cole.

Sousa-Poza, J.F., & Rohrberg, R. (1977). Body movement in relation to type of information (person- and nonperson-oriented) and cognitive style (field independence). *Human Communication Research, 4,* 19–29.

CHAPTER FOUR

Proxemic Communication

The way we use space clearly communicates meaning. Different meanings are communicated in many different ways throughout the world. The beliefs, values, and, ultimately, the meaning of a culture are communicated by the way people handle space. The German culture, for example, has long emphasized orderliness and clearly defined lines of authority. Hence, Germans object to individuals who literally "get out of line," or those who disregard signs such as "keep out" and "authorized personnel only," which are intended to stipulate the approved use of space (Hall, 1969).

Americans are inclined to think of space, and to react to it, as "empty." In contrast, in Japan it is space—and not objects—that communicates meaning. The Japanese customarily assign specific meanings to specific types of spaces. For this reason, intersections are given names in Japan, but not streets. The particular space, with its functional characteristics, is the thing. The space available in a single room serves a number of functions because the Japanese use movable walls and separators to create the kinds of spaces that serve specific functional objectives. In fact, the Japanese cope with the problem of limited available space by miniaturizing parts of their environment. The gardening practices that produce bonsai plants are a case in point (Altman, 1975).

Whereas Americans covet privacy by demanding their own offices, and maintain their distance from others through the use of large and elevated desks, the Arabs know no such thing as "privacy" in public, and they are offended by anything less than intimacy of contact while carrying on a conversation. Such conversations (Hall, 1969) characteristically feature "the piercing look of the eyes, the touch of the hands, and the mutual bathing in the warm moist breath during conversation [which] represent

FIGURE 4.1

stepped-up sensory inputs to a level which many Europeans find unbearably intense" (p. 158). In effect, the Arab's use of space and olfactory stimuli communicates two meanings. It invites and demands intense involvement in interpersonal communication, and it assures the withdrawal of those who reject this method of relating.

Meanings communicated by the use of space are not confined to the sometimes gross differences among cultures. Differences within cultures are probably of more practical importance, and they abound. Spatial needs seem to vary dramatically among citizens of a nation, residents of a city, and even members of a family. To satisfy these needs, some people define and protect a set of spatial boundaries with a persistence and vigor that would put the family dog or cat to shame. The stone wall around one's property may be interpreted by some to be the narcissistic attempt of a socially alienated person to find privacy; others may interpret the wall as an enlightened response to the overcrowding of urban living. The fact that one person's spatial boundaries may intrude upon another person's territory accounts for the distinctive type of communication problem that is associated with spatial needs and their frustrations.

In our use of space, we must remember that there is often a great disparity between the meanings we intend to communicate and the meanings we actually do communicate. For example, another professor engaged my wife in conversation at a cocktail party. While so doing, he stood so close to my wife that she became extremely uncomfortable and, unconsciously, began backing away. Later, she noted that she was eventually backed up against a wall on the other side of the room, and, in her continuing attempts to maintain a comfortable distance, made a run in one of her stockings. By his use of space, the professor probably intended to communicate a sense of involvement, pleasure, and vigor; however, by his inadvertent violation of my wife's invisible spatial boundaries, he had communicated a drastically different set of meanings—most noticeably, an unseemly aggressiveness.

The ways to use space, as well as the ways we react to how others use space, can have a profound impact on the image we project. The judgments people make about how friendly, likable, personally attractive, honest, and empathic we are may be strongly affected by the way we relate to people spatially. As we shall see in subsequent chapters, our success in the job interview, in the selling situation, and in cross-cultural communication can be affected in important and readily identifiable ways by our use of space. In short, the impression manager must carefully consider the types of proxemic behavior that should and should not be exhibited in various contexts.

The need to understand the meaning and functions of specific kinds of bodily movement resulted in specialized research known as *kinesics*; the need to understand how humans communicate through their use of space resulted in research which is known as *proxemics*. Edward T. Hall, the pioneer of proxemic research, coined the term *proxemics* because it suggests that proximity, or lack of it, is a vitally important factor in human interaction.

In its broadest perspective, Hall defines proxemics as the study of how people structure and use microspace (1968). Proxemics focuses not only on the ways individuals orient themselves to other individuals and objects in their immediate physical environment, but on the perceptual and behavioral impact of these spatial orientations. For our purposes, *proxemics* is defined as the *study of how individuals use space to communicate.*

The Proximate Environment

We use space to communicate. When we use the space that can be perceived directly, we are communicating within the *proximate environment.* The proximate environment includes everything that is physically present to the individual at a given moment. The proximate environment of a student in a classroom includes the student's desk, the other students, the teacher, the blackboard, the windows, and the doorway. The student's proximate environment does *not* include the soccer team practicing outside, or students in another classroom (Sommer, 1966).

There is no single concept that adequately describes how we communicate in our proximate environment. Because terms such as *space, distance,* and *territory* are clearly related in a conceptual sense, there is a tendency to treat them as synonyms. They are not synonyms, however, and should not be treated as such. *To understand what and how we com-*

municate via our proxemic behavior we must understand the meaning of five interrelated concepts: space, distance, territory, crowding, and privacy.

Space

The concept of visual space in nonverbal communication is somewhat analogous to the concept of silence in verbal communication. Though both are, in a sense, devoid of content, the ways we use them may be rich in communicative significance. Edward Hall, for example, contends that our culture places severe constraints on the ways in which we may use space. In fact, he maintains that there are basically three types of space: fixed-feature, semifixed-feature, and informal space (1969). Rapoport (1982) has amplified Hall's classificatory scheme and modified his terminology. He identifies three major types of space that have communicative significance in our society: *fixed-feature, semifixed-feature,* and *nonfixed-feature space.*

Fixed-feature space refers to the characteristic arrangement of rooms by function. Within the home, for example, formal meals are rarely served in the bedroom and bookcases rarely line the walls of the bathroom. Ironically, the fixed-features that define how space is to be used in the home are often quite dysfunctional. Hall (1969) cites the kitchen as a particular problem. He emphasizes that "the lack of congruence between the design elements, female stature and body build (women are not usually tall enough to reach things), and the activity to be performed, while not obvious at first, is often beyond belief" (p. 105).

The problem may not be as severe as it seems for the upwardly mobile woman in our society because it is important that she foster the perception that she spends little time in the kitchen. Rapoport (1982) emphasizes that "In the case of the Puerto Rican culture, status is gained during a party through a hostess being seen to produce food, being seen in the kitchen, and 'performing' in front of an audience of her peers; in Anglo culture, a woman is seen as a good hostess when she apparently does no work, yet food appears as though by magic" (p. 94).

Semifixed-feature space refers to the placement of objects in the home, office, conference room, and other proximate environments. The objects we use in these types of spaces may include furniture, plants, screens, paintings, plaques, and even birds and animals. The objects we choose—to demarcate the boundaries and to accent the meanings of the semifixed-feature spaces in which we interact—are important because often they are a direct extension of our personality. Our choices of curtains, interior colors, shutters, mailboxes, and decorative planting may reveal more about us than our handwriting or our IRS file.

The semifixed objects we choose to use do more than shape perceptions of presumed personality characteristics. The choice of objects and their placement in semifixed feature space can have a strong impact on the credibility of the occupant of a home or office. Important as these communicative functions are, perhaps the most important communicative function of semifixed-feature space is the degree to which it promotes *involvement* or *withdrawal* among the individuals who are using the space.

Nonfixed-feature space is a concept with which all of us should be rather familiar. This is the space, immediately surrounding our body, that each of us perceive to be ours. We use no physical objects to mark the boundaries of our "personal space" because these boundaries are invisible. The amount of personal space that we claim as ours may vary, depending on our size, current emotional state, status, and sex. Malandro and Barker also emphasize (1983) that people may vary with regard to the amount of personal space, both in front of and in back of them, that they claim to be theirs.

As we consider the communicative implications of the three major kinds of space, we should pay particular attention to semifixed-feature and nonfixed-feature space. This is true because we have little opportunity to modify the nature of most fixed-feature environments. In contrast, we can consciously consider the communicative implications of the objects we choose to place in semifixed-feature space, and we can contemplate the advantages and disadvantages of claiming and defending a "personal space" of a given size and dimension.

Semifixed- and nonfixed-feature space can be used in a variety of ways to transmit meanings. Although the uses vary widely, they frequently serve one of two communicative functions. Either they bring people together and stimulate involvement (in which case they are serving a sociopetal function), or they serve to keep people apart and promote withdrawal (in which case they are serving a sociofugal function). Sommer, who has been a leader in research on the sociopetal and sociofugal uses of microspace, maintains that we transmit very different connotative meanings by the way we use space. He refers to the sociofugal function as "sociofugal space," and finds that sociofugal spatial arrangements or conditions suggest the following meanings: (a) large; (b) cold; (c) impersonal; (d) institutional; (e) not owned by an individual; (f) overconcentrated; (g) without opportunity for shielded conversation; (h) providing barriers without shelter; (i) isolation without privacy; and (j) concentration without cohesion (1967). By contrast, the sociopetal use of space promotes involvement, communicative interaction, and a feeling of involvement. Figure 4.2 illustrates the contrasting uses of space. The opposing sets of chairs in the doctor's waiting room represent a sociofugal use of space, and the conversation pit in the home satisfies the sociopetal use of space.

Distance

At least in theory, space has no finite barriers and becomes a tangible concept only when people or objects occupy space and when individuals attempt to define its boundaries. In contrast, distance is a relational concept and is usually measured in terms of how far one individual is from another.

FIGURE 4.2

Once again, Hall has done pioneering work in attempting to identify and classify the distances people use to separate themselves from others in order to satisfy their various needs. Hall identifies four types of informal distance: *intimate, personal, social-consultative,* and *public.*

Type 1, or intimate distance, is easily distinguishable because of the number and intensity of sensory inputs, of which the communicators are intensely aware. Intimate distance has both a close and a far phase. In the close phase, we engage in intimate activities such as lovemaking, which requires extensive contact of head and the erogenous zones of the body. By contrast, the distance that separates people in the far phase (6 to 18 inches) means that it is difficult to make contact between intimate parts of your own and your partner's body. Intimate distance of either type is considered inappropriate in public by the typical middle-class American (Hall, 1969). The fact that people have rather well-defined proxemic expectations about appropriate distance for different types of communication implies that violation of those expectations can have a very disruptive effect on subsequent communication. If you have ever been in a packed elevator, you should be able to appreciate the disruptive effect—each person in the elevator is violating someone else's proxemic expectations.

Type 2, or personal distance, is the distance that individuals customarily place between themselves and others. This distance is particularly important, for several reasons. The personal distance one characteristically assumes may be a reliable clue to one's self-confidence as well as to one's felt privacy needs. Successful communicators will be sensitive to the personal distances that others maintain when interacting with them.

At the close phase of personal distance ($1^1/_2$ to $2^1/_2$ feet), the three-dimensional quality of objects becomes readily apparent. American proxemic expectations dictate that husband and wife can, and often should, communicate at this distance. For a husband or wife to consistently communicate at this distance with some other member of the opposite sex is to invite gossip, rumors, and certainly the ire of the involved spouse. In contrast, the far phase of personal distance ($2^1/_2$ to 4 feet) precludes truly intimate interaction, no matter what the identity of the interactants.

Type 3, or social distance, separates interactants far enough so that communication reflects an impersonal quality. The close phase of social distance (4 to 7 feet) is the characteristic communicating distance of people who work together or are attending a casual gathering. At the far phase of social distance (7 to 12 feet), people are far enough away from each other to avoid sustained eye contact between subordinates and superordinates, and people can give the impression of not seeing someone else without appearing to be rude.

Finally, the shift from social to public distance has tangible and important implications for interpersonal communication. At the public distance of 12 to 25 feet, the types of nonverbal meanings that one attempts to transmit and the meanings that can be perceived vary rather dramatically. At the close phase of public distance (12 to 25 feet), alert communicators can give the appearance that they have received no message, or they can remove themselves physically from the situation. If individuals do communicate at this distance, they will find that the interaction is of a very formal nature.

The far phase of public distance (25 feet or more) can have a particularly disruptive impact on interpersonal communication. Beyond 25 feet the voice loses much of its potential to transmit meanings accurately, and facial expressions and movements must be rather expansive in order to be recognized. As Hall (1969) emphasizes, "much of the nonverbal part of communication shifts to gestures and body stance" (p. 125).

The normative distance zones developed by Hall are illustrated in Figure 4.3. Hall maintains that members of our culture must stay within certain prescribed distances when they engage in different kinds of communication: *intimate* (0-$1^1/_2$ feet); *personal* ($1^1/_2$–4 feet); *social-consultative* (4–10) feet); and *public* (10 feet to infinity).

Hall's distance zones have been widely cited as the guidelines we should use to assume proper spatial orientations vis-à-vis other individ-

FIGURE 4.3

uals, but recent research suggests that these distance zones should be subjected to more careful scrutiny. In fact, Burgoon and Jones (1976) argue convincingly that *distance zones* or *"expected distancing"* are *determined not only by the normative expectations of our culture but by the idiosyncratic preferences of individual communicators.* They contend that "Expected distancing in a given context is a function of (1) the social norm and (2) the known idiosyncratic spacing patterns of the initiator" (p. 132).

The personality profile of individuals clearly has an impact on the distance they prefer to maintain when interacting with intimates, friends, business associates, or casual acquaintances. We know, for example, that extroverts approach others more closely and maintain shorter communicating distances than do introverts. We know also that people with a high level of communication apprehension and a low level of self-confidence and self-esteem prefer to maintain much greater separation when communicating than do their more confident counterparts. Recent research (Burgoon, 1978) has provided additional support for the idea that expected distancing in a given situation is determined *both* by culturally derived proxemic distancing norms and by the personal preferences of the interactants with regard to what are comfortable interaction distances.

The culturally determined distancing zones identified by Hall do not necessarily represent comfortable interaction distances for all communicators. Thus, Hayduk (1981) found that subjects experienced extreme discomfort at an interaction distance of 11.7 inches, moderate discomfort at 19.5 inches, and only slight discomfort at 27.3 inches. More importantly, Hayduk found that preferred interaction distances for individual communicators vary. Individuals who prefer greater interaction distances become uncomfortable much sooner, as a stranger approaches them, than individuals who prefer shorter interaction distances. Of the former group, 50 percent became moderately uncomfortable at a distance of 4.4 feet. Of the latter group, 50 percent became moderately uncomfortable at a distance of 1.3 feet.

In short, results from recent research "generally suggest that people seek an *optimal range of distance* for interaction, and departures from this range that leave either too large or too small distances result in discomfort and dissatisfaction" (Sundstrom & Altman, 1976, p. 54). If we know and like an individual, for example, we are apt to prefer an interaction distance that is closer than the culturally prescribed norm. When we interact with an individual we dislike, preferred interaction distance is usually greater than that indicated by the cultural norm.

Territory

The concept of *territory* has vast implications for interpersonal communication, and many of these implications remain unexplored. Much of our knowledge of the concept comes from studies which illustrate how animals identify and defend clearly delineated territories by means of instinct. Territoriality in this sense is a basic concept in the study of animal behavior; it is defined as behavior by which an organism characteristically lays claim to an area and defends it against members of its own species, and in so doing assures the propagation of the species by regulating density (Hall, 1969).

Sommer recognizes that the concept of territoriality now has great relevance for the study of human behavior, even if humans do not define their territories exclusively or even primarily by instinctual means. He sees *territory* as *an area controlled by an individual, family, or other face-to-face collectivity, with the emphasis on physical possession, actual or potential, as well as defense.* The essential nature of territoriality is captured by Sommer's delightfully homespun ruminations on the concept:

> *Since human communication is based largely on symbols, territorial defense relies more on symbols such as name plates, fences, and personal possessions than on physical combat, or aggressive displays. . . . Salesmen have, and actively defend, individual territories. One criterion of territoriality is . . . the home team always wins . . . [and] an animal on its own territory will fight with more vigor. . . . [Hence] a male on its own territory is almost undefeatable against males of the species. (Sommer, 1966, p. 61)*

Territorial behavior, therefore, is defined by attempts to mark the boundaries of territories that are "owned" by individuals or groups. Through the use of personalized markers, we strive either to regulate social interaction within territories perceived as ours, or to prevent unauthorized individuals from entering the territory. *The more personal the markers used to delineate territorial boundaries the more effective they are in controlling or preventing interaction* (Altman, 1975).

If territories serve so central a function in regulating human interaction, the obvious question is: What types of territories are typically defined and defended? Writing from a broad perspective, Lyman and Scott (1967) observe that there are four kinds of territories: *public, home, interactional,* and *body.*

Public territories are those areas where individuals may enter freely. Great constraints are placed on human interaction within public territories, however, because of explicit laws and social traditions. The struggles to desegregate buses, restaurants, and beaches suggest that the term *public territory* can have a very restricted connotation for some individuals who choose to enter and attempt to interact with others within the territory.

By contrast, home territories feature freedom of interaction by individuals who claim the territory. Home territories are defined in part by the distinctive markers used to assure boundary maintenance. Examples include reserved chairs, drinking mugs, and even the cat's own litter. Fraternities, private clubs, and even gay bars all constitute home territories. In each of these, distinctive territorial markers are used to limit usage by outsiders.

Interactional territories are areas where individuals congregate informally. A party, a local pool hall, and an informal meeting on campus may all be associated with interactional territories. Although every territory has boundaries that are maintained, interactional territories are unique in that they have movable boundaries.

Finally, *body territories* consist of *space that is marked as reserved for use by our bodies.* Goffman has developed and supported the provocative thesis that "eight territories of self" exist, and their changeable boundaries are a function of both variability in individual behavior and in environmental conditions. These territories of self are: (a) personal space; (b) stalls; (c) use-space; (d) turns; (e) sheaths; (f) possessional territory; (g) informational preserves; and (h) conversational preserves (Goffman, 1971).

Of the eight territories of self identified by Goffman, five seem particularly relevant and important for interpersonal communication. First, the *stall* is space with clear-cut boundaries that individuals claim exclusively for their own use. Telephone booths and parking places are obvious examples of stalls. Unlike personal space, stalls have highly visible and fixed boundaries which can easily be protected from intruders.

Stalls identify themselves by their structure, but use-space identifies itself by its function. *Use-space* is that space immediately surrounding us which we must have in order to perform personal functions, such as lighting our cigarette or swinging at a golf ball. Our claim to use-space is usually respected by others in close proximity to us because they realize that they would require similar space to perform similar functions.

The *turn* represents a territorial claim based on both structure and function. Expressions such as "take your turn" and "get in line, Bud" suggest the nature of this type of territorial behavior. We have been socially conditioned to expect that such territorial claims will be honored.

The *sheath*, which consists of both the skin covering and the clothes we wear, functions to afford us with the desired degree of privacy. Much like the sheath, *possession territory* is closely identified with the human body. Rather than skin or clothes as coverings for the body, *possessional territory* is defined by the set of objects that we claim as our own and that we array around us wherever we are. Objects such as gloves and handbags often function as markers to delineate the boundaries of possessional territory. Only the most insensitive individual will attempt to move such territorial markers.

Crowding

Crowding is a concept of central importance to the study of proxemic communication. To begin, crowding should be clearly differentiated from density. *Density* is a concept that is defined strictly in physical terms. Density refers to the *number of people per unit of space.* Crowding, in contrast, is a psychological concept. *Crowding is that condition which exists when an individual's attempts to achieve a desired level of privacy have been unsuccessful, in the sense that more social contact continues to occur than is desired* (Altman, 1975).

The sensation of being crowded is uncomfortable. This sensation is subjective, of course, in that it is dependent on *who* else is involved, *when* and *where* it occurs and *why* and *how* it occurs. When we do experience the sensation of crowding, however, we usually find interpersonal communication to be less than satisfying. In any given situation, we may or may not have the opportunity to modify our own proxemic behaviors (or the proxemic behaviors of persons with whom we interact) in ways that will minimize or eliminate the sensation of crowding. We should recognize, nonetheless, that the frequency with which we experience crowding has been cited as one reliable barometer of the skill we exhibit in using our spatial resources (Baldassare, 1978).

The feeling of being crowded seems to have a negative impact on our ability to establish and maintain satisfying relationships with other individuals. McCarthy and Saegert (1978) compared the behaviors of individuals living in a fourteen-story apartment building and in a three-story walkup: the residents of the high-rise building felt much more crowded than residents of the walk-up. The individuals who reported that they felt crowded had greater difficulty in establishing relationships with their neighbors, were less socially active, felt more detached from their place of residence, belonged to fewer voluntary groups, and felt they had less power to exercise influence on the decisions made by the management of the apartments. In fact, there is even some evidence to indicate that dorm residents who experience an uncomfortable degree of crowding make more frequent visits to their physicians, and do not perform as well academically as individuals who do not feel crowded (Stokols, Ohlig, & Resnick, 1978).

The potential for perceptions of crowding to negatively affect our feelings about, and our relationship with, other individuals should not be overemphasized, however. Feelings of overcrowding clearly result in some elevation in anxiety and stress levels (Altman, 1975). We know little about the long-term effects of crowding but the impact on interpersonal relationships is apt to be severe.

Privacy

Altman (1975) quite clearly establishes the importance of privacy to an understanding of the communicative implications of our proxemic behaviors. He writes that *"the concept of privacy is central to understanding environment and behavior relationships; it provides a key link among the concepts of crowding, territorial behavior, and personal space.* Personal space and territorial behavior function in the service of privacy needs and, as such, are *mechanisms* used to achieve desired levels of 'personal or group privacy' " (p. 6). He goes on to emphasize that crowding results from ineffective or unsatisfactory use of space, distance, and territory, with the result that individuals achieve inadequate levels of privacy.

Privacy may be defined as *selective control of access to one's self or to one's group* (Altman, 1975). To a considerable degree, we control access to ourselves and to groups that are important to us by our use of space. Our needs for privacy must of course be balanced against our needs to be perceived as friendly and outgoing individuals who seek interaction with oth-

FIGURE 4.4

ers. Neither the hermit nor the member of the commune has achieved the balance necessary for most of us to be effective communicators in the real world.

As Figure 4.4 suggests, some individuals place a high premium on privacy. Rare indeed is the individual who views the bathroom as the appropriate place for social interaction in the home. On the other hand, some individuals make a practice of walking around nude in their own home. Privacy, therefore, is defined by the felt needs of those who assert specialized types of claims to it.

The concepts of crowding and privacy are both useful if we are to understand why we react as we do to the violation of proxemic norms and expectations. By understanding the characteristic ways in which individuals seek to cope with such violations, we enhance our capacity to use our spatial resources effectively.

The Disruptive Effects of Violating Proxemic Norms and Expectations

Whether we are talking about the concept of space, distance, territory, crowding, or privacy, individuals have well-developed expectations. These expectations specify what is acceptable proxemic behavior in a given situation. Because many of these expectations are sufficiently stable and enduring, and are shared by so many people, that they might be called *proxemic norms.* Although it is difficult to generalize about proxemic behavior, one generalization has consistently been supported by empirical research. Simply put, *the violation of proxemic expectations, or norms, results in consistently disruptive effects on the communication between two or more people.*

So long as we maintain a distance perceived as "comfortable" or appropriate by persons with whom we interact, we know that close physical proximity is consistently associated with positive affect, friendship, and attraction. Close physical proximity that does not violate the interactants' notion of "comfortable interaction distance" serves to signal liking and is viewed as a sign of friendliness. However, both the "violated" and the "invadee" become visibly uncomfortable when interaction is attempted at inappropriately close distances (Sundstrom & Altman, 1976).

Under certain conditions, it may actually be advantageous to initiate interaction at a distance closer than the cultural norm would dictate. Burgoon (1978) maintains that many individuals respond in a favorable manner if one person moves closer to another than is ordinarily viewed as appropriate. This is true, however, only when the "violator" is perceived positively as someone who can provide desired rewards, and when the "violator" does not move so close as to approach or exceed the "threat threshold" of that person.

By contrast, individuals who perceive the "violator" as someone who is apt to provide them with negative rewards will react negatively when the "violator" moves closer to them than the proxemic norm dictates. Violators seen as possessing negative-reward power are judged to be threatening at much greater distances than violators possessing positive-reward power. As a result, negatively rewarding individuals would be well advised to maintain a communicating distance greater than that specified by the proxemic norm.

Unfortunately, only a limited number of studies have focused directly on the specific communicative effects of the violation of spatial expectations and preferences. Many of the studies that have been undertaken were conducted in the somewhat antiseptic and unreal environment of classrooms, libraries, and mental hospitals. In the classroom and library studies, a "plant" is typically used and one or more unsuspecting subjects is approached. In one typical library study, where a person trained by the experimenter violated the spatial expectations of library users, only 18 of 80 subjects actually left during the 10-minute period when they were intruded upon (Patterson, Mullens, & Romano, 1971). A relatively small number of individuals resort to "flight" when their proxemic expectations are violated, but many use elbows, knees, books, and personal artifacts as barriers to prevent further violation(s) of their personal space.

Successful communication requires that we be sensitive to the spatial needs of those with whom we communicate. In fact, we must remember that nationality, race, age, and sex may all be determinants of preferred interaction distances.

In one of the few highly realistic studies of proxemic behavior outside of the laboratory, Baxter (1970) observed dyads at the Houston city zoo in order to determine the preferred interaction distances of subcultural groups in the United States. He found that Mexican-Americans, of all age and sex groupings, interacted "most proximally"—were consistently closest together; Anglos were intermediate, and blacks stood most distant. He also found that children interacted more proximally than adults; male-female groups interacted most proximally, female-female groups were intermediate, and male groups were most distant.

The communicative impact of violating (or conforming) to spatial expectations has been measured largely in quantitative terms. The questions are straightforward. How many people will physically withdraw from a social situation if their spatial boundaries have been violated? How many people in rather close proximity to a person will that person tolerate? How much space do people require to separate themselves from others? At what point does the violation of proxemic norms lead to the sensation of crowding, with resultant efforts to achieve greater privacy?

Distance between individuals seems to have its greatest impact on the development of interpersonal relationships. Individuals who use mutually preferred interaction distances facilitate the development of satisfying interpersonal relationships. Beware of increasing the distance between yourself and another individual as you interact. This practice will probably create a negative impression and may help to destroy interpersonal trust.

One interesting study directly examined impression formation as a function of interpersonal physical distance. As distances between individuals increased, their personal impressions of each other became more negative. Individuals not only viewed each other as less socially active, as distance between them increased, but as less friendly, aggressive, extroverted, and dominant (Patterson & Sechrest, 1970).

To minimize the distance you maintain between yourself and the individuals with whom you communicate can be highly beneficial. In fact, one researcher (Willis, 1966) went so far as to suggest that communicating at appropriate distances is one way of operationally defining satisfying interpersonal relationships. To attempt to communicate at uncomfortably close distances, from the perspective of the "invadee," however, must be avoided.

Two recent studies (Kmiecik, Mausar, & Banziger, 1979; Smith & Knowles, 1979) support the view that physically unattractive persons should attempt more distant communication than physically attractive persons. Subjects waiting at a stoplight to cross a street were "threatened" by the approach of a physically unattractive pedestrian at much greater distances than by the approach of a physically attractive pedestrian; they crossed the street more quickly as the physically unattractive pedestrian approached.

The important point to remember is that the violation of proxemic norms is disruptive. Violation of proxemic norms is a sort of "noise," because it diverts the attention of the interactants from their communication objectives. In fact, we know that the violation of proxemic norms is almost always uncomfortable for both the violator and the invadee. Violations are particularly discomforting and stressful when the invadee neither expects nor desires interaction with the invader (Sundstrom & Altman, 1976).

If the violations of individually preferred distance orientations typically produce identifiably disruptive effects on interpersonal communication, the effects of violating territorial boundaries are often more extreme.

The boundaries of public, home, and interactional territories are clearly delineated by personal markers. Violations of territorial boundaries are disruptive. Territorial encroachment usually results in defensive reactions designed to defend or to reestablish one's territory. Fences, hedges, "private property" signs and guards are all examples of markers used to identify the boundaries of home territories. Reaction to the violation of home territory is so strong that on numerous occasions violators have been shot. Violations of public and interactional territories are typically handled by more subtle means. Books and clothing are used to reserve spaces in public; hostile glances and unpleasant facial expressions are used to warn violators that they are not welcome; groups may resort to in-group jargon or in-group languages to signal intruders that they have violated territorial boundaries; and the ultimate response to territorial encroachment may be aggression and fighting (Altman, 1975).

The sort of territorial violation that seems to produce the most visceral response is the violation of body territories. Goffman (1971) emphasizes that territories reserved for the use of our bodies represent the "central claim in the study of co-mingling. . . . The central offense is an incursion, intrusion, encroachment, presumption, transgression, defilement, besmearing, contamination—in short a violation" (p. 45).

Goffman (1971) identifies at least five types of territorial violation that seem particularly important: (a) the closer placement of your body to another individual than your status allows; (b) the use of your body, and hands, to "touch" and "defile the sheath or possessions of another"; (c) the use of the penetrating gaze to transgress or circumvent societal expectations; (d) the use of the voice, or other sounds, to intrude upon someone's auditory preserve; and (e) bodily excreta which violate social expectations because of spatial proximity of the violator to the person being violated.

The disruptive effect of each of these five types of territorial invasions on interpersonal communication can be rather clearly illustrated. First, the physical distance that should separate you and the person with whom you are communicating is a function of social distance. In a high proportion of instances, when superordinates and subordinates communicate, the subordinate approaches the superordinate. The status of the subordinate determines how closely he or she may approach the superordinate. The offices of major business executives are usually arranged to provide cues to subordinates as to proper approaching distance, and, consequently, warn the subordinate of that point at which the executive's personal territory has been violated. Second, the body and hands can be used to violate the territorial preserve of another. Rape is the most extreme example, and unsatisfactory conformance to your host's conception of rules of etiquette is perhaps one of the least significant types.

Third, territories can be violated through the penetration of the eyes. "Although in our society the offense that can be committed by intrusive looks tends to be slighter than other kinds of offensive incursions, the distance over which the intrusion can occur is considerable, the directions multiple, the occasions of possible intrusion very numerous and the adjustments required in eye discipline constant and delicate" (Goffman, 1971, p. 45). Not only is the penetrating glance often perceived as a type of behavior that is demeaning, but it is also behavior that can be used to establish dominance at the expense of the individual to whom it is directed.

Fourth, violation of personal territories by high-volume sound, or otherwise objectionable sounds, is becoming an increasingly pervasive and insidious form of disruption. Such violations may occur in an intimate encounter when the sound level is considered inappropriate, or when sounds are simply insinuative because of sexual or other connotations. As any city planner knows, this type of territorial invasion may occur in a much larger setting. Citizens groups in virtually every major city are attempting to tighten restrictions against noise from commercial jet airliners, noise from motorbikes, or just plain vehicular traffic. Many cities have become the defendants in large lawsuits as the result of their alleged violations of the plaintiff's auditory territory or preserves.

Finally, bodily excreta can be a particularly disruptive type of territorial violation. It is important to note that odor, a direct byproduct of bodily excreta, "operates over a distance, and in all directions; unlike looking, it cannot be cut off once it violates and may linger in a continued place after the agency has gone" (Goffman, 1971, p. 47). Although spittle, snot, perspiration, food particles, blood, semen, vomit, urine, and fecal matter are perhaps not disruptive in themselves (when confined to the original source of excretion), they can be extremely odious when present while individuals are attempting to communicate at the intimate or even personal distance.

The violation of proxemic norms may result in more intense social stimulation than a person desires. When the desired level of privacy exceeds the actual level of privacy, the sensation of crowding results. Baldassare (1978) emphasizes that if "there is not enough room or privacy to conduct desired roles alone and with others, competition for space use may occur. Undoubtedly, the possibilities of incomplete role performances, intrusions, and the blocking of desired role enactments are heightened" (p. 47).

Resentment, conflict, and withdrawal frequently result when an individual's felt need for privacy is frustrated by the violation of their proxemic expectations. In our society, certain groups of individuals have difficulty in maintaining desired levels of privacy. For example, the personal space of short people is much more frequently violated than the personal space of tall people. In one study (Caplan & Goldman, 1981) the personal space of short males (5' 5") was invaded 69 percent of the time, and the space of tall males (6' 2") was invaded only 31 percent of the time. Furthermore, women are at a disadvantage when they use space to try to achieve desired levels of privacy. This is true in part because the "private territory" claimed by males as their own is significantly larger than for females (Mercer & Benjamin, 1980).

In short, our use of space represents an important communicative medium. When we conform to the proxemic expectations of those with whom we interact, we enhance our capacity to communicate successfully. When we violate proxemic expectations, we can anticipate that we will encounter resentment, resistance, and conflict in our interpersonal relationships. Successful communicators exhibit the capacity to interpret accurately the spatial expectations of other persons and adjust their own proxemic behaviors so that they are compatible with those expectations.

Summary

Proxemics is defined as the study of how individuals use space to communicate. To understand the communicative effects and implications of our proxemic behaviors we must understand the significance of *space, distance, territory, crowding,* and *privacy.* The successful communicator must be able to recognize and adjust to the normative expectations that have been developed for each of these types of proxemic behavior.

The three major types of space that have communicative significance are *fixed-feature, semifixed feature,* and *nonfixed-feature space.* Because the nature of semifixed-feature and nonfixed-feature space can be controlled by the communicator, they are especially important. These two types of space can be used to satisfy the *sociopetal* function to promote communicative interaction, or to satisfy the *sociofugal* function, which inhibits communicative interaction.

Normative distances have been established for intimate, personal, social-consultative, and public communication. Over and above cultural norms, comfortable distances for individual communicators vary. To determine comfortable interaction distances, we must take into account both cultural norms and the idiosyncratic preferences of persons with whom we communicate.

The boundaries of public, home, interactional, and body territories are delineated by personal markers. To disregard such markers is to run the risk of being perceived as both insensitive and inept. Violations of body territory have a particularly disruptive impact on interpersonal communication.

When proxemic expectations are violated, individuals frequently experience the sensation of crowding. One result may be that a person's needs for adequate privacy are frustrated. Finally, the person who violates proxemic expectations creates negative impressions; runs the risk of personal rejection; promotes conflict; and contributes to the deterioration of interpersonal relationships.

References

Altman, I. (1975). *The environment and social behavior.* Monterey, CA: Brooks/Cole.

Baldassare, M. (1978). Human spatial behavior. *Annual Review of Sociology, 4,* 29–56.

Baxter, J. C. (1970). Interpersonal spacing in natural settings. *Sociometry, 33,* 449–454.

Burgoon, J. K. (1978). A communication model of personal space violations: Explication and an initial test. *Human Communication Research, 4,* 129–142.

Burgoon, J. K., & Jones, S. B. (1976). Toward a theory of personal space expectations and their violations. *Human Communication Research, 2,* 131–146.

Caplan, M. E., & Goldman, M. (1981). Personal space violations as a function of height. *Journal of Social Psychology, 114,* 167–171.

Goffman, E. (1971). *Relations in public.* New York: Harper.

Hall, E. T. (1968). Proxemics. *Current Anthropology, 9,* 83.

Hall, E. T. (1969). *The hidden dimension.* New York: Doubleday.

Hayduk, L. A. (1981). The permeability of personal space. *Canadian Journal of Behavioural Science, 13,* 274–287.

Kmiecik, C., P., Mausar, & Banziger, G. (1979). Attractiveness and interpersonal space. *Journal of Social Psychology, 108,* 277–278.

Lyman, S. M., & Scott, M. B. (1967). Territoriality: A neglected sociological dimension. *Social Problems, 15,* 237–241.

Malandro, L., & Barker, L. L. (1983). *Nonverbal communication.* Reading, MA: Addison-Wesley.

McCarthy, D., & Saegert, S. (1978). Residential density, social overload, and social withdrawal. *Human Ecology, 6,* 253–272.

Mercer, G. W., & Benjamin, J. L. (1980). Spatial behavior of university undergraduates in double-occupancy residence rooms: An inventory of effects. *Journal of Applied Social Psychology, 10,* 32–44.

Patterson, M. L., Mullens, S., & Romano, J. (1971). Compensatory reactions to spatial intrusion. *Sociometry, 34,* 116–120.

Patterson, M. L., & Sechrest, L. B. (1970). Interpersonal distance and impression formation. *Journal of Personality, 38,* 166.

Rapoport, A. *The meaning of the built environment.* (1982). Beverly Hills: Sage.

Smith, R. J., & Knowles, E. S. (1979). Affective and cognitive mediators of reactions to spatial invasions. *Journal of Experimental Social Psychology, 15,* 437–452.

Sommer, R. (1966). Man's proximate environment. *Journal of Social Issues, 22,* 60.

Sommer, R. (1967). Sociofugal space. *American Journal of Sociology, 72,* 655.

Sommer, R. (1974). *Tight spaces: Hard architecture and how to humanize it.* Englewood Cliffs, NJ: Prentice-Hall.

Stokols, S., Ohlig, W., & Resnick, S. M. (1978). Perception of residential crowding, classroom experiences, and student health. *Human Ecology, 6,* 233–252.

Sundstrom, E., & Altman, I. (1976). Interpersonal relationships and personal space: Research review and theoretical model. *Human Ecology, 4,* 46–67.

Willis, F. N. (1966). Initial speaking distance as a function of the speaker's relationship. *Psychonomic Science, 5,* 221–222.

CHAPTER FIVE

Personal Appearance

Appearance communicates meaning. In an age that gives lip service to the cliché that beauty is only skin deep, one might surmise that personal appearance represents a secondary and superficial value, and that few people devote attention or time to their personal appearance. Exactly the reverse is true. Our personal appearance has a pervasive impact on our self-image and on the image we communicate to others. As such, it is a major factor in shaping our behavior and the behavior of those with whom we interact.

In *Orpheus Descending*, Tennessee Williams wrote that "we're all of us sentenced to solitary confinement inside our own skins for life." For many Americans, that can be a severe sentence. Our "skin," or overall personal appearance, does, in many cases, dictate that we cannot date or marry a person more attractive than we are. If our personal appearance is subnormal, our childhood peers ridicule and ostracise us. Our social and sexual success is heavily dependent on our physical attractiveness. Moreover, personal appearance can be used to predict vocational success.

There is a well-developed physical-attractiveness stereotype in our society which is based on the assumption that beauty is good (Dion, Berscheid, & Walster, 1972). Adams and Crossman (1978) capture the essence of the physical-attractiveness stereotype when they write that:

> *Enough information is available to support the existence of a wide ranging physical attractiveness stereotype. . . . The message is that beauty implies goodness, talent, and success. Therefore, attractive people should be able to walk with their heads held high since everyone sees them in a socially desirable way. Also, when they are perceived as failing, this is construed merely as a case of stumbling but not falling. (p. 17).*

A billion-dollar cosmetics industry testifies to the fact that millions of Americans recognize the importance of accentuating the attractive features of their personal appearance. In fact, the increasing prominence of plastic surgeons in our society serves to highlight the importance of personal appearance. Kurt Wagner, a plastic surgeon, and Gould (1972) write that "it used to be the great truism that it was the inner qualities that counted and the outer ones were superficial—as in the old saying that beauty is only skin deep. But we know now that there is no such thing as separating the mind from the body" (p. 22).

There is no more intimate form of communication than personal appearance. *Our visible self functions to communicate a constellation of meanings which define who we are and what we are apt to become, in the eyes of others. In interpersonal communication, the appearance of the participants establishes their social identity.* From a communication perspective, personal appearance has great functional significance.

Our visible self plays a major role in shaping our social identity. Once established, our social identity—as perceived by others and by us—places identifiable limits on how, when, and where we are expected to engage in interpersonal communication. Our social identity carries with it the implicit responsibility to communicate in such a way as to meet the expectations of those for whom that identity has meaning. When we violate those expectations, our communication with others is apt to become ineffective and unsatisfying.

The impact of personal appearance on social identity became even more obvious to me when I walked into one of my classes dressed in a bathrobe and tennis shoes. My hair, which had just received a wild treatment from a dryer, was sticking out in all directions; much of it was combed down to obscure my face. I was wearing sunglasses and smoking a long, black cigar. Placing my bare legs and tennis shoes ostentatiously on my desk, I began my remarks to the students by asserting that "appearance communicates meaning."

Because the meanings communicated by my altered appearance conflicted so strikingly with the meanings associated with my social identity, the students became rather disoriented. They were at first uncertain, and seemed not to know whether to laugh, or to refuse to acknowledge the incongruous sight in front of them. A few laughed, many squirmed, and the rest tried to be cool. Later, when they realized that they were being put on, my appearance triggered an intense and fascinating discussion of the communicative functions of personal appearance.

This chapter begins by identifying those facial and bodily features that are almost universally recognized in our society as physically attractive. As I mentioned before, there is in our society a commonly accepted perspective which suggests that what is beautiful is talented, good, and socially desirable. We have little difficulty in judging objectively the level of physical attractiveness of those with whom we interact. Accurately assessing our own level of physical attractiveness is another matter, however. Because we recognize that we are apt to suffer severe perceptual and behavioral penalties if our personal appearance is much below normal, we often distort our own image (our physical features) so that, in our mind, they approximate the cultural ideal.

Features of Physical Attractiveness

The societal stereotype for personal appearance dictates what is and is not beautiful. Adams (1977) emphasizes the strength of the stereotype, and the implicit guidelines for judging physical attractiveness, when he writes that "the evidence suggests the stereotype is seldom mediated by environmental contexts, and that physically attractive persons are differentiated from their less attractive peers across a variety of experiences which are typical of various stages in the life cycle" (p. 219).

As we consider the defining features of physical attractiveness, two facts should be kept in mind. Americans have a much more detailed stereotype, or mental picture, of the physical features that define beauty for women than for men. In addition, Americans are much more precise in identifying physical features associated with facial beauty than in identifying physical features associated with bodily attractiveness.

Facial Attractiveness

The *ideal* face has been described objectively and in specific detail. The noted plastic surgeon, Dr. Kurt Wagner, and Helen Gould (1972), write that the German sculptor, Gottfried Schadow (1764–1850), geometrically laid out his ideal of facial beauty in the nineteenth century. In so doing, Schadow "formulated the facial proportions for a prevailing standard of symmetry which the occidental world accepts as the ideal. . . . Our own eyes automatically accept the standard of what is aesthetically pleasing. Take any super example—from Greta Garbo to Rock Hudson—to even *any* example of the good-looking individual, and you know they pass the Schadow test before you apply the calipers" (p. 45).

Schadow's model of perfect facial features and proportions has been adopted by plastic surgeons because it accurately reflects the detailed standards in our society that are used in assessing facial attractiveness. When clients approach a plastic surgeon with a request that they undergo facial surgery, for example, they begin their treatment with profile analysis. The term *profile analysis* correctly suggests that plastic surgeons agree on a very specific ideal for facial beauty. The profile analysis "indicates the necessity for a definite proportion between the forehead, nose, lips, and chin. To correct a nose alone, without considering the related features, is going on a fool's journey" (Wagner & Gould, 1972, p. 47).

By using the profilometer to determine exactly how far a patient's facial features deviate from the perfect profile or ideal face, the plastic surgeon can project with precision the degree of correction needed on one or more facial features. The *profilometer*, a special instrument that resembles and functions like the protractor, is used to measure the length and angles of the nose, from the tip, through the bridge, to the top, in centimeters. "The ideal nose for a man . . . is straight with a bridge angle of 30 to 35 degrees and an 8- to 12-degree tip angle. As to length, the nose should roughly correspond to the man's height measured in feet. Thus, a 6-foot man would ideally have a nose of about six centimeters (2.35 inches) in length" (Routh, 1974, p. 39).

The larger your facial features the more unattractive they will probably be perceived. *Large facial features are typically considered less attractive than smaller facial features* (Staat, 1977). Large noses are a good case in point. I have observed a mother smile at one son, a six-year-old with a cute, small, button nose, and then scowl at her eight-year-old son, who had an abnormally long, large nose. She remarked to the younger son, "You are so cute; you have mommy's small nose." The eight-year-old son may have been comforted by the realization that he is well-equipped to do a Bob Hope imitation, but he was probably hurt by his mother's cruel stereotyping. If you doubt that oversized facial features make a bad impression, consider the picture of a well-known politician struggling throughout life to conceal his jumbo-sized ears.

A single unattractive facial feature does not of course mean that you have a physically unattractive face. Dr. Kurt Wagner stressed this point during a tape-recorded interview done with me in his home in the Hollywood hills. If most of your facial features conform to the ideal profile for facial attractiveness, you may still be perceived as a winner. Dr. Kurt Wagner claimed that:

> the reasons that you know [what the ideal model or profile is for beauty] is that people still have a good idea of what is beautiful. OK. Now you might not like Elizabeth Taylor, or her life-style, or what she stands for, but nobody is going to deny that Elizabeth Taylor is beautiful. OK. You take the males and push them in the profile . . . We tend to go for real anti-heroes now. Right now, it is just a rebellion against male beauty—where you have Charles Bronson or Richard Boone. Yet, they have strong, square faces, except their nose is a little weird, but even their nose isn't too weird. Redford, very popular. James Coburn, very popular. OK. Ah, Rock Hudson, perfect. All right, perfect. . . . There never has been a successful leading man who has no chin [author's italics]. (Wagner, 1973)

Bodily Attractiveness

The physical features that differentiate one human body from another often differ drastically. Both common and uncommon persons have recognized this fact for centuries. Shakespeare, a man of uncommon insight, expressed in *Julius Caesar* what common people have long recognized.

Caesar: *Let me have men about me that are fat;*
Sleek-headed men, and such as sleep o'nights:
Yond Cassius has a lean and hungry look;
He thinks too much: such men are dangerous. . . .

Antony: *Fear him not, Caesar; he is not dangerous.*
            He is a noble Roman and well given.
Caesar: *Would he were fatter! . . .*

People have known for centuries that human bodies differ in appearance, but they made few systematic efforts to measure the differences. Ernst Kretschmer, a professor of psychiatry and neurology, probably made the first comprehensive effort to record differences in bodily appearance. In 1925, Kretschmer published the first edition of *Physique and Character: An Investigation of the Nature of Constitution and of the Theory of Temperament*. Kretschmer concluded that individuals who share morphological similarities may be classified into three major groups: (a) *asthenic* (skinny, bony, narrow body); (b) *athletic* (muscular body); and (c) *pyknic* (fat body).

Sheldon's follow-up research has established the empirical practice of *somatyping*—classifying people as to body type. Sheldon's classification is now widely used. According to Sheldon (1954), there are three body types: (a) *endomorphic* (soft, fat, and so on); (b) *mesomorphic* (bony, athletic, and so on); and (c) *ectomorphic* (thin, fragile, and so on).

When we classify individuals by body type it is easiest to conjure up simplistic images of someone such as football star Herschel Walker, who is clearly mesomorphic, or a *Vogue* fashion model, who is clearly ectomorphic. To accurately describe a person's body type, however, you need to assign them three numbers on a seven-point scale. The numbers refer to the degree of endomorphy, mesomorphy, or ectomorphy. Herschel Walker would probably get a rating of 1/7/1, and the skinny fashion model would be rated 1/1/7.

Sheldon theorized that there is a relationship between body type and temperament, or personality characteristics. In Sheldon's view, the person with the endomorphic body type will probably exhibit a *viscerotonic* temperament—a laid-back, relaxed, and even indolent personality. Mesomorphic body types are associated with a *somatotonic* temperament—a highly confident, task-oriented, aggressive person. Finally, the ectomorphic body type is associated with the *cerebrotonic* temperament—individuals who are tense, fussy, and critical of others (1954).

Although Sheldon's theory, and his system for body typing have both been criticized, body typing (or somatyping) represents an undeniably useful way of describing a dominant set of physical features that differentiate one body from another. As we shall see, the impact of a person's body type on his or her self-perceptions and behaviors, as well as on the perceptions of those with whom they interact, is substantial.

In our society, it is more important for a woman than for a man to have bodily features that are physically attractive. Relatedly, Americans seem to have a more detailed notion of what constitutes bodily beauty for women than for men. *For females, slenderness is a particularly important feature of bodily attractiveness, and waist width and hip width correlate negatively with perceptions of physical attractiveness* (Horvath, 1979). *The bigger a woman's waist and the hippier she is, the less attractive she is perceived to be.* When considered either from the perspective of male or female perceivers, female physiques that emphasize great curvature (e.g., very large breasts and a very small or a very large waist) are seen as less physically attractive than breasts and waists of moderate size.

The ideal body type of men features reasonably broad shoulders and muscular chests (Horvath, 1981). The "traditional female" places a high priority on such stereotypically masculine features as well-muscled upper arms and a tapering upper trunk. Nontraditional females attach much less importance to muscle-development. But traditional and nontraditional women agree, however, that males who have small chests and arms, an "unmasculine physique," are physically unattractive (Lavrakas, 1975).

In short, there is nothing ambiguous about the proportions of the face and body that distinguish the physically attractive from the unattractive person. The profile for physically attractive women is more complete than the profile for physically attractive men, and, partially as a result of this fact, women attach a higher priority to physical attractiveness than do men.

Body Image

Our conception of our personal appearance begins with the general evaluative assessment we make of our own personal appearance. *Body-cathexis* is the *degree of feeling of satisfaction or dissatisfaction with the various parts or processes of our body* (Secord & Jourard, 1953). Empirical research has confirmed the hypothesis that *body-cathexis* or image is *integrally related to the self-concept.* Furthermore, body image has been found to have significant behavioral implications.

People with low body-cathexis, or a negative body image, are predisposed to be anxious, concerned with pain, disease, and bodily injury, and they are insecure (Secord & Jourard, 1953). By contrast, individuals with a positive body concept (based in part on their self-perceptions as mesomorphs) have a much more sophisticated conception of their own body (Sugerman & Haronian, 1964). From such findings we might infer that individuals with negative body images attempt to avoid the negative connotations of such an image by deliberately maintaining a fuzzy or incomplete image of their own body.

Persons with negative body images have understandable reasons for developing an inaccurate image of their own body. The practice of distorting one's physical features in one's own mind is known as *body distortion* (Malandro & Barker, 1983). People with negative body concepts experience unusual difficulty in visualizing accurately the physical features of their personal appearance, and often have unrealistic notions about their personal appearance.

Obese individuals, for example, do not have to search for reasons for engaging in body distortion. The obese probably recognize that "once the endomorphic phenotype is firmly established, stigmatization sets in and blocks the exit to normal acceptance in interpersonal relationships" (Cahnman, 1968, p. 297). If you realized that fat persons are frequently characterized as uninteresting, lazy, and unsocial (Worsley, 1981), you might subconsciously engage in some body distortion in order to slim down your bodily proportions—at least in your own mind.

Individuals seem most inclined to distort self-perception of the bodily features that are most central to notions of physical beauty. Thus, females have consistently exhibited a propensity to distort estimates of their own bust, waist, and hip sizes so that their estimates more closely approximate the physical features of the *ideal female figure* (Singer & Lamb, 1966).

There is little disagreement as to what the physically attractive female and male *should* look like; this is *ideal body image.* There is also a good deal of evidence to suggest that most persons can make accurate judgments about how physically attractive *other* individuals actually are. Although perceptions of physical attractiveness are far from being a subjective matter, there are some variables that seem to affect *how* physically attractive we judge others to be.

There is some evidence to suggest that people who are perceived to be highly intelligent, and to have similar attitudes and values as the perceiver, will be judged to be more physically attractive than their less intelligent peers, those with dissimilar attitudes and values. This evidence is far from conclusive, however (Newman, 1982). One study did support the view that the relative attractiveness of a person's personality affects judgments of their level of physical attractiveness. Newman (1982) found that subjects with a "positive personality" were rated as significantly more physically attractive than subjects with a "negative personality."

Newman's experimental conditions were so strong, however, that it would have been surprising if the stimulus persons with "negative personalities" did not receive extremely negative ratings on almost any conceivable dependent measure. Their personalities seemed to include some of the worst traits of Machiavelli, the master manipulator. Thus, in this study, the stimulus persons with "negative personalities" were losers in almost every sense of the word. They took pride in foisting their dirty clothes on their mothers, and noted that "Doing laundry is what mothers are here for. Besides, I can't stand going to coin-operated laundromats. Have you ever seen the wretched people that hang out there" (p. 62)?

Body Image: Self, Other, and Reflective

The communicator must be prepared to deal with at least three types of body image. Each of us has an image of our own body, which varies both with respect to our feelings about our personal appearance and with regard to how detailed that image is. As indicated, the more positive our feelings about our body image, the more detailed that image is apt to be. Moreover, our friends, associates, and others with whom we interact also have an image of our bodies. Finally, there is the *reflective* image. The reflective image represents a completely objective and accurate description of our facial and bodily features, as measured by instruments such as the profilometer and the X-ray.

Mike and Marvin Westmore recognize the importance of making individuals completely aware of the features of their reflective image. (The Westmore brothers are sought-after consultants to the movie industry, in Hollywood; they own and operate their own cosmetic studio.) When I taped an interview with the Westmore brothers in their office, they emphasized that they begin a series of consultations with a client by describing in detail a client's reflective image. They do so because the reflective image reveals, in an objective and precise manner, the undistorted features of the individual's personal appearance. Mike Westmore told me that they "are interested in the impact of the reflective image on the self-image. And the self-image relationship with social intercourse. Because this is what we are dealing with, we are working on a reflective image but the impact is on the self-image. And the self-image determines our place in society" (1973).

Effective communication based on fact rather than fantasy puts a premium on our ability to perceive accurately the defining features of our personal appearance. We must recognize that our actual (or reflective) body image may be different in important respects from our own image of our body, or the image our friends and associates have of our bodies. We must have an objective basis for comparing and constrasting these three images of our body before we decide whether to modify our appearance.

The Body Image Test

The Body Image Test has been devised to provide you with a practical means of developing a complete evaluation profile of the important features of your personal appearance. Although this test is different in form and function from the survey they developed, many of the terms for the body parts are from the body-survey research by Berscheid, Walster, and Bohrnstedt (1973).

The Body Image Test

To develop a complete image of your own body, begin by considering the eight bipolar scales in Table 5.1. Then provide an overall rating of your face in the blanks provided in Table 5.2. If you think that your face is extremely beautiful, you should put a 1 in the first blank. In contrast, if you feel that your face is extremely ugly, you should put a 7 in the first blank; if you feel your face is average, put a 4 in the first blank. Use all eight scales to rate the physical features of your face and body. After you have rated your own physical features, ask a group of business associates to use the same test to rate your physical features. Finally, ask a specialist, such as a dermatologist or a plastic surgeon, to use the same test to rate your physical features. By comparing the three sets of ratings, you will have complete profiles of the three body images most relevant to you.

TABLE 5.1   Scales 1–8

	1	2	3	4	5	6	7	
SCALE #1	BEAUTIFUL							UGLY
SCALE #2	HARD							SOFT
SCALE #3	STRONG							WEAK
SCALE #4	PLEASANT							UNPLEASANT
SCALE #5	ANGULAR							ROUNDED
SCALE #6	ROUGH							SMOOTH
SCALE #7	GOOD							BAD
SCALE #8	APPEALING							UNAPPEALING

Once the Body Image Test has been completed, you have an objective basis for determining whether the physical features of your personal appearance represent an asset or a liability. The ratings of your physical features may indicate that you should draw attention to your best feature (perhaps your complexion) in order to divert attention from a relatively unattractive feature (perhaps your chin). As I will indicate in the chapter on impression formation and management, a number of concrete options are available to the person who wishes to accentuate certain features of personal appearance.

The Matching Hypothesis

Consider carefully the personal appearance profile that has been revealed by The Body Image Test. How realistic has your image of your own body been? Have you made repeated attempts to date others who are markedly more, or less, physically attractive than you are? If so, you are running the risk of rejection, or the risk of developing interpersonal relationships that are less than satisfying.

Success in the development of intimate relationships seems to be based, at least in part, on the ability to seek out opposite-sex individuals who match your own level of physical attractiveness. In fact, individuals who have a realistic image of their body frequently seek to associate with others with similar levels of physical attractiveness. This is particularly true for dating relationships.

The *Matching Hypothesis* has been developed to explain the role of physical attractiveness in the selection of dating partners. This hypothesis is based on the assumption that individuals of similar levels of physical desirability seek each other out as dating partners and, eventually, as mar-

TABLE 5.2 Face-Body Parts and Scale Blanks

Part of Body	Number of Evaluative Scale							
	1	2	3	4	5	6	7	8
A Face (overall)	___	___	___	___	___	___	___	___
A(1) Hair	___	___	___	___	___	___	___	___
A(2) Eyes	___	___	___	___	___	___	___	___
A(3) Ears	___	___	___	___	___	___	___	___
A(4) Nose	___	___	___	___	___	___	___	___
A(5) Mouth	___	___	___	___	___	___	___	___
A(6) Teeth	___	___	___	___	___	___	___	___
A(7) Chin	___	___	___	___	___	___	___	___
A(8) Complexion	___	___	___	___	___	___	___	___
B Extremities B(1) Shoulders	___	___	___	___	___	___	___	___
B(2) Arms	___	___	___	___	___	___	___	___
B(3) Hands	___	___	___	___	___	___	___	___
B(4) Feet	___	___	___	___	___	___	___	___
C Mid Torso C(1) Abdomen	___	___	___	___	___	___	___	___
C(2) Buttocks	___	___	___	___	___	___	___	___
C(3) Hips	___	___	___	___	___	___	___	___
C(4) Thighs	___	___	___	___	___	___	___	___
C(5) Legs	___	___	___	___	___	___	___	___
C(6) Ankles	___	___	___	___	___	___	___	___

riage partners (Adams & Crossman, 1978). There is considerable empirical evidence to support the validity of the Matching Hypothesis. In fact, we may safely conclude that *individuals are likely to be attracted to other individuals who are similar to them in body build or type, dress, facial and bodily features, and overall physical attractiveness* (Archer, 1980).

The Matching Hypothesis may not apply of course when other factors prove to be more important than physical attractiveness. As you consider the individuals on the sofa (Figure 5.1), you will see that the physically attractive person may be drawn to the physically unattractive person who is wealthy, or who has a compensating virtue. There is evidence to suggest, however, that even among friends of the same sex, similarity in degree of physical attractiveness exceeds chance expectations (Cash & Derlega, 1978).

Do you have the ability to match up dating couples simply by assessing their level of physical attractiveness? Will the Matching Hypothesis be supported if we consider the physical attractiveness of dating couples at a major university? The Matching Test that follows is not intended to be a comprehensive and valid test of the Matching Hypothesis. It is intended, however, to increase your awareness of the Matching Hypothesis and its implications for the development of intimate relationships.

Your task is to determine which of the individuals in the photographs of Figure 5.2 are "dating couples." The photographs are of University of Georgia students who were waiting to see a movie at the Tate Student

FIGURE 5.1

" YOU DID SAY YOU WERE WORTH TWENTY MILLION DOLLARS DIDN'T YOU ? "

FIGURE 5.2

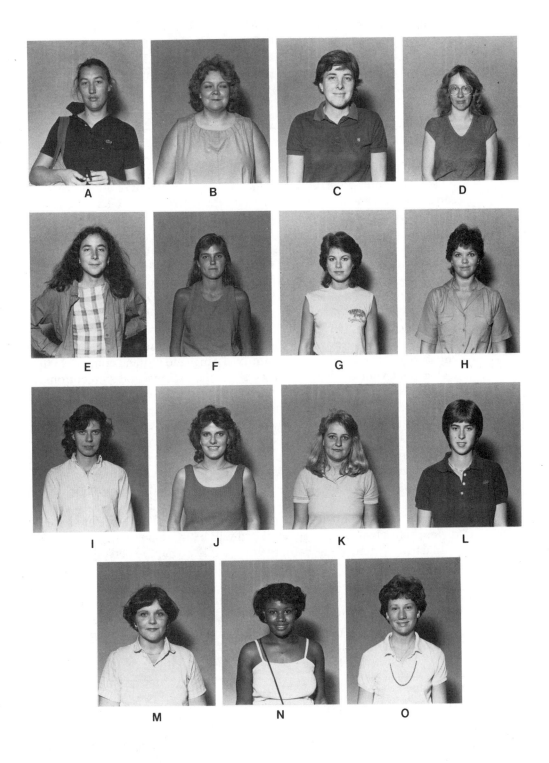

A   B   C   D

E   F   G   H

I   J   K   L

M   N   O

Center. Study the physical features of Female A and decide which of the males was her partner. In Table 5.3, put the appropriate number for the male you chose in the blank across from Female A. Follow the same procedure as you consider Female B, C, and so on. Photographs of the couples are shown in Appendix A.

Effects of Personal Appearance

Personal appearance has repeatedly been found to exert a major influence on social impressions. Our personal appearance strongly affects the personality traits and personal qualities that are attributed to us. As a result, personal appearance is an influential determinant not only of first impressions but also of our long-term image in the eyes of others.

We know that personal appearance exerts a significant impact on perception and behavior in almost every setting in which its effects have been studied; physically attractive persons consistently receive preferential treatment. As we shall see, *physically attractive persons seem to be discriminated against only when they take obvious advantage of their personal appearance.*

Adams and Crossman (1978) have identified some of the more salient effects of appearance in school, family, dating, and clinical contexts. Physical attractiveness clearly affects the expectations and perceptions of teachers and parents. In school settings, teachers seem to expect physically attractive children to be more succesful, academically and socially. As a result of this expectation, a physically attractive child often becomes "teacher's pet." In the family setting, too, parents' perceptions are often affected by their child's level of physical attractiveness. Thus, parents are inclined to attribute the misbehavior of unattractive children to personality flaws but dismiss the misbehavior of physically attractive children as a temporary aberration. Such parental behavior may reflect a general expectation: that physically attractive children will have better attitudes toward school and life in general, and will be more popular.

In dating situations as well, the physically attractive person clearly has the advantage. They are usually better liked, are seen as more desirable, and are approached more often. Even in the clinical setting, the physically attractive person is apt to receive preferential treatment. Thus, physically unattractive individuals are more likely than their physically attractive peers to be referred to a psychiatrist, and are more likely to be diagnosed as extremely maladjusted.

Perceptual Effects

The perceptual impact of our level of physical attractiveness begins with our self-concept. There is a strong positive relationship between physical attractiveness and self-concept. In simple terms, *the more physically attractive we are perceived to be, the more positive our self-concept is apt*

TABLE 5.3.   The Matching Test

	Couple #1	
Female A		Male _____
	Couple #2	
Female B		Male _____
	Couple #3	
Female C		Male _____
	Couple #4	
Female D		Male _____
	Couple #5	
Female E		Male _____
	Couple #6	
Female F		Male _____
	Couple #7	
Female G		Male _____
	Couple #8	
Female H		Male _____
	Couple #9	
Female I		Male _____
	Couple #10	
Female J		Male _____
	Couple #11	
Female K		Male _____
	Couple #12	
Female L		Male _____
	Couple #13	
Female M		Male _____
	Couple #14	
Female N		Male _____
	Couple #15	
Female O		Male _____

to be. The impact of physical attractiveness on self-concept is particularly pronounced for adolescents. In view of the rapid growth spurts and skin disturbances that are characteristic of the teenage years, it is not surprising that many teenagers become preoccupied with their personal appearance. However, both mature college students and adults also find that self-concept is strongly affected by personal appearance.

Physical attractiveness affects not only self-perceptions but the ways others perceive us. Dion, Berscheid, and Walster (1972) found, for example, that physically attractive individuals were perceived to be more likely to be sexually warm and responsive, sensitive, strong, and sociable than less attractive persons. Similarly, physically attractive counselors have been viewed as more intelligent, competent, trustworthy, assertive, and likable than less attractive counselors (Cash, Begley, McCown, & Weise, 1975).

A person's level of physical attractiveness also markedly affects the judgments that are made about the person's behavior. A number of studies have shown a relationship between an individual's personal appearance and the judgments made about the quality of work he or she produces. Landy and Sigall (1974) found, for example, that male readers of essays gave comparable grades to high-quality essays written by physically attractive and unattractive females. When the quality of the essay was inferior, however, unattractive females received significantly lower grades. Anderson and Nida (1978) found that physically attractive essay writers received the highest evaluations from members of the opposite sex, but individuals of moderate physical attractiveness received the highest ratings from members of their own sex.

Perhaps most importantly, essay writers of the lowest level of physical attractiveness received the lowest evaluations of all. Finally, attractive female essay writers have been judged, by male judges, to be significantly more "talented" than less attractive female essay writers (Kaplan, 1978). In short, the physically unattractive woman who does high-quality work may find that she receives relatively objective evaluations by men. When the physically unattractive woman produces work of marginal or low quality, however, she can expect much more negative evaluations by males than her more attractive female counterpart.

Physical attractiveness seems also to affect the dispensation of justice. This is particularly true when the plaintiff or defendant is a woman. Jurors, at least in a mock trial, who are exposed to an attractive plaintiff and an unattractive defendant find more often in favor of the plaintiff. They also award more money to the physically attractive as opposed to the physically unattractive plaintiff (Kulka & Kessler, 1978). Furthermore, attractive women are convicted less often for crimes they are accused of committing and in general receive more lenient sentences. Physically attractive female defendants seem to lose their edge in court only when they have taken advantage of their personal appearance to commit a crime. Thus, physically attractive females convicted of swindling receive stiffer sentences than their less attractive counterparts. If the conviction is for burglary, the unattractive female is apt to receive the harsher sentence (Adams, 1977).

Finally, there is some evidence to suggest that the morality of a person's behavior is affected by his or her level of physical attractiveness. In one interesting study, subjects were shown photographs of Barb and John. They were told that John invited Barb to his apartment and asked her to have sexual intercourse. Barb accepted the invitation. No matter what their attitude toward "casual sex," subjects judged the sexual behavior of the "highly attractive Barb" to be *less* moral than the behavior of the "quite unattractive" Barb. This study represents one of those rare instances where physical attractiveness seems to be a disadvantage. Because the attractive female might be viewed as having more opportunities for socially acceptable sexual outlets than the unattractive female, she is apparently expected to set and meet higher standards of morality in her sexual conduct (Hocking, Walker, & Fink, 1982).

Behavioral Effects

Our level of physical attractiveness affects not only our own behavior but the behavior of those with whom we interact. Ultimately, the nature of our relationships with other individuals is affected in important ways by our level of physical attractiveness.

The impact of our level of physical attractiveness is perhaps manifested most strongly in its effect on our self-concept. As I have already indicated, the more physically attractive we are, the more positive our self-concept is likely to be. Adams (1977) has examined the physical attractiveness/ self-concept relationship in detail, and has found that the behavioral profiles for physically attractive and physically unattractive persons do differ significantly in effectiveness of communication. For example, both physically attractive females and males exhibit *greater resistance to conformity pressure, more independence,* and more *self-disclosure* than their less attractive peers.

Attractive facial features have a particularly pronounced effect on the behaviors of those who possess such features. Females with attractive facial features are *more confident, experience little anxiety about having their own actions evaluated,* and are *highly resistant to peer pressure to conform.* Males with attractive facial features are more apt to exhibit *initiative, have a higher level of self-esteem,* and are *less likely to be critical of self and others* (Adams, 1977).

The potential of personal appearance to affect an individual's behavior is strikingly illustrated by the case of Rebecca Richardson. Becky Richardson came from a family with a history of congenital cleft palates. Her own condition was so bad that she had undergone 17 operations on her face to correct both articulatory and appearance problems associated with her cleft palate. After the final operation, she went to Mike and Marvin Westmore for professional cosmetic treatment of her face. When the Westmores began their cosmetic treatment, Becky Richardson's self-confidence was very low; she was withdrawn, and it was difficult to sustain communicative interaction with her. In the words of Mike Westmore (1973) "She was twenty-two years old and obvioulsy not getting her share of social intercourse with male members of society."

After she received a full set of aesthetic cosmetic treatments from the Westmore brothers, which produced a dramatic improvement in the attractiveness of her facial features, Becky Richardson's behavior changed dramatically. She was once withdrawn and uncommunicative, and she became a confident and sought-after young woman who assumed an active role in many social activities. She developed to the point where she actually became socially aggressive, in some situations. In Becky Richardson's case, the change in her reflective image produced a significant, highly beneficial change in her self-image and, consequently, in her behavior. Not only did she become a much more effective communicator, she also became a much more effective and satisfied human being.

The physical appearance of our body also seems to have important behavioral implications. We expect people with given body types to behave in distinctive ways. For example, the stereotypical expectation is that *mesomorphs* will be more assertive, mature, and self-reliant than individuals with other kinds of body types. *Endomorphs* are stereotyped as relatively lazy, warm-hearted, sympathetic, good-natured, and dependent. *Ectomorphs* are viewed stereotypically as suspicious, tense, nervous, pessimistic, and reticent. Although not conclusive, there is evidence to support the view that persons with each of these body types do indeed behave in ways that conform to their stereotype (Wells & Siegel, 1961).

The behavioral impact of body type may be stronger for children than for adults; we know that teenagers are particularly concerned about their personal appearance. In one study, the author (Walker, 1963), who had reliably classified children by body type, was able to confirm two-thirds of the predictions he made about the children's behavior, based solely on their body type. Girls' behaviors could be predicted from body type much more accurately than boys' behaviors. This finding is understandable in view of the fact that society attaches more importance to the physical attractiveness of females than males.

Parents' actual description of the behaviors of their children indicated that *endomorphic* girls are eager to please, even-tempered, friendly, and relaxed. By contrast, *ectomorphic* girls are tense, jealous, unpredictable, moody, suspicious, worried, and afraid of failure. The behaviors of mesomorphic children could not be predicted with a high degree of accuracy (Walker, 1963). Subsequent research indicates, however, that adolescents with *mesomorphic* body builds have a much stronger achievement need than either *endomorphs* or *ectomorphs* (Cortes & Gatti, 1966, 1970).

In short, individuals who are perceived to be physically attractive do behave differently. In general, persons who are *physically attractive* have a more positive self-image than persons who are not. Their behavior is characterized by *self-confident and assertive efforts to achieve demanding goals; by an independence of thought and action; and by an ability to resist the kinds of conformity pressure that would have the effect of diminishing their uniqueness as individuals.*

Because our physical attractiveness has such marked effects on our self-perceptions, behaviors, and on the perceptions of those with whom we interact, it is not surprising that physical attractiveness also affects our interpersonal relationships and interpersonal communication with others. The fact that the physically attractive are more highly regarded in our society means that they have greater opportunity for developing satisfying heterosexual relationships.

Physically attractive persons of both sexes have more opportunities to interact with members of the opposite sex. They have more dates, they go to more parties, they spend more time conversing with members of the opposite sex, and they spend less time on nonsocial, task-oriented activities. Perhaps most importantly, *both physically attractive females and males report that they are more satisfied with their opposite-sex relationships over an extended period of time than their less physically attractive peers* (Reis, Nezlek, & Wheeler, 1980).

Whether one is a casual or a serious dater, the more physically attractive a person is the greater the availability of opposite-sex partners. Also, attractive persons are less inclined to worry about the involvement of their partner with members of the opposite sex (White, 1980). In short, not only do physically attractive persons have more social interaction with members of the opposite sex, but the quality of that social interaction tends to be superior, from their perspective (Reis, Wheeler, Spiegel, & Kernis, 1982).

The physical attractiveness stereotype emphasizes that physically attractive individuals are more socially desirable. As a result, many of us exhibit a desire to identify with, to associate with, and to be similar to physically attractive persons. The net result is that physically attractive persons receive preferential tretment in the initiation and development of interpersonal relationships.

We know, for example, that more positive personality characteristics are attributed to a female when she is associated with a physically attractive male (Strane & Warts, 1977). We are *more self-disclosing* when in the presence of a physically attractive person. We *exhibit a greater willingness* to reward physically attractive individuals monetarily (Mathes & Edwards, 1978). We are *more willing to extend help* to those who are *physically attractive* (Wilson, 1978). We view our attitudes as being more similar to physically attractive than to physically unattractive persons (Mashman, 1978).

Finally, there is a strong tendency to judge the physically attractive as more credible and, ultimately, as more persuasive. Because you are viewed as being physically attractive does not of course assure that you will always be more persuasive than a less attractive person (Chaiken, 1979; Whaley, 1983), but it provides you with a decided advantage in a great variety of communicative situations. As I will emphasize in the chapter on impression formation and management, personal appearance is frequently a major determinant of both first impressions and our more enduring image.

Modification of Personal Appearance

Personal appearance is clearly a powerful medium of communication. The individual who meets or exceeds the standards for acceptable personal appearance in our society has many advantages. Unfortunately, many of us must face the realization that our overall personal appearance, or a specific physical feature, is deficient. We are left, at that point, with two options: We can brace ourselves to suffer the rather severe perceptual and behavioral penalties already described in this chapter, or we can use artifacts to modify those parts of our physical image that are subject to modification.

When I use the term *artifact*, I do not refer to the esoteric findings that came from an archaeological dig. I refer instead to *those things that humans can wear on their body, or do to their body, in order to modify personal appearance.* Chief among the artifactual means to modify our personal appearance are clothing, hairstyle, eyeglasses, contact lenses, and plastic surgery.

Clothing represents a particularly important artifact. By our choice of clothing, we can strongly affect the impressions people form of our authoritativeness, trustworthiness, and likability. We can help shape perceptions of our social standing as well as our sensitivity to the dress codes and preferences of those with whom we interact. We can, by our choice of clothing, emphasize the attractive features of our personal appearance and de-emphasize the unattractive features. The distinctive features of our personal appearance serve as an important source of information others use to determine how socially desirable we are.

In *The Winning Image,* Gray (1982) graphically illustrates how clothing and other artifacts can be used to enhance one's physical image. He cites the example of Michelle, a middle-aged businesswoman with a stocky frame. Michelle is six feet tall. Her endomorphic body build, combined with a short, severe hairstyle and large-frame glasses, make her seem intimidating and dominating to her clients.

Gray emphasizes that Michelle was able to make highly functional changes in the professional image she projected by changes in her choice of artifacts:

> Michelle made her appearance more relaxed and less dominating by exchanging the glasses for contacts and by wearing lighter, less authoritative dresses to deemphasize her build and low-heeled shoes to decrease her height.... Not only does she feel more comfortable but her client list is starting to grow. (p. 44)

In his enlightening book, Gray develops detailed clothing guidelines for the tall, muscular male; the tall, commanding female; the tall, thin male;

the tall, thin female; the short male; the short female; the hefty male; and the hefty female. The subject of what clothing and other artifacts a person should wear to project the desired image is one that I treat in detail in the chapter on impression management. As a beginning orientation to this important subject, however, the reader may wish to check a number of excellent sources (Gray, 1982; Leathers, 1981; Linver, 1983; Martel, 1984).

The choice of highly personalized artifacts, such as cosmetics, hairstyle, eyeglasses or contact lenses, and even orthodontal devices, clearly requires the aid of a professional image consultant. It is perhaps sufficient to say that the cosmetic aspects of some of these artifacts are often judged to be more important to the wearer than the medical health aspects. We do know, for example, that the interpersonal attractiveness of adolescent females who received orthodontic treatment increased significantly (Korabik, 1981).

Finally, plastic surgery is perhaps the most drastic means of modifying unattractive features. Plastic surgery is no longer undertaken exclusively for therapeutic purposes—reconstructing the face of the victim of an automobile crash, or rebuilding the skin of a burn victim. Each year, millions of Americans now elect to have aesthetic plastic surgery because they are not satisfied with their physical image.

Almost without exception, individuals who seek plastic surgery have a negative image of their own body. They may be upset by the social stigma of ethnic facial features, excessive fatty tissue, or sagging skin. Their own sense of identification is fuzzy at best and extremely self-deprecating at worst. Many of these individuals start with a negative sense of identification and seem to make a conscious effort to make others aware of their feelings of inferiority. Thus, Dr. Kurt Wagner, who served part of his residency performing plastic surgery on inmates in a prison in Oklahoma, has observed that "many inmates feel ugly, or they don't feel accepted or they have been made fools of . . . With tatoos, they go out of their way to mark themselves and further isolate themselves" from society (1973).

The motivation of those who seek plastic surgery, the resultant changes in their image, and the impact on their communicative behavior is a subject I have treated in detail elsewhere (Leathers, 1976). The considerable expense that is usually associated with plastic surgery, and the pain and discomfort that sometimes results, seem simply to emphasize the high priority that many Americans attach to an acceptable personal appearance.

Summary

In our society, a well-developed physical attractiveness stereotype suggests that what is beautiful is talented, good, and socially desirable. Persons who deviate from the cultural ideal for physical attractiveness frequently suffer severe penalties in terms of self-concept, the undesirable personal traits attributed to them, and the relatively limited social rewards they are able to derive from interpersonal relationships.

The facial and bodily features that differentiate the physically attractive from the physically unattractive person are almost universally recognized in our society. Societal standards that are used to define beauty are more detailed for women than for men; and definitions for facial features are more detailed than those for bodily features. A precise profile exists that identifies the facial features that define facial attractiveness. In general, the smaller our facial features the more attractive they are judged to be. Bodily attractiveness depends in part on whether one's body type is *mesomorphic, ectomorphic,* or *endomorpic.* For women, slenderness of body and body parts is an important feature of bodily attractiveness. For males, the unmasculine physique is viewed as particularly unattractive.

Body cathexis is the concept which reflects how satisfied or dissatisfied we are with our own body. To the extent that we are unsatisfied with the appearance of our own body, or parts of it, we are apt to engage in *body distortion.* Body distortion is the distortion of our own estimates of the size of certain of our physical features, usually those which deviate from the cultural ideal. In order to determine how realistic our own body image is when compared with the reflective image and the image our friends have our bodies, we should take The Body Image Test.

Our personal appearance has a major impact on not only our self-perceptions and behaviors but on the perceptions and behaviors of those who interact with us. The perceptual impact of personal appearance is perhaps strongest on self-concept; the more physically attractive we are perceived to be the more positive our self-concept is apt to be. From a perceptual perspective, physical attractiveness also affects the kind of person we are perceived to be; it markedly affects judgments made about the quality of work we produce; and it affects the way we are treated by the judicial system.

The behavioral impact of personal appearance is also striking. Individuals who are viewed as physically attractive *do* behave differently. They are self-confident and assertive in their effots to attain demanding goals; they exhibit independence in thought and action; and they exhibit an ability to resist conformity pressure, which is not characteristic of the physically unattractive person. When the physically attractive person mingles with others, there are greater opportunities for interaction with the opposite sex, and the nature of the interaction tends to be more satisfying.

Persons who do not meet the standards which are used to define acceptable personal appearance may wish to modify their personal appearance by using artifacts. Artifacts are those things that humans wear on their body, or do to their body, in order to modify their personal appearance. Clothing, cosmetics, hairstyle, eyeglasses and contact lenses, and plastic surgery are among the major artifactual means that may be used to exercise control over one's personal appearance.

References

Adams, G. R. (1977). Physical attractiveness research: Toward a developmental social psychology of beauty. *Human Development, 20,* 217–239.

Adams, G. R., & Crossman, S. M. (1978). *Physical attractiveness: A cultural imperative.* Roslyn Heights, NY: Libra.

Anderson, R., & Nida, S. A. (1978). Effects of physical attractiveness on opposite- and same-sex evaluations. *Journal of Personality, 46,* 410–413.

Archer, D. (1980). *How to expand your social intelligence quotient.* New York: Evans.

Berscheid, E., Walster, E., & Bohrnstedt, G. (1973). The happy American body, a survey report. *Psychology Today, 7,* 123.

Cahnman, W. J. (1968). The stigma of obesity. *Sociological Quarterly, 9,* 297.

Cash, T. F., Begley, P. J., McCown, D. A., & Weise, B. C. (1975). When counselors are heard but not seen: Initial impact of physical attractiveness. *Journal of Counseling Psychology, 22,* 237–239.

Cash, T. F., & Derlega, V. (1978). The matching hypothesis: Physical attractiveness among same-sexed friends. *Personality and Social Psychology Bulletin, 4,* 240–243.

Chaiken, S. (1979). Communicator physical attractiveness and persuasion. *Journal of Personality and Social Psychology, 37,* 1387.

Cortes, J. B., & Gatti, F. M. (1966). Physique and motivation. *Journal of Consulting Psychology, 30,* 408–414.

Cortes, J. B., & Gatti, F. M. (1970). Physique and propensity. *Psychology Today, 4,* 42.

Dion, E., Berscheid, E., & Walster, E. (1972). What is beautiful is good. *Journal of Personality and Social Psychology, 24,* 285–290.

Gray, J., Jr. (1982). *The winning image.* New York: AMACOM.

Hocking, J. E., Walker, B. A., & Fink, E. L. (1982). Physical attractiveness and judgments of morality following an immoral act. *Psychological Reports, 51,* 111–116.

Horvath, T. (1979). Correlates of physical beauty in men and women. *Social Behavior and Personality, 77,* 145–151.

Horvath, T. (1981). Physical attractiveness: The influence of selected torso parameters. *Archives of Sexual Behavior, 2.*

Kaplan, R. M. (1978). Is beauty talent? Sex interaction in the attractiveness halo effect. *Sex Roles, 4,* 195–204.

Korabik, K. (1981). Changes in physical attractiveness and interpersonal attraction. *Basic and Applied Social Psychology, 2,* 59–65.

Kretschmer, E. (1970). *Physique and character,* 2nd ed. New York: Cooper Square.

Kulka, R. A., & Kessler, J. B. (1978). Is justice really blind? The influence of litigant personal attractiveness on juridicial judgment. *Journal of Applied Social Psychology, 8,* 366–381.

Landy, D., & Sigall, H. (1974). Beauty is talent: Task evaluation as a function of the performer's physical attractiveness. *Journal of Personality and Social Psychology, 29,* 299–304.

Lavrakas, P. J. (1975). Female preferences for male physiques. *Journal of Research in Personality, 9,* 324–344.

Leathers, D. G. (1976). *Nonverbal communication systems.* Newton, MA: Allyn.

Leathers, D. G. (1981). Communication in the premium audit. In Robert J. Gibbons, Coordinating Author, *Principles of Premium Auditing,* Vol. 2. Malvern, PA: Insurance Institute of America.

Linver, S. (1983). *Speak and get results.* New York: Summit.

Malandro, L. A., & Barker, L. (1983). *Nonverbal communication.* Reading, MA: Addison-Wesley.

Martel, M. (1984). *Before you say a word: The executive guide to effective communication.* Englewood Cliffs, NJ: Prentice-Hall.

Mashman, R. C. (1978). Effect of physical attractiveness on the perception of attitude similarity. *Journal of Social Psychology, 106,* 103–110.

Mathes, E. W., & Edwards, L. L. (1978). Physical attractiveness as an input in social exchanges. *Journal of Psychology, 98,* 267–275.

Newman, D. A. (1982). The effects of positive and negative personality characteristics on perceptions of physical attractiveness. Unpublished master's thesis, University of Georgia, Athens, Ga.

Reis, H. T., Nezlek, J., & Wheeler, L. (1980). Physical attractiveness in social interaction. *Journal of Personality and Social Psychology, 38,* 604–617.

Reis, H. T., Wheeler, L., Spiegel, N., & Kernis, M. H. (1982). Physical attractiveness in social interaction: II. Why does appearance affect social experience? *Journal of Personality and Social Psychology, 43,* 979–996.

Routh, J. R. (1974). Cosmetic surgery is for men, too. *The Atlanta Journal and Constitution Magazine,* April 7, p. 39.

Secord, P. F., & Jourard, S. M. (1953). The appraisal of body-cathexis: Body-cathexis and self. *Journal of Consulting Psychology, 17,* 347.

Sheldon, W. H. (1954). *Atlas of man: A guide for somatyping the adult male at all ages.* New York: Harper.

Singer, J. E., & Lamb, P. R. (1966). Social concern, body size, and birth order. *Journal of Social Psychology, 68,* 144–147.

Staat, J. C. (1977). Size of nose and mouth as components of facial beauty. *Dissertation Abstracts International,* Doctoral dissertation, University of Oklahoma, Norman, Oklahoma.

Strane, K., & Warts, C. (1977). Females judged by attractiveness of partner. *Perceptual and Motor Skills, 45,* 225–226.

Sugerman, A. A., & Haronian, F. (1964). Body type and sophistication of body concept. *Journal of Personality, 32,* 393.

Wagner, K., & Gould, H. (1972). *How to win in the youth game: The magic of plastic surgery.* Englewood Cliffs, NJ: Prentice-Hall.

Walker, R. N. (1963). Body build and behavior in young children: II. Body build and parents' ratings. *Child Development, 34,* 20–23.

Wells, W. E., & Siegel, B. (1961). Stereotypes somatypes. *Psychological Review, 8,* 78.

Whaley, L. J. (1983). The effects of physical attractiveness on persuasion. Unpublished master's thesis, University of Georgia, Athens, Ga.

White, G. L. (1980). Physical attractiveness and courtship progress. *Journal of Personality and Social Psychology, 39,* 660–668.

Wilson, D. W. (1978). Helping behavior and physical attractiveness. *Journal of Social Psychology, 104,* 313–314.

Worsley, A. (1981). In the eye of the beholder: Social and personal characteristics of teenagers in their impressions of themselves and fat and slim people. *British Journal of Medical Psychology, 54,* 231–242.

CHAPTER SIX

Vocalic Communication

Sounds communicate meaning. The meanings exchanged by sound are vitally important in communicating the emotional state, the perceived personality characteristics, and, ultimately, the image of the communicator. If you doubt the truth of this assertion, listen to the audiotapes of President Franklin Roosevelt's Fireside Chats, during World War II.

The expressed purpose of Roosevelt's extemporaneous speeches was to allay the fears of the nation, and FDR's consummate use of sound as a communication medium was highly instrumental in helping him achieve his purpose. Imagine for a moment the following situation: Roosevelt's voice comes over the radio, he is speaking in a high-pitched, quavering voice, at an extremely rapid rate. He stutters repeatedly and fills his frequent pauses with perceptible sighs. If this had been the case, the nation might have experienced a real panic. Americans might have been as fearful of an emotionally distraught president as they were of the Nazis.

In fact, Roosevelt recognized what many subsequent studies have verified. The voice can be a powerful instrument for transmitting the emotional state of the communicator. Perhaps more important, to the person concerned with projecting a desired image, the voice can be used as a major force in shaping the perceived personality characteristics and credibility of the communicator. FDR used his voice to communicate the image of a vigorous, confident, and decisive leader who was completely in control of his emotions. Not-so-incidently, he used his voice to mold a political personality which successfully withstood the critical scrutiny of four presidential campaigns.

At least intuitively, most individuals recognize the role of the voice in shaping the image they project. The point was demonstrated graphically in my class on communication and conflict. Former Secretary of State Dean Rusk was once a guest in this class. The students asked him many questions, and each was obviously concerned with putting his or her best personality forward. Significantly, each student's vocal pattern was very different when addressing Rusk than it had been previously in the class. Almost invariably, the students paused before addressing Rusk. Usually, the pitch of the voice was much lower, the rate was much slower, the cadence more measured, and the nonfluencies less frequent. Clearly, the students wanted to be perceived as serious and thoughtful observers of the international scene, who were in control of their emotions. They knew that Rusk's perception of them would be affected materially by their use of their voice.

Vocal cues can of course serve many functions. The sound of the voice can be used to signal liking or disliking, dominance or submission, to reveal turn-taking preferences, and to provide information that may reveal gender, age, and race (Scherer, 1982). The voice functions most effectively, however, to communicate information about a person's emotions, presumed personality characteristics, and image. This chapter focuses on those primary functions of vocalic communication.

The Semantics of Sound

The semantics of sound is not a simple matter. We do know, however, that the vocal cues of communicators can be differentiated on the basis of attributes of sound uniquely associated with each communicator's vocal cues. *Vocal cues consist of all attributes of sound that can convey meanings and which have some measurable functions in interpersonal communication.* The *sound attributes* that give any vocal cue its unique characteristics are: (a) *loudness;* (b) *pitch;* (c) *rate;* (d) *duration;* (e) *quality;* (f) *regularity;* (g) *articulation;* (h) *pronunciation;* and (i) *silence.*

Loudness, or the power of the human voice, is perhaps the most basic attribute, because if a voice cannot be heard none of its other attributes can be used to convey meaning. Loudness is defined in terms of *decibels,* a measure of the acoustic energy reaching the receiver at a given second.

The quiet whisper at 10 decibels can be just as disruptive to interpersonal communication as the construction worker's hammer blows on steel plate, at 114 decibels. Very often, as individuals experience anxiety while they are delivering a speech or engaging in interpersonal communication, the power of their voice drops quickly and they are talking in a whisper which is unintelligible to the individual(s) with whom they are trying to communicate. On one occasion, I had a student who might very aptly been nicknamed Whispering Smith. A prominent and affluent businessman, the man (whom we shall simply call Smith) experienced great anxiety when giving a public speech. As his anxiety increased, Smith's volume dropped until he was whispering, and his audience was left in silent exaspration.

In spite of the fact that studies have been conducted on a great variety of conditions in big companies which use the assembly-line technique, few have focused on the damaging effects of excessive noise. The noise level in an average factory is 10 decibels above the noise level of a big-city street. This fact was dramatically emphasized for me when, with a group of my students, I toured an assembly plant of one of the world's largest auto manufacturers. In response to my question, the personnel director indicated that he had no idea what the noise level on the assembly line was, but that he knew for certain that his assembly line was really rather quiet, and that his company had never been sued for job-related hearing disability. Interestingly, communication with the personnel director, who was 3 to 6 feet away as we toured the assembly line, was often impossible, because of the noise level.

Anyone who has played a musical instrument is familiar with the concept of pitch. *Pitch* is the musical note that the voice produces. When you strike middle *C* on the piano, the *C*-string is vibrating at the rate of 256 times per second. Likewise, a human voice that produces the middle-*C* note is conveying the same pitch. Communicators have a *modal* pitch, i.e., one that occurs more frequently than any other pitch in their extemporaneous speech. You can easily identify your own modal pitch by recording a brief sample of your speech and matching the pitch of the sound that occurs most frequently with the appropriate note on your piano keyboard.

The communicator should note that a number of factors affect modal pitch. Most importantly, "emotion affects modal pitch. A person who is sad or stunned is likely to use a lower modal pitch. Excitement and gaity are normally shown by higher modal pitch. The quietly angry individual may use a low pitch, but the volatile type of anger may be high-pitched. We tend to associate low pitch with affection between sexes, but higher pitch with talking to babies" (Fisher, 1975, p. 155).

Your speaking or communicating *pitch range* is a measure of the musical interval (the number of notes) between the high and low pitch, which you use in speaking. Fisher notes that the range we employ in speaking depends on our intent, and on the content of what we are attempting to communicate. Factual communication has a much more limited pitch range than emotional communication, and emotional communication is apt to be high-pitched because most of it falls above your modal speaking range. Apathetic and apparent monotone speech both have a very narrow range (Fisher, 1975).

Rate is the third sound attribute of vocal cues that may facilitate or disrupt the transfer of meaning. Rate refers to the number of sounds emitted during a given unit of time—usually one second. Of course, when the communicator uses sounds to produce speech, speaking rate can have a vitally important impact on the quality of communication. Irregular rate may result in the communicator's combining words into units which are unconnected phrases rather than thought units.

Intelligibility and/or comprehension decline when rate of utterance exceeds 275 to 300 words per minute, although individuals can learn to comprehend material presented at faster rates through training in simple listening routines (Orr, 1968). Although we recognize that the average individual's thought rate is considerably faster than his or her speech rate, an accelerated rate of utterance is not always desirable. People differ substantially as to the optimum rate of utterance which they as listeners prefer. If the rate is too slow or the pauses too long, communicators will lose the attention of the person(s) with whom they are trying to communicate.

Finally, rate is a variable of primary interest to the paralinguists because it helps determine how fluent or dysfluent the communicator is and, hence, how effective the communicator is.

The attributes of rate and duration are integrally related because the length of time a communicator takes to emit a given sound or sounds is a major factor in determining the short-term, and often, the long-term, rate at which sounds are emitted. Duration is sometimes treated as a component of rate, but it is treated separately here because duration is an identifiable attribute of sound and, as such, may either hinder or help the communicator in attempts to transmit distortion-free meanings.

Quality, the fifth attribute of sound, has a variety of connotations and is difficult to define precisely. However, there is general agreement among students of vocalic communication that voice quality refers to those dominant vocal characteristics that allow you to differentiate one person's voice from another.

More than one authority now maintains that an individual's voice qualities are so distinctive that an expert can identify a given individual's voice from a tape of the voices of many other individuals. In the past few years, *voiceprints* have been used increasingly in criminal trials, in an attempt to provide positive identification of a suspect.

One of the foremost students and proponents of the voiceprint technique is Lawrence G. Kersta of New York, a retired technical specialist for Bell Laboratories and president of Voiceprint Laboratories, Inc., of New York. Kersta has appeared frequently as an expert witness for the prosecution and has attempted to identify the accused. Probably his most famous appearance involved the trial of a defendant who admitted to a network newsman—in an interview put on audiotape—that he had committed arson during the Watts riots in Los Angeles. The newsman would not reveal the identity of the arsonist, on the grounds that the confidentiality of his sources of news had to be protected. Kersta was brought in to the trial and asked to identify the arsonist by matching the voice in the taped interview with known samples of the alleged arsonist's voice, which was included among samples of a number of other voices. Although the identification of the defendant by voiceprints was not used by the jury as a piece of evidence to convict him, voiceprints have been used as admissible and persuasive evidence in subsequent trials.

The dominant *quality* of a person's voice strongly affects the impression that person makes. Addington's research (1968), for example, indicates that individuals with *flat* voices are apt to be perceived as masculine, sluggish, cold, and withdrawn. The *breathy* female voice reinforces the stereotypical conception that breathy females are superficial and shallow individuals. Finally, the *nasal* voice is particularly undesirable because it is associated with a substantial number of socially undesirable personal qualities.

The sound attribute of *regularity* refers to whether your production of sound has a rhythmical, and possibly even a predictable quality. If you have ever listened to newscaster Walter Cronkite, you know what is meant by regularity of sound, and sound pattern. In contrast, comedian Dick Smothers has made a lot of money by emphasizing the arhythmic or irregular nature of his sound production. Depending on the communicative situation, the sound attribute of regularity can be highly desirable or undesirable.

Articulation involves the use of movable parts at the top of the vocal tract, such as tongue, jaw, and lips, to shape sounds and, in speech communication, to make transitions between individual sounds and words. Although primarily physiological, articulation represents an attribute of sound, much like loudness, which must be present in acceptable form or communication virtually ceases to exist. If you remember saying "Peter Piper picked a peck of pickled peppers" in your grade-school days, you know that very careful articulation was necessary or the listener would not be able to determine the exact nature of Peter's task.

Pronunciation is defined by specific vowel or consonant sounds in words, and by the syllable that is emphasized. If you pronounce a word in a way that is inconsistent with general usage, or usage among the social groups with which you associate, it almost surely will result in confusion, at minimum. Perhaps more importantly, in terms of its long-range effect on the communicator, consistent mispronunciation of words may impair a speaker's credibility and communicative effectiveness. For example, *irrelevant* is probably one of the most commonly mispronounced words in our society. Often irrelevant is pronounced *irrevelant.* If such mispronunciation occur frequently, this will markedly lower the quality of an individual's communication.

In the strictest technical sense, *silence* is not an attribute of vocal cues because silence assures that none of the eight defining attributes of vocal cues can be present. On the other hand, any sensitive observer of interpersonal communication recognizes that silence is a variable that is closely related to the other eight attributes of vocalic communication; therefore, silence serves important functions in interpersonal communication. We may give someone the "silent treatment" if we do not wish to acknowledge his or her presence; we may become silent when we become unbearably anxious; or we may remain silent in order to exhibit emotions such as defiance or annoyance (DeVito, 1983).

Communicating Emotional Information

Vocal cues represent an important medium of emotional communication. Mehrabian (1981), for example, maintains that 38 percent of the emotional information transmitted by a given message may be attributed to vocal cues. Facial expressions, as the predominant medium of emotional communication, account for 55 percent of the total feeling in a message and words account for only 7 percent.

In order to assess the potential of vocal cues as a medium of emotional communication, researchers have used a number of techniques to eliminate the effective impact of the words uttered. Subjects have been asked to read ambiguous passages from texts that have no readily identifiable meaning, to utter nonsense words and syllables, and to speak in a foreign language. Electronic "filters" have also been applied to speech samples, to eliminate the sounds of higher frequencies. This practice renders the verbal message unintelligible and leaves the vocal message relatively intact.

Fairbanks and Pronovost (1939) were among the earliest experimenters in speech communication who attempted to determine whether individuals could communicate significant emotions solely by vocal cues, and if so, how accurately various emotions could be communicated. They used the technique of an ambiguous text, in an attempt to assure that the meanings communicated were solely the result of the sound attributes of the vocal cues used in reading the passage.

Six competent actors were asked to read the following passage repeatedly:

> *You've got to believe it in time to keep them from hanging me. Every night you ask me how it happened. But I don't know! I don't know! I can't remember. There is no other answer. You've asked me that question a thousand times, and my reply has always been the same. It always will be the same. You can't figure out things like that. They just happen, and afterwards you're sorry. Oh, God, stop them . . . quick . . . before it's too late.*

As the actors repeated the passage to a group of 64 student judges, they were to vary the nature of the vocal cues in such a way that they believed they were accurately conveying the emotions of contempt, anger, fear, grief, and indifference.

The experiment demonstrated not only that all *emotions could be conveyed accurately by vocalic communication, at a level that greatly exceeds chance, but that the vocal cues that conveyed the different emotions had readily identifiable and distinctive sound attributes.* Average accuracy of identification for the five emotions was: 88 percent for indifference; 84 percent for contempt; 78 percent for anger and grief; and 66 percent for fear.

Contempt was communicated by extreme variations in inflections at the ends of phrases, a low median pitch level, and a wide total pitch range. Anger was associated with the greatest variability in all sound attributes, the widest mean extent of all pitch shifts, and the most downward pitch shifts. Fear was associated with the highest median pitch level, the widest total pitch range, and the fewest pauses within phrases at which shifts of pitch were not made. Grief exhibited the least variability among the attributes of sound; the presence of vibrato, the shortest duration of sound, and the slowest rate of pitch change. Indifference was communicated by the lowest pitch, the narrowest total pitch range, and shortest duration of sound when downward or upward inflections occurred.

Recent research (Scherer & Oshinsky, 1977) identified similar but not identical relationships between specific emotions and the sound attributes that are used to express them. For example, sadness is expressed by downward inflections, low pitch, and slow speaking rate. Anger is expressed by wide variations in pitch, downward inflections, and fast speaking rate.

Probably the most detailed and enlightening contemporary research on the use of vocal cues to communicate specific emotions has been done by Davitz and Davitz. They gave graduate students at Columbia University a list of ten emotions and asked them to communicate these emotions by reciting the alphabet. Subjects were then asked to identify the emotions communicated via separate recitations of the alphabet by the graduate students. Judges were asked to make 240 total judgments. The number of correct identifications expected by chance would be 24. The number of correct identifications for each emotion expressed was: (a) anger, 156; (b) nervousness, 130; (c) sadness, 118; (d) happiness, 104; (e) sympathy, 93; (f) satisfaction, 74; (g) and (h) fear and love, 60; (i) jealousy, 59; and (j) pride, 50 (Davitz & Davitz, 1959).

Subsequent research by Davitz (1964) and by Scherer (1979), as well as an extensive review and assessment of this type of research (Harper, Wiens, & Matarazzo, 1978), clearly supports the conclusion that vocal cues are an effective medium for the communication of specific emotions. In fact, the human voice has the potential to communicate specific kinds of information about emotions experienced by individual communicators that is exceeded only by the human face.

The fact that the human voice can be used as a powerful medium for the communication of emotions does not of course mean that everyone uses it effectively for this purpose. In fact, we know that *individuals' ability to encode and decode emotional information via vocal cues varies substantially.* Levy (1964) found significant differences among individuals in terms of the accuracy with which they were able to encode and decode vocally expressed emotions. Individuals even differed significantly in their ability to identify their own feelings, which had previously been expressed in their own voice on audiotape.

The practical implications of this finding are clear for the person who wishes to be a successful communicator. We must be able to use our own voice effectively to express our feelings and emotions. We must also be able to identify accurately the emotions that others express vocally.

The Vocalic Meaning Sensitivity Test (VMST) has been developed both to test and to develop the accuracy with which individuals can communicate and perceive emotional meanings conveyed solely by vocal cues. The personal testimony of many classroom instructors who have used the VMST suggests that it is a useful measurement and training tool. Individuals who take the test almost always become very involved in the learning experience it provides. Many of these same individuals have emphasized that the VSMT gives them a much better appreciation of the functions of vocalic communication, and with repeated use it significantly improves both their encoding and decoding abilities.

To use the Vocalic Meaning Sensitivity Test in its simplest form you must do two things. First, have a friend or acquaintance attempt to communicate disgust, happiness, interest, sadness, bewilderment, contempt, surprise, anger, determination, and fear solely by the vocal cues used in reading the following sentences: *"There is no other answer. You've asked me that question a thousand times, and my answer is always the same."*

Your friend should repeat the two sentences ten times, and each time he or she should be trying to communicate a different meaning by varying sound attributes such as pitch, loudness, and rate. Randomize the order in which attempts are made to communicate each class of vocalic meaning. For example, *sadness* may be the first meaning he or she attempts to communicate, and determination the *second*. To separate one reading from another, your friend should begin each reading by saying, "This is vocal message number 1," then, "This is vocal message number 2," and so on.

If your friend is particularly interested in communication of the highest possible quality, he or she may want to practice and record the best efforts on audiotape—then, rather than listening to your friend speaking in person, you will listen to the tape. When attempting to communicate vocally before a live audience, the communicators should sit with his or her chair turned away from the audience. Ideally, the communicator should sit behind a screen, to prevent the audience from seeing kinesic or other nonverbal cues.

Second, you should take the Vocalic Meaning Sensitivity Test by following the directions given. When you identify the vocal message of others, your own decoding skill is being measured. When others attempt to identify your vocal messages, your own encoding skill is being measured.

The Vocalic Meaning Sensitivity Test

The communicator you are listening to—either live or on a tape recording—is attempting to communicate ten different classes or kinds of meaning to you. Each attempt to communicate a class of meaning will begin with the words "This is a vocal message number—." You are to listen very carefully, and in Table 6.1 place the number of the vocal message in the blank across from a word, such as disgust or happiness, whichever comes closest to representing the meaning just communicated to you vocally. Follow the same procedure for each of the ten vocal messages.

To test your ability to communicate meanings accurately as opposed to testing your ability to perceive meanings transmitted by vocal cues, you should attempt to communicate the ten emotions which comprise the VMST by making a tape recording and then giving the test to a group of people of your own choice.

Students' ability to communicate the ten emotions which comprise the

TABLE 6.1*

Class of Vocalic meaning	Number of Vocal Message
Disgust	_____
Happiness	_____
Interest	_____
Sadness	_____
Bewilderment	_____
Contempt	_____
Surprise	_____
Anger	_____
Determination	_____
Fear	_____

*You may use an expanded form of the test if you desire. The ten terms used here were used for two reasons: They have previously been used in tests of vocalic communication, and they are the same terms used in Step 1 of the Facial Meaning Sensitivity Test. Therefore, the reader can make direct comparisons between his or her ability to perceive and communicate meanings by facial and vocal means. Simply compare accuracy of identification scores for Step 1 of the FMST with scores on the VMST. If you want to make a more extended test of your ability to perceive and transmit meanings vocally, however, you should add ten terms to the test. These terms, also frequently used in tests of vocalic communication, are *indifference, grief, anxiety, sympathy, pride, despair, impatience, amusement, satisfaction,* and *dislike.* By adding these terms to the VSMT, you have a more comprehensive and demanding test of vocalic skills.

VMST vary dramatically (6 correct choices out of 10 is 60 percent accuracy of identification). The scores of the "vocal communicators" in my classes have ranged from 85 percent to 30 percent; the scores of the "vocal perceivers" have been in about the same range. As a rule of thumb, you can assume that a score of 70 percent or above is excellent; 69 to 50 percent is average; and below 50 percent is poor.

Repeated use of the VMST usually leads to marked improvement in both the ability to encode and decode messages conveyed by sound. You have the potential to improve your scores on the test by at least 20 percent. If you set realistic goals for yourself, the VMST can be a great help to you in attaining them.

Communicating Perceived Personality Characteristics

Clearly, vocal cues represent an effective medium for the communication of emotional meanings. The functions of vocalic communication are hardly limited to the exchange of emotional meanings, however. Another function may be even more important to some readers. *Communicators can make marked changes in their personaliaty, as it is perceived by others, by their use of vocal cues.* The implications of this finding are striking for individuals who wish to emphasize or de-emphasize certain perceived characteristics of their personality.

This statement could, of course, be misinterpreted. A course or two in voice training is not apt to result in a startling transformation of your actual personality. Indeed, the calculated use of your voice is not apt to change your basic personality, but it may result in marked differences in the *ways others perceive your personality.*

Interest in the possible relationships between vocal cues and personality characteristics can be traced to the early days of radio, when massive national audiences were first attracted to it. Not surprisingly, many radio listeners beccame convinced that they could form accurate personality profiles of radio performers simply by listening to their voices. Other listeners were convinced that they could also accurately predict what announcers looked like by listening to them.

Stimulated by the intense curiosity of radio listeners, Pear (1931) analyzed the reaction of over 4,000 radio listeners to nine trained radio voices and concluded that listeners consistently identified certain patterns of vocal cues with certain occupations, such as clergymen and judges. Pear also found, however, that listeners consistently agreed that certain "vocal stereotypes" identified certain professions, although they made a number of errors in the application of such stereotypes.

In 1934, Allport and Cantril conducted the first major study specifically designed to examine the question of *whether, and to what extent, the natural voice is a valid indicator of personality.* Their results strongly affirmed a positive relationship. The authors wrote that the voice definitely conveys "correct information concerning inner and outer characteristics." Specifically, they found that the sound attributes that comprise vocal cues are accurate indicators of the important personality dimensions of *introversion/extroversion* and *ascendance/submission.*

Although the pioneering study by Allport and Cantril did suggest a strong relationship between the nature of vocal cues and dimensions of the speaker's personality, the authors were bothered by the apparent fact that a limited number of vocal cues seemed to create a stereotype of the speaker in the mind of the listener. Initially, the tendency of listeners to deal in stereotypes suggested that the listeners took a limited number of vocal cues and erroneously concluded that a large group of people, who conveyed vocal cues with the same sound attributes, had the same personality characteristics.

The concern that "vocal stereotypes" might invalidate research that attempts to predict personality characteristics from vocal cues has persisted up to the present. Such concern seems unwarranted for a number of reasons: (a) Stereotypes, although sometimes inaccurate, are often accurate; (b) When the vocal stereotypes are inaccurate, the judges typically make the same error. Thus, as Crystal (1969) writes, "such consistency in error may well be indicative of the existence of unformulated but none the less systematic voice-quality/trait correlations, or *vocal stereotypes,* as they are usually called in the literature, and is an important piece of evidence justifying the psychologists' optimism that a systematic basis for personality in vocal cues does exist"(p. 70); (c) *The accuracy of an audience's or individual's inferences about a speaker's real personality characteristics is not as important as an audience's agreement about a speaker's perceived personality characteristics.*

As Pearce and Conklin (1971) write, "it should be noted that the accuracy of audience inferences about a speaker is not particularly important in this context. Experienced public speakers develop characteristic manners of presentation that lead audiences to draw desired or undesired inferences about them which, *whether accurate or not* [author's italics], affect the continuation and effectiveness of the communication situation. If a speaker is perceived as effeminate, arrogant, unscrupulous, or incompetent because of vocal cues . . . his actual personality and credibility may be superfluous" (p. 237).

In spite of the great promise of the Allport and Cantril research, World War II, and perhaps the cyclical rhythms of researchers, resulted in a period of almost twenty-five years when little effort was made to examine the relationship between vocal cues and perceived personality characteristics.

Addington has conducted perhaps the most exhaustive research on the question of which specific attributes of sound are indicators or predictors of specific personality characteristics. In work for his doctoral dissertation (1963), he attempted to simulate a number of vocal qualities (breathy, thin, flat, nasal, tense, throaty, and orotund), to manipulate rate and to introduce variety in pitch. Judges consistently agreed on the personality attributes associated with the different sound attributes in the vocal cues. Judges' agreement was highest on the feminine–masculine ratings of personality (.94) and lowest for the extroverted–introverted ratings (.81). The most uniformly perceived personality dimensions were feminine–masculine, young–old, enthusiastic–apathetic, energetic–lazy, good-looking–ugly, cooperative–uncooperative, unemotional–emotional, talkative–quiet, intelligent–stupid, interesting–unintresting, and mature–immature.

Male communicators were seen as varying along four relatively unique personality dimensions: (a) lanky–dumpy; (b); hearty–glum; (c) potent–impotent; and (d) soft-hearted–hard-hearted. In contrast, female communicators were seen as varying along five personality dimensions: (a) social–antisocial; (b) aggressive–unresisting; (c) urbane–coarse; (d) passionate–dispassionate; and (e) wise–foolish. Thus, personalities of males were perceived, from vocal cues, in terms of physical characteristics and females were evaluated in more social terms.

Pitch, rate, and the distinctive overall quality of communicators' voices are attributes of vocal cues that determine which personality characteristics are attributed to the communicators. For both male and female speakers, those who use greater variety in *pitch* are thought to be *dynamic* and *extroverted*. Both male and female speakers who use variety in *rate* are thought to be *extroverted*; males are also seen as *animated*, but females are seen as *high-strung, inartistic,* and *uncooperative* (Addington, 1963).

Specific sound attributes seem, in the minds of the listeners, to be associated with very specific personality characteristics. For example, *both* males and females with flat voices were evaluated as *sluggish, cold,* and *withdrawn,* and both males and females with nasal voices were evaluated as *unattractive, lethargic,* and *foolish.* Other vocal qualities were associated with very different personality characteristics for males and females. For example, males with breathy voices were perceived as *youthful* and *artistic,* and females with breathy voices were viewed as *feminine,* but *callow* and *high-strung.* Males with tense voices were perceived as *cantankerous,* but females with tense voices were perceived as *high-strung* and *pliable.* Even more strikingly, the male with a throaty voice was evaluated as *suave,* but a female with a throaty voice was evaluated as *oafish,* or a "*clod*"; males with orotund voices were perceived as *vigorous* and *aesthetic* but the female with an orotund voice was perceived as a "*clubwoman.*"

Certainly, "this study has made it quite evident that it is possible for a speaker, through a variety of vocal changes, to make gross or subtle alterations in his personality as it is perceived by listeners cued only by a sample of the speaker's speech. . . . For those speakers interested in creating a perceived personality they would be pleased to claim as their own, and for those interested in character interpretation, vocal dexterity is a mandatory skill" (Addington, 1963, p. 163).

Research conducted since Addington's comprehensive efforts has consistently confirmed the idea that the nature of vocalic communication materially affects the personality characteristics that listeners identify with the communicator. In addition, specific sound attributes—such as rate, pitch, or nasality—are consistently associated with the same specific personality traits by the listener. In further interpreting and refining his earlier research, Addington (1968) concluded that "judgments of listeners ascribing personality from samples of speakers' voices tended to be uniform," and that this relationship was "well supported in the present findings" (p. 498).

When considered in the aggregate, empirical research has established that perceivers consistently attribute specific personality characteristics to communicators on the basis of the sound of their voices (Aronvitch, 1976). We now know, for example, that we can speak with the "voice of social attractiveness" by systematically controlling the sound attributes that are dominant in our vocal cues (Street & Brady, 1982).

Our vocal cues are particularly important determinants of how *self-confident, self-assured,* and *dominant* we are perceived to be. The confident voice is defined by substantial but not excessive volume, a rather rapid speaking rate, expressiveness, and fluency. Communicators who exhibit a "confident" as opposed to a "doubtful" voice are perceived as significantly more *enthusiastic, forceful, active, dominant,* and *competent* (Sherer, London, & Wolf, 1973).

Conversely, we attribute unacceptable levels of anxiety to individuals who speak nonfluently. Nonfluencies include "ah," sentence changes, word repetitions, stuttering (repeating the first syllable of a word), incomplete sentences, tongue slips, and intruding incoherent sounds, such as tongue clicks (Prentice, 1972). From a perceptual perspective, nonfluencies are, in the mind of the perceiver, strongly associated with high levels of anxiety (Jurich & Jurich, 1974).

The sound attributes which must be emphasized and de-emphasized in order to speak with the "voice of social attractiveness" have been rather clearly identified. One note of caution is warranted, however. We are more apt to be judged as socially attractive by others if our voices sound similar, in important respects, to *their* voices. For example, individuals tend to respond more favorably to a communicator when the communicator's speaking rate is similar to his or her own voice (Street & Brady, 1982). Our characteristic speaking rate, pitch, and volume must fall within ranges that are viewed as socially acceptable, however, in order for others to judge us as more socially attractive simply because we sound like them.

Communicating the Desired Image

In our society, there is a well-developed vocal stereotype that specifies how communicators must sound if they are to be viewed as credible (Thakerar & Giles, 1981). The dimension of credibility most apt to be affected by the sound of our voice is *competence*. We know, for example, that individuals who exhibit standard or prestigious accents, pause only briefly before responding, speak fluently, exhibit suitable variation in pitch and volume, and speak at a relatively fast rate are usually perceived as more competent than individuals who are associated with contrasting vocal cues (Street & Brady, 1982).

To speak with the "voice of competence," you must pay particular attention to those attributes of sound that are know to markedly affect judgments of credibility. In separate chapters—on selling yourself nonverbally and on impression formation and management—I will identify in detail those sound attributes that you should and should not exhibit if you wish to speak with the voice of competence. In a variety of applied contexts, such as the sales and selection interview, it is clear that the sound of your voice will go a long way to establish or destroy your personal credibility (Gray, 1982).

Vocal cues affect not only perception of communicators' credibility but also perceptions of their power and status. A moderately fast rate, high volume, and full resonance all reinforce perceptions of power and status (Burgoon & Saine, 1978). Schlenker emphasizes "that an image of power can be communicated to an audience through paralanguage in several ways. When people are anxious and lacking in confidence, they speak with lower volume and exhibit more speech disturbances, such as stuttering, omitting portions of a word or sentence, failing to complete a sentence, and taking longer pauses between words and sentences—seeming to grope for the correct word but unable to find it. People who are self-confident do not display such awkward paralanguage" (p. 252).

Vocal cues clearly have the potential to play a major role in helping an individual communicate the desired image. We know that vocal cues are a major determinant of the first impression that we make (Kleinke, 1975). This is true in part because others intuitively distrust the calculated first impression that communicators try to project through the words that they utter. More importantly, our long-term image can be strongly affected by the image traits that are attributed to us because of the sound of our voices.

We know that individuals with whom we interact make judgments about the kind of person we are presumed to be on the basis of our affective reaction to them, the personality characteristics they attribute to us, and on the basis of our personal credibility. The voice is a potentially powerful medium of communication, one which can strongly affect these kinds of person-oriented judgments. As a result, we must carefully consider the value of speaking with the "voice of competence" and the "voice of social attractiveness" if we are to communicate an image that is both desired and desirable.

Summary

Vocal cues consist of all attributes of sound that can convey meanings and have some measurable functions in interpersonal communication. The sound attributes that differentiate one person's vocal cues from another's are: (a) loudness; (b) pitch; (c) rate; (d) duration; (e) quality; (f) regularity; (g) articulation; (h) pronunciation; and (i) silence.

Vocal cues are an important medium of emotional communication. Their potential to provide specific information about a communicator's emotional states is exceeded only by facial expressions. We do know, however, that individuals' ability to encode and decode emotional information via vocal cues varies substantially. Successful communication puts a premium on the development of these important nonverbal communication skills. The Vocalic Meaning Sensitivity Test (VMST) presented in this chapter should be used both to test and develop the accuracy with which individuals can communicate and perceive emotional meanings conveyed solely by vocal cues.

Vocal cues strongly affect the specific kinds of personality characteristics and personal qualities that are attributed to the communicator. Pitch, rate, and the overall quality of our voices determine which personality characteristics are attributed to us. Persons who exhibit little variation in pitch and rate, for example, are typically viewed as introverts, lacking dynamism and assertiveness. Persons who exhibit a nasal quality are likely to have a wide array of undesirable personality characteristics attributed to them.

Communicators who speak with the "voice of social attractiveness" usually exhibit substantial but not excessive volume, a rather rapid speaking rate, expressiveness, and fluency. Sound attributes such as these are characteristically exhibited by communicators who are judged to be self-confident and self-assured.

Finally, vocal cues can be very important in helping an individual communicate a desired image. There is a well-developed vocal stereotype in our society that specifies how credible persons sound. Vocal cues can exert great impact on not only an individual's personal credibility but on the power and status they are presumed to have. In short, the impressions we make are so strongly affected by the way we sound that we cannot expect to communicate a desired image until we sound both socially attractive and competent.

References

Addington, D. W. (1963). The relationship of certain vocal characteristics with perceived speaker characteristics. (Doctoral dissertation, University of Iowa, 1963).

Addington, D. W. (1968). The relationship of selected vocal characteristics to personality perception. *Speech Monographs, 35,* 492–503.

Allport, G. W., & Cantril, H. (1934). Judging personality through voice. *Journal of Social Psychology, 5,* 40–51.

Aronovitch, C. P. (1976). The voice of personality: Stereotyped judgments and their relation to voice quality and sex of speaker. *Journal of Social Psychology, 92,* 207–220.

Burgoon, J. K., & Saine, T. (1978). *The unspoken dialogue.* Boston: Houghton.

Crystal, D. (1969). *Prosodic systems and intonation in english.* Cambridge, MA: Cambridge University Press.

Davitz, J. R. (Ed.), *The communication of emotional meaning.* New York: McGraw-Hill.

Davitz, J. R., & Davitz, L. J. (1959). The communication of feelings by content-free speech. *Journal of Communication, 9, 9.*

DeVito, J. A. (1983). *The interpersonal communication book,* 3rd ed. New York: Harper.

Fairbanks, G., & Pronovost, W. (1939). An experimental study of the durational characteristics of the voice during the expression of emotion. *Speech Monographs, 6,* 88–91.

Fisher, H. B. (1975). *Improving voice and articulation,* 2nd ed. Boston: Houghton.

Gray, J., Jr. (1982). *The winning image.* New York: AMACOM.

Harper, R. B., Wiens, A. N., & Matarazzo, J. D. (1978). Nonverbal communication: The state of the art. New York: Wiley.

Jurich, A. P., & Jurich, J. A. (1974). Correlations among nonverbal expressions of anxiety. *Psychological Reports, 34,* 199–204.

Kleinke, C. L. (1975). *First impressions.* Englewood Cliffs, NJ: Prentice-Hall.

Levy, P. K. (1964). The ability to express and perceive vocal communications of feeling. In J. R. Davitz (Ed.), *The Communication of Emotional Meaning.* New York: McGraw-Hill.

Mehrabian, A. (1981). *Silent messages,* 2nd ed. Belmont, CA: Wadsworth.

Orr, D. B. (1968). Time compressed speech—A perspective. *Journal of Communication, 18,* 288–291.

Pear, T. H. (1931). *Voice and personality.* London: Chapman and Hall.

Pearce, W. B., & Conklin, F. (1971). Nonverbal vocalic communication and perception of a speaker. *Speech Monographs, 38,* 235–241.

Prentice, D. S. (1972). The process effects of trust-destroying behavior on the quality of communication in the small group. (Doctoral dissertation, University of California at Los Angeles.)

Scherer, K. R. (1979). Nonlinguistic vocal indicators of emotion and psychopathology. In C. E. Izard (Ed.), *Emotions in personality and psychopathology.* New York: Plenum,

Scherer, K. R. (1982). Methods of research on vocal communication: Paradigms and parameters. In K. R. Scherer & P. Ekman (Eds.), *Handbook of methods in nonverbal behavior research.* Cambridge, MA: Cambridge University Press.

Scherer, K. R., London, H., & Wolf, J. J. (1973). The voice of confidence: Paralinguistic cues and audience evaluation. *Journal of Research in Personality, 7,* 31–44.

Scherer, K. R., & Oshinsky, J. S. (1977). Cue utilization in emotion attribution from auditory stimuli. *Motivation and emotion, 1,* 331–346.

Schlenker, B. R. (1980). *Impression management.* Monterey, CA: Brooks/Cole.

Street, R. L., Jr., & Brady, R. M. (1982). Speech rate acceptance ranges as a function of evaluative domain, listener speech rate, and communication context. *Communication Monographs, 49,* 290–308.

Thakerar, J., & Giles, H. (1981). They are—So they spoke: Noncontent speech stereotypes. *Language and Communication, 1,* 255–261.

CHAPTER SEVEN

Tactile Communication

Touch communicates meanings. Touch has substantial communicative potential, but this potential has been little explored. Our lack of knowledge about touch can be attributed to a number of factors. First, many individuals have accepted the misconception that touch is a primitive sense and has limited value in the transmission and reception of meanings in interpersonal communication. Second, ironic as it may seem, in an age that has seen the rise of the Esalen Institute—with its nude encounter and sensitivity-training sessions—ours is a society with strong inhibitions and taboos about touching others. This is true particularly if our status is low, or if we are female. Finally, only a limited amount of empirical research has been done on touch. Consequently, we lack a sufficiently precise terminology to describe either the modalities used to touch others or to describe fully the impact of touch on the toucher and the touched.

We should not underestimate the important impact of touch on successful interpersonal communication, however. Touch cannot communicate the highly specialized emotions that can be communicated by facial expressions or vocal cues, but this should not obscure the fact that touch often serves as the last medium available to the elderly and to the critically ill to communicate feelings. As a means of communicating caring, comfort, affection, and reassurance, touch is the preeminent sense. As we shall see, touch can serve important functions in interpersonal communication, functions which are not served at all, or frequently are not served as well, by any other nonverbal medium of communication.

The Nature of Touch

We are just beginning to realize that the skin is a sense organ of great value in interpersonal communication. In fact Scott (1973) maintains that: "the skin is the greatest sense of all. There are those physiologists, in fact, who consider touch the only sense. Hearing begins with sound waves touching the inner ear; taste with a substance touching the taste buds; and sight with light striking the cornea. All the other senses are therefore really derivations of touch as an expression of stimulation to the skin, muscles, and blood vessels" (p. 12). The great applied communication value of touch can be illustrated by the experience of Helen Keller. More than one authority has argued that if Helen Keller had lost her sense of touch, even while regaining hearing and sight, it is doubtful whether her spirit and talent would have left such a mark (Montagu, 1971).

Until recently, we knew little about what could be communicated by touch. For some time, however, serious students of the skin have known that the amount and kind of touching received by both animals and humans as they matured have a great impact on their behavior. The effect of touching on behavior is strongly associated with the fact that "the sense of touch, 'the mother of the senses,' is the earliest to develop in the human embryo. When the embryo is less than an inch long from crown to rump, and less than eight weeks old, light stroking of the upper lip or wings of the nose will cause bending of the neck and trunk away from the source of stimulation" (Montagu, 1971, p. 1).

The skin is such a sensitive organ because its surface area has a tremendous number of sensory receptors that receive stimuli of heat, cold, pressure, and pain. Montagu (1971) estimates that there are 50 receptors per 100 square millimeters; that tactile points vary from 7 to 135 per square centimeter; and that the number of sensory fibers which connect the skin with the spinal cord is well over half a million. The number and importance of sensory stimuli experienced through the skin is much greater than most people realize. The acuteness and variety of sensations experienced via the skin is explained in part by the surprising size of the tactile areas of the brain. A disproportionate amount of cerebral space is devoted to the processing of sensory stimuli that come from the lips, the index finger, and the thumb.

We have known for some time that baby monkeys do not develop properly without physical intimacy, and that lack of caressing is positively associated with a high death rate among nursery babies (Young, 1973). Harlow (1958) in his famous experiments exposed baby monkeys to two types of surrogate mothers. One "mother" was made of wire and provided milk and protection to the infant monkeys; the other "mother" was made of rubber and terry cloth but provided no milk or protection. The infant monkeys consistently chose the terry cloth "mother," so it seems obvious that the need to be touched was overriding. Harlow concluded, therefore, that a monkey's access to physical contact was a crucial variable in the development of normal adult behavior—assuring normal affectional responsivity and normal sexual behavior. Subsequent studies on other monkeys, rats, lambs, and other animals have supported the same central conclusion: Touching is a requirement for the healthy development of animals.

Many of the animal experiments seemed to be designed to support the inference that suitable maturation of human beings also requires an extensive amount of touching, in the form of fondling, stroking, caressing, or even licking. Hence, when we speak of "skin (cutaneous tactile) stimulation, we are quite evidently speaking of a fundamental and essential ingredient of affection and equally clearly of an essential element in the healthy devleopment of every organism" (Montagu, 1971, p. 31).

Adult behavior is also markedly affected by one's tactile history. For example, Hollender (1970) found that some women's need to be held is so compelling that it resembles addiction. Those deprived of tactile stimulation earlier in their lives used both direct and indirect means (i.e., sexual enticement and seduction) to obtain the holding or cuddling desired. Not surprisingly, half of Hollender's sample was composed of female psychiatric patients. Their behavior supported his conclusion that the need or wish to be held is a relevant consideration in the treatment of several psychiatric disorders. Similarly, Hollender, Luborsky, and Scaramella (1969) studied the correlation between the intensity of the need to be held or cuddled and the frequency with which sexual intercourse is bartered for this satisfaction. They found that every high scorer on the body-contact scale (those with a great need to be touched) used sex in order to be held, whereas not a single low scorer did so.

The behavioral effects of quantitative and qualitative insufficiency of touch in childhood are numerous and generally accepted. The communicative potential of the skin has remained a mystery until recently, however. Slowly, we have begun to recognize that the skin is not only our most sensitive organ, but also our first means of communication.

As a reader, you may remain skeptical. You may think that it is fine to talk of touch as a mode of communication, but can anything of importance really be communicated solely through the medium of touch? Using electrodes attached to the fingers, to monitor the electrical messages which the skin transmits to the brain, Brown (1974) has demonstrated the remarkable capacity of the skin as a communication *sender*. In contrast, Geldhard (1968) has documented the skin's great value as a communication *receiver*. In so doing, he has established that the skin is capable of decoding a set of electrical impulses into specific symbols, words, and thoughts. He has developed a language of the skin.

The Skin As a Communication Sender

Can the skin send or transmit meaning? Barbara B. Brown answers *yes*, emphatically. The mind boggles at the possibility that the skin may be capable of sending messages that convey rather specific information and meanings. Such seems to be the case, however. "All that is necessary to listen to the skin's emotional talk is several small electrodes taped to the skin, and a proper recording instrument. Then you listen. The skin will tell you when there is emotion, how strong the emotion is, and even just how emotional a person you are. It also will very likely tell you when you are lying" (Brown, 1974, p. 52).

Polygraphers and medical researchers have long recognized the potential of the human skin as a communication sender. The polygraph exam is based on the assumption that changes in the liar's internal states at the moment of deception will be reflected in machine-monitored changes in skin-conductance, in pulse, and in heart rate, for example. Similarly, physicians and medical technicians monitor the condition of the heart, brain, and other bodily organs by decoding the electrical messages that are transmitted via the skin.

A series of experiments have been conducted which suggest that the skin more than the eye, for example, will much more accurately signal the brain as to what events are being perceived in the environment. Because the skin operates at the subconscious level, it is not biased by group-conformity pressures and other external stimuli that might affect the accuracy with which our various senses perceive events and stimuli in our external environment.

The skin's sending capacity, when aided by machines, has perhpas best been demonstrated in the area of subliminal perception. In one experiment, "naughty" and "emotion-arousing" words were flashed on the screen so briefly that the subjects could not report what they had seen. Neutral words were mixed in with the arousing words. Although the subjects could neither see the words nor recognize them consciously, the skin reflected the difference in the emotional meaning of the words. There was an orienting response by the skin to every naughty word, but an absence of tactile response to neutral or bland words (Brown, 1974).

Such research and the results seem astounding. Nonetheless, Brown reports that simple electrodes attached to an individual's fingers will pick up the electricity of the skin and separate the slow from the fast activity. Slow activity is converted into a signal that represents the level of emotional response; fast activity reflects the type of emotional response. Obviously, this newly discovered communicative capacity of the skin has many practical applications. The foremost application, currently employed during psychotherapy, is to use the messages sent by the skin to pinpoint emotional difficulties. Obviously, many other applications are possible, including the determination of whether and when the communicator is lying, and whether the emotion the skin indicates an individual is really experiencing is consistent with the emotion he or she attempts to convey by some other means, such as facial expressions.

The Skin As a Communication Receiver

Few people would argue that the skin has no communicative value. Is there anyone who does not receive a message from the bite of an insect, from an angry jab in the ribs, or from a light touch on the thigh? We can and do recognize that the skin functions as a crude form of communication. Furthermore, as the examples suggest, most of us tend to think of the skin as a communication receiver. It is doubtful, however, whether very many of us have thought of the skin as a sophisticated receiving instrument which is capable of deciphering complex ideas and emotions transmitted by an outside source.

Thanks to the research of Frank A. Geldhard, at Princeton's Cutaneous Communication Laboratory, we now know that the skin does have amazing communicative capabilities as well as potential. Geldhard (1960) emphasizes that the skin is the body's only communication receiver that can handle both spatial and temporal distinctions fairly effectively; the skin

> can make both temporal and spatial discriminations, albeit not superlatively good ones in either case. It is a good "break-in" sense; cutaneous sensations, especially if aroused in unusual patterns, are highly attention-demanding. It is possible, therefore, that the simplest and most straightforward of all messages—warnings and alerts—should be delivered cutaneously. . . . If we add the clear superiority of touch (when vision and hearing are lacking or impaired) to the remaining modalities, the chemical senses, smell and taste, we have a formidable set of properties to utilize in cutaneous message processing—a list that ought to challenge us to find ways to capitalize on it. (p. 131)

In order to make reasonably effective use of the skin's communicative potential, it soon became obvious to Geldhard and his associates that a means for sending electrical impulses to different parts of the body would be necessary. In effect, these electrical impulses would symbolize thoughts and emotions which the skin would have to decode by assigning meanings to groups of symbols. Given this means of message transmission, the central question was how many different ways could the electrical impulses be used to transmit messages? In a very real sense the problem was analogous to that faced by Morse as he contemplated telegraphic communication. Morse's deductions were simple but important. Variation in the length of time the telegraph key was held down, and variation in the periods of time between the striking of the key, could be used to send messages by a code which was understandable to a communication receiver on the other end of the telegraph line.

Geldhard developed a langue of the skin, *vibratese*, consisting of electrical impulses transmitted to the skin that vary in intensity, duration, and frequency. Each letter in Geldhard's *Optohapt Alphabet* is represented by an electrical impulse with distinctive stimulus properties. An *Optohapt* (an instrument with a standard typewriter keyboard) is used to transmit cutaneous messages, in the form of electrical vibrations, to the skin of a receiver. Electrodes are attached to nine different places on the body (Geldhard, 1968).

The details of Geldhard's tactile communication system are explored in detail in his own research reports; however, the essence of the system can be described concisely. Letters of the alphabet are *each assigned a signal representing a unique combination of duration, intensity and location. The times were kept short—0.1, 0.3, 0.5 second for short, medium, and long, respectively. The most frequently occurring language elements werre assigned shorter durations, enabling the system to "fly" at a rapid pace. This proved quite efficient, since the all-important vowels were assigned each to its own vibrators, and since letters followed each other promptly, with none of the wasteful silences that are built into International Morse. (Geldhard, 1968, p. 45)*

While research continues, the use of machines such as the Optohapt to transmit messages to the skin suggests that the skin is capable of decoding at least simple ideas as well as differentiating between emotions. The full potential of the skin as a communication receiver has clearly not been explored, however.

Most readers will probably marvel at the ingenuity and attention to detail which is reflected in the research of Geldhard and his associates. Nonetheless, the reader may be bothered by two unanswered questions. First, does Vibratese as transmitted by the Optohapt have much practical, communicative value? Second, can the process of transmitting messages to the skin be modified in such a way that human beings can transmit as well as receive messages by Vibratese?

The first question can probably be more readily answered than the second. Certainly Vibratese can have great value in accurately communicating to individuals whose major senses, such as sight and hearing, are temporarily impaired. The most obvious example is the airplane pilot. Consider the case of the commercial jet that plunged into the Pacific Ocean upon takeoff from Los Angeles International Airport, killing all aboard. The main and auxiliary generators both ceased to function, and all lights in the airplane went out, including those in the cockpit. Suddenly, bereft of his primary means of determining distance, the pilot apparently became highly disoriented and flew the plane straight into the ocean. There is good reason to believe that he could have averted the disaster had his body been equipped with the nine vibrators that are used to receive tactile messages. The vibrators would have enabled the air traffic controller at Los Angeles to use his radar screen to give the pilot specific flight directions via electrical impulses sent by remote control; a pilot trained in Vibratese could easily have understood such tactile messages and could have maintained level flight while in a darkened cockpit. This is hardly a far-fetched idea. During World War II, research was conducted to determine if warning signals could be built into seat cushions so that a pilot could literally hear and fly by the seat of his pants.

Clearly, Vibratese can be used as a warning system; as a means of supplementary information about one's environment; as a sophisticated language for the blind or deaf; and as a command system for pilots, auto drivers, and others. Of course, the possible applications in the area of surveillance and spying are enough to make an intelligence agent's mouth water. All of the foregoing applications are based on the assumption that a wireless means of activating the vibrators on the body will be developed. Such an invention should hardly tax the creativity of the modern engineer.

The greatest deficiencies of Vibratese, as a language of the skin, are that an individual must be wired, and impulses must be transmitted to a human receiver in order for communication to take place. Obviously, this places great restrictions on the receiver's mobility, and the wires and vibrators may be so distracting as to alter the nature of messages perceived. In addition, it is obvious that Vibratese gives an individual only a receiving capacity; he or she has no independent capacity to transmit messages to the skin. Solutions to these problems are not available at this moment, but they should not take long in coming. Anyone who has seen policemen communicating by walkie-talkie or radio will realize that the same principles can be applied to tactile communication. There is no reason why messages in the form of electrical impulses can not be sent by remote control and received by another individual who is not hampered by wires. Once this goal is achieved, tactile communication by electrical impulse will have almost the same flexibility as kinesic communication. Certainly, the potential for practical application will be greatly expanded.

Touching Norms

Tactile and proxemic communication are similar in one important respect. Both tactile and proxemic behavior are governed by an implicit set of norms that specify what types of behavior are acceptable in our society. When we violate either touching or proxemic norms, we usually make those with whom we interact uncomfortable. The absence of touching of a person by others may be taken as a sign that the untouched person is insignificant and unimportant. Paradoxically, the person who is touched too much is apt to be labeled as a person of inferior status.

Ours is a noncontact society, where limited touching in public is the norm. Touching norms dictate that even friends and intimates are expected to refrain from anything beyond perfunctory touching in public; touching among strangers is deemed to be deviant. Walker (1975) demonstrated the strength of touching norms in our society by asking strangers to touch each other during encounter-group exercises. He found that strangers who were forced to touch each other perceived the tactile contact as difficult, stress-producing, and psychologically disturbing..

Touching norms that have developed in our society have been most strongly influenced by two factors: *the region of the body that is touched, and the demographic variables that differentiate one communicator from another* (i.e., *sex, race, age,* and *status*). Successful communicators will not only exhibit an awareness of what regions of the body may be touched in specific contexts but will also understand that the sex, race, age, and status of the interactants dictate what type and how much touching is socially acceptable.

Jourard (1966) has divided the body into the 24 regions that may be touched. His research indicates that it is the norm for opposite-sex friends to touch all body regions. Touching of the head, shoulders, and arms occurs most frequently but touching in other regions of the body is also acceptable. In general, touching of same-sex friends should be confined to shoulders, arms, and hands. Touching norms for males and females are different, however, and this difference seems to be reflected in their tactile behavior. Walker (1975) found, for example, that the amount of nonreciprocal touching exhibited by female pairs in sensitivity groups increased as the groups continued to meet, but touching of male pairs decreased over time. Males are reluctant to touch or to be touched by another male because their masculinity is threatened by the homosexual connotations of tactile contact.

Although touching norms dictate that intimates may touch "personal regions" of the body, nonintimates must confine touching to "impersonal regions" of the body. Communicators generally conform to this touching norm (Willis, Rinck, & Dean, 1978). Accordingly, touch among strangers should be confined primarily to the hand-to-hand contact associated with greetings and farewells. Touching norms that specify what regions of the body may be touched by whom seem to have remained relatively constant over time, although recent research suggests that opposite-sex friends are now engaging in an increasing amount of touching in the body areas between the chest and knees (Major, 1981).

Appropriate tactile communication requires familiarity with the demographic variables that exert a major influence on touching norms. These touching norms dictate that the sex, race, age, and the status of the interactants must all be considered before we are in a position to exhibit socially appropriate tactile behavior.

Sex is clearly an important variable. The normative expectation is that the most touching should occur among opposite-sex friends. In both intimate and professional relationships men are expected to touch women much more frequently than they are touched by women, and they do so. Male to female touch is the most frequent type of touch, even though females touch children of both sexes more frequently than do men (Majors & Williams, 1980). In same-sex interaction, touch among women is more frequent than among men. Whatever the sex of the interactants, the cultural norm dictates that the amount of touching may be increased as our relationship with another person becomes more personal (Major, 1981).

Henley (1977) maintains that the different touching norms for men and women perpetuate the idea that men have superior power and status. Women who touch men in professional settings must be aware that such touching is often interpreted as a sign of unseemly sexual advance. In contrast, the disproportionate amount of touching of women by men gives men the edge in asserting their dominance over women.

Race is also an important determinant of touching norms. Tactile contact is much more frequent among blacks than among whites. In one study of racial touching patterns (Smith, Willis, & Gier, 1980), blacks touched each other on the average 29.03 times per hour and whites touched each other only 9.87 times per hour. Consistent with previous findings, white males touched each other less frequently than any other sex-race dyad. However, black males touched each other more frequently than any sex-race dyad. Black females touched each other almost twice as often as white females. The touching pattern that emerges is clear. When interacting with each other, blacks prefer and exhibit more touching than whites. However, both blacks and whites touch members of their own race much more frequently than they touch members of the other race (Smith et al., 1980; Willis et al., 1978).

Age has also proven to be an important factor in the development of touching norms. Age-related touching norms specify that high rates of touching are most appropriate for the young and the old. As might be expected, rates of touching are high during the first five year's of a child's life. Frequency of touching has been observed to decrease from kindergarten through junior high, however. This finding may be attributable in part to the fact that the identity crisis experienced by young people makes the initiation of communication difficult. Because tactile communication is one of the most intimate forms of communication, the initiation of tactile contact may be doubly difficult. Finally, the amount of touching characteristically exhibited during the adult years seems to remain relatively constant until retirement age approaches. At that point, frequency of touching behavior increases markedly (Major, 1981).

The last demographic variable that exerts a major influence on touching norms is *status*. High-status individuals touch low-status individuals much more frequently than they are touched by low-status individuals. Henley (1977) maintains that the "touching privilege" not only reliably identifies the high-status person but is reserved almost exclusively for their use.

The status of the toucher seems to affect directly the amount of non-reciprocal touching they initiate. Watson (1975) studied the amount of touching of patients by staff, in a home for the elderly. He found that *the higher the rank of the nursing person the greater the amount of touching of the patients.* Nurses touched patients much more frequently than aides and aides touched patients much more frequently than orderlies. Low-status individuals seem intuitively to recognize that the touching norm specifies that the amount of touching they initiate should be limited. Thus, Watson (1975) concluded that "the frequent omissions of touching behavior by orderlies suggested a clear relation between low status in the nursing hierarchy and social constraint against touching" (p. 107).

The Semantics of Touch

As I have already indicated, the skin can serve important communicative functions when its sensory capacity is enhanced by the use of machines. Most of us are probably more concerned about the communicative functions served by one person touching another, however. Heslin (1974) maintains that human touch serves five major functions: (a) *functional–professional*; (b) *social–polite*; (c) *friendship–warmth*; (d) *love–intimacy*; and (e) *sexual arousal.* The first function is associated with the nurse's touch of a patient, or the hairdresser's touch of a customer, which is designed to achieve some specific instrumental objective. Although the first function is instrumental, the other four functions serve essentially communicative functions in that they involve the use of touch to communicate specialized types of meanings.

The semantics of touch is not of course a simple matter. In a professional setting the touch of a man by a woman may communicate a distinctively different meaning than the touch of a woman by a man. The meanings of touch are affected not only by who touches whom but by the *type of touch:* We still lack a complete description or understanding of the types of touching that may be used in interpersonal communication. However, Nguyen, Heslin, and Nguyen (1975) have identified four different types of touches: a *pat*, a *squeeze*, a *brush*, and a *stroke.* The squeeze and the brush seem to communicate meaning that varies with the context. In contrast, a pat is usually interpreted to mean that the toucher is playful and friendly, while the stroke signals affection and sexual desire.

Touch can affect the way we are perceived by others. The limited amount of research that has been done on this subject suggests, however, that touch is apt to play a secondary role in shaping the image we project. We do know that counselors who touch clients are more positively perceived than those who do not. They are also judged to be more empathic (Pattison, 1973). Similarly, subjects form more favorable impressions of engaged couples who touch each other than those who do not (Kleinke, Meeker, & LaFong, 1974).

Touch does seem to play a relatively important role in persuasion. Studies have repeatedly shown that communicators who touch those persons they are trying to persuade are more successful than those who do not. Kleinke (1977) found that subjects who were touched by a "telephone caller" returned a dime left in a phone booth significantly more often to the caller who touched them than to the caller who did not. Similarly, Willis and Hamm (1980) report that touching behavior is linked to persuasive effectiveness. Experimenters who approached shoppers at a shopping center in Kansas City, asked the shoppers to either complete a brief rating scale or to sign a petition; half of the shoppers were touched lightly on the upper arm and half were not touched. The shoppers who were touched complied with the requests significantly more often than those who were not touched.

The role that touch can play in impression management and persuasion is important and deserves further study. At the moment, however, those communicative functions of touch seem to be much less important than two others. Touch seems to function most effectively to *communicate specialized kinds of emotional meanings* and to influence *perceptions about the perceived power of communicators.*

Emotion Cues

Touch has proven to be an effective medium for communicating information about specific emotions that individuals experience. Facial expressions and vocal cues are a more sophisticated medium to communicate
emotion than touch. Many more emotional meanings and nuances of
emotional meaning can be communicated by facial expression and vocal
cues than by touch. Tactile communication assumes primary importance,
however, when we wish to emphasize feelings of *warmth, reassurance,* or
comfort.

As emotion cues, tactile messages have been found to be particularly
effective in providing reassurance and support to those who need emotional support. Tactile messages seem to serve the therapeutic function
better than any other means of communication. Jourard (1966) is convinced that the therapeutic function of touch is the most important of all.
He emphasizes that he has "found that some form of physical contact with
patients expedites the arrival of this mutual openness and unreserve. So
far, I have only held hands with a patient, put an arm around a shoulder,
or given a hug—all in the context of unfolding dialogue. I believe we are a
nation of people who are starved for physical contact" (p. 65).

In their insightful book, *Nonverbal Communication with Patients:
Back to the Human Touch* (1977), Blondis and Jackson make quite clear
that in nursing touch can serve a more important therapeutic role than
any other kind of nonverbal communication. They emphasize that our
"first comfort in life comes from touch—and usually our last, since touch
may communicate with the comatose, dying patient when words have no
way of breaking through" (p. 6). Patients who have lost all verbal capacity
can ordinarily feel a gentle touch and be moved by the message of caring
and reassurance that it represents. Some terminal patients lose the power
to speak. When this is the case, a tactile code is sometiems worked out
where one squeeze of the nurse's hand by the patient means yes, and two
squeezes mean no. In these instances the tactile message represents the
patient's sole surviving means of communicating with the outside world.

Whether working in pediatrics, geriatrics, or the emergency receiving
room, the nurse and other members of a medical team recognize that
touch is frequently their most effective medium of emotional communication. This is probably true because the trauma associated with birth and
critical illness strongly reinforces the patient's insecurities and fears,
while placing a premium on the empathic response, which provides reassurance. Thus, a "patient may reach out to grasp the nurse's hand,
seeking comfort and reassurance through the sense of touch. The positive
feelings of sympathy, reassurance, understanding, and compassion are
transmitted through touch—just as are the negative feelings of anger, hostility, and fear. To be truly therapeutic, tactile communication must be
used at the appropriate time and place" (Blondis & Jackson, 1977, p. 9).

Given the therapeutic power of touch, it is a sad fact that many individuals who most need touch are the least likely to receive it. Results from

one study indicate that severely impaired patients are touched much less frequently by members of a medical team than those with less severe impairments. Similarly, patients who have had a breast removed or who have undergone a sex-change operation are less likely to be touched than those who have received less drastic medical treatment (Watson, 1975).

Tactile messages may of course communicate many different kinds of emotional meanings. Touch seems to function best, however, when it is used to provide comfort, caring, and reassurance to those in emotional need, and as a means of expressing warmth, affection, intimacy, and sexual desire in interpersonal relationships (Major, 1981). In fact, one investigator has gone so far as to describe the 24 steps in the "courtship dance." In the courtship dance, different kinds of socially approved touching represent the sole medium for the communication of, and development of, intimacy (Nielsen, 1962).

Power Cues

Touch probably functions most effectively to delineate the relative power and status of interacting individuals. Henley, in her fascinating research (1977), has established quite clearly that the frequency with which we touch and are touched by others is a reliable indicator of our perceived power. Results from her research show that "people reported more likelihood of their touching subordinates and coworkers than bosses; of touching younger or same-age people than older ones; and of touching sales clerks than police officers. Likewise, their expectations of others' touching them also reflected their hierarchical relationship: for example, they reported more probability of boss and coworker touching them than of a subordinate doing so" (p. 104). In short, the powerful person is apt to be the toucher and the powerless person the touched. Because of this relationship, the power of touch is a privilege reserved for the powerful. This relationship applies even to the "untouchable" castes of India. They are called *untouchable* because their low status dictates that they may not touch members of a higher caste.

Touch is so effective a medium for the communication of power cues that touchers are perceived to have more power and status than the touched, regardless of the gender of the toucher or the touched (Scroggs, 1980). Touchers have consistently been perceived as more dominant and assertive than nontouchers (Major, 1981). Finally, observers who have looked at photographs of male-female dyads, some who were touching and some who were not touching, rated the *touchers* as significantly more powerful, strong, superior, and dominant (Summerhayes & Suchner, 1978).

In her insightful summary of research on the meaning of touch, Major (1981) emphasizes that touch strongly and reliably shapes perceptions of one's power. She writes that empirical research strongly supports Henley's theory that *touching implies power. Across experiments, the initiator of touch is seen as more powerful, dominant, and of higher status than the recipient. Furthermore, it appears that touch affects the balance of power in a relationship by simultaneously enhancing that of the toucher and diminishing that of the recipient. (p. 26)*

Quite clearly, touchers are perceived as more powerful than the touched, and this relationship holds without regard to the gender, age, or status of the interactants. Furthermore, the failure to touch others consistently results in a diminution of one's perceived power.

Summary

Touch can and frequently does play a central role in our maturational development, from cradle to grave. The sending and receiving capacity of the human skin, when accentuated with the use of machines, is remarkable. With the aid of electrodes attached to the skin, tactile messages reveal when a person is experiencing an emotion, how strong the emotion is, and even whether the person is lying. When aided by machines, the skin as a communication receiver is capable of decoding both ideational and emotional messages. These messages can serve vitally important functions when other senses are impaired or inoperative.

Rather detailed touching norms have developed in our society, and these norms specify who may touch whom, and in what context. The nature of *touching norms* depends not only on the *region of the body* that is being *touched*, but on the *sex, race, age,* and *status* of the interactants.

Touching norms shaped by sex dictate that opposite-sex friends should touch the most, and males should touch each other the least. Men often use the touching privilege, which allows them to touch women more frequently than they are touched by women, to assert their dominance over women. Racial touching norms result in a higher rate of touching among blacks than whites but a lower rate of interracial touching. Touching norms based on age specify that it is appropriate for the young and old to engage in the most frequent tactile contact. Finally, status dictates that the high-status person is the toucher and that the low-status person the touched.

In interpersonal communication touch can and should serve an important therapeutic function. As a medium of emotional communication, touch functions effectively to communicate feelings of warmth, reassurance, and comfort. Touch also plays an important role in interpersonal relationships, in the development of affection and sexual desire. Finally, touch may function most forcefully to delineate the relative power and status of the interactants. The frequency with which we touch and are touched by others is a reliable indicator of our perceived power.

References

Blondis, M. N., & Jackson, B. E. (1977). *Nonverbal communication with patients: Back to the human touch.* New York: Wiley.

Brown, B. (1974). Skin talk: A strange mirror of the mind. *Psychology Today, 8,* 52–74.

Geldhard, F. A. (1960). Some neglected possibilities of communication. *Science, 131,* 1583–1587.

Geldhard, F. A. (1968). Body English. *Psychology Today, 2,* 45.

Harlow, B. F. (1958). The nature of love. *American Psychologist, 13,* 678–685.

Henley, N. M. (1977). *Body politics: Power, sex, and nonverbal communication.* Englewood Cliffs, NJ: Prentice-Hall.

Heslin, R. (1974, May). *Steps toward a taxonomy of touching.* Paper presented at the meeting of the Midwestern Psychological Association, Chicago.

Hollender, M. H. (1970). The need or wish to be held. *Archives of General Psychiatry, 22,* 445–453.

Hollender, M. H., Luborsky, L., & Scaramella, T. J. (1969). Body contact and sexual enticement. *Archives of General Psychiatry, 20,* 188–191.

Jourard, S. M. (1966). An exploratory study of body-accessibility. *British Journal of Social and Clinical Psychology, 5,* 221–231.

Kleinke, C. L. (1977). Compliance to requests made by gazing and touching experimenters in field settings. *Journal of Experimental Social Psychology, 13,* 218–223.

Kleinke, C. L., Meeker, F. B., & LaFong, C. (1974). Effects of gaze, touch, and use of name on evaluation of engaged couples. *Journal of Research in Personality, 7,* 368–373.

Major, B. (1980). Gender patterns in touching behavior. In C. Mayo & N. M. Henley (Eds.), *Gender and nonverbal behavior.* New York: Springer-Verlag.

Major, B., & Williams, L. (1981). Frequency of touch by sex and race: A replication of touching observations. Unpublished paper, State University of New York at Buffalo.

Montagu, A. (1971). *Touching: The human significance of the skin.* New York: Perennial.

Nielson, G. (1962). *Studies in self-confrontation.* Copenhagen: Munksgaard.

Nguyen, T., Heslin, R., & Nguyen, M. L. (1975). The meanings of touch: Sex difference. *Journal of Communication, 25,* 92–103.

Pattison, J. E. (1973). Effects of touch on self-exploration and the therapeutic relationship. *Journal of Consulting and Clinical Psychology, 40,* 170–175.

Scroggs, G. F. (1980, April). *Sex, status, and solidarity: Attributions for nonmutual touch.* Paper presented at meeting of the Eastern Psychological Association, Hartford, CT.

Scott, B. (1973). *How the body feels.* New York: Ballantine.

Smith, D. E., Willis, F. N., & Gier, J. A. (1980). Success and interpersonal touch in a competitive setting. *Journal of Nonverbal Behavior, 5,* 26–34.

Summerhayes, D. L., & Suchner, R. W. (1978). Power implications of touch in male-female relationships. *Sex Roles, 4,* 103–110.

Walker, D. N. (1975). A dyadic interaction model for nonverbal touching behavior in encounter groups. *Small Group Behavior, 6,* 308–324.

Watson, W. H. (1975). The meanings of touch: Geriatric nursing. *Journal of Communication, 25,* 104–112.

Willis, F. N., Jr., & Hamm, H. K. (1980). The use of interpersonal touch in securing compliance. *Journal of Nonverbal Behavior, 1,* 49–55.

Willis, F. N., Rinck, C. M., & Dean, L. M. (1978). Interpersonal touch among adults in cafeteria lines. *Perceptual and Motor Skills, 47,* 1147–1152.

Young, M. G. (1973). The human touch: Who needs it? *Bridges not walls.* Reading, MA: Addison-Wesley.

PART TWO

Developing the Successful Communicator

CHAPTER EIGHT

Selling Yourself Nonverbally

In an interview presented by CBS television on November 4, 1979, CBS correspondent Roger Mudd asked Senator Ted Kennedy, "What's the present state of your marriage, Senator?" Kennedy replied, "Well, I think that, uh, it's a, uh, uh, uh, we've had um, uh, some uh, difficult uh, uh, times but I think we uh, have uh, uh, oof, I think been able to make some uh, very good progress and uh, uh, it's uh, uh, I would say that it's uh, uh, it's it's um delighted that we're able to, to share, share the time and the, the relationship that we do share." ("CBS Reports: Teddy," 1979)

The vocal image Kennedy projected was highly undesirable for a man trying to sell himself as a credible presidential candidate. Consider for a moment how Kennedy's vocal message may have affected his credibility in your eyes. Did his frequent hesitations, stammering, and speech errors make him seem more or less competent, trustworthy, and dynamic? Did his vocal message help convince you that he was seeking to give Mudd a forthright and honest answer?

Kennedy's credibility was seriously damaged because he projected an image he quite clearly did not wish to project. Students of mine who have analyzed Kennedy's interview with Mudd approach unanimity in the judgments they make. Kennedy's vocal cues assumed a central role in communicating an image of evasiveness and indecision that is unacceptable for a presidential candidate. The student analysts became convinced that the negative impression that Kennedy made was shaped primarily by his nonverbal communication rather than by the words that he uttered.

If you disagree with these judgments, think once again about Senator Kennedy's response to Roger Mudd's question. Kennedy did not say that the question made him uncomfortable to the point of being anxious; he did not say that he would be forced to be indirect, evasive, and untruthful

147

in his response; and he did not say that his marriage was irreparably broken. Nonetheless, these messages were all clearly communicated. They were communicated unintentionally and implicitly through the communicative medium of Kennedy's vocal cues.

The Kennedy interview serves to dramatize the potentially powerful impact of nonverbal cues on one's credibility. Nonverbal factors are known to be particularly important for the person who wishes to be perceived as a leader. In fact, perceptions of leadership potential and leadership qualities are often more strongly affected by nonverbal than verbal cues (Gitter, Black, & Fishman, 1975). Both frequency and specific kinds of nonverbal cues exhibited have been shown to exert a strong influence on perceptions of leadership (Baird, 1977).

Successful communication requires the development of personal credibility. As James Gray, Jr., writes in *The Winning Image* (1982), "your image is a tool for communicating and for revealing your inherent qualities, your competence, abilities, and leadership. It is a reflection of qualities that others associate with you, a reflection that bears long-lasting influence in your bid for success" (p. 6). You need not be a presidential candidate to be concerned about the impact of your credibility on your bid for success.

My work as a communication consultant in a presidential campaign and as a communication trainer of corporate salespeople has convinced me that successful communicators must master the art of selling themselves nonverbally. You will not vote for the politician or buy from the salesperson unless you find them to be sufficiently credible.

This chapter focuses on the role of nonverbal communication in the development of personal credibility. The nonverbal communicative behaviors of presidential candidates and corporate sales representatives are used here to illustrate the specific perceptual effects of such behaviors on credibility. Specific guidelines for developing credibility are presented, and the nonverbal profile of the credible communicator is highlighted.

If you doubt the importance of credibility in personal selling, consider the case of the agritech salesperson in the Rio Grande Valley of Texas. The prospect is a vegetable farmer in the Valley, who has over 50,000 acres under cultivation. The salesperson must try to persuade the farmer to purchase a liquid hormone that will be sprayed on his vegetables and will allegedly increase his yield by up to 25 percent. Because the liquid hormone is a new product, results from field research are still limited. The farmer recognizes that a decision to use the salesperson's product on all of his vegetables will cost him many thousands of dollars. He does not want to make the wrong decision.

Salespeople in the Rio Grande Valley who actually find themselves in such a selling situation tell me that their personal credibility is frequently the critical issue. The credibility of their company may have been important in arranging the sales call, but it is their personal credibility that is of most concern to the farmer. Does the farmer find them to be knowledgeable enough and trustworthy enough to buy from them? One farmer told an agritech salesperson, "I can't buy from you. I give old Ned all of my business. He knows what he is doing. I trust him. I give Ned all of my business because he has never done me wrong."

The farmer found "old Ned" to be credible because he found him to be believable. Credibility is a measure of how believable you are to those with whom you interact. The development of high credibility does not of course provide any assurance that you will achieve your objectives. Many other factors may also affect persuasive effectiveness (Brembeck & Howell, 1976). Generally, however, the higher your credibility, the greater your chances for success as a persuader (Burgoon & Saine, 1978).

Dimensions of Credibility

Credibility is defined by three major components: *competence, trustworthiness*, and *dynamism* (Brembeck & Howell, 1976). How competent, trustworthy, and dynamic a communicator one is judged to be will vary, depending upon such factors as personal reputation, organizational affiliation, personal appearance, and, most importantly, communicative behaviors exhibited. Although individuals have the potential to exercise considerable control over their perceived credibility, we should recognize that credibility is not defined by inherent personal qualities or characteristics of the source. On the contrary, credibility or believability is the perception of the message sender by the *receiver*.

A person's perceived competence, trustworthiness, and dynamism may be positively or negatively affected in a given situation by the person's communication. For example, professors who provide inaccuate information in their lectures will lower their perceived competence. An individual's perceived competence, trustworthiness, and dynamism may vary from extremely high to extremely low in a given situation, therefore these terms may be properly identified as *dimensions of credibility.*

Competence

Competence is an important dimension of credibility. Individuals who are recognized as experts on a given subject inspire confidence. Conversely, *incompetence* is a word with unflattering connotations. In our society, competence is associated with excellence. For example, universities that are widely recognized for their academic excellence receive such recognition in large part because their faculty members have been judged to be unusually competent.

As Table 8.1 suggests, an individual's perceived level of competence may be assessed by rating tht individual on a set of scales that reflect how competent, qualified, well-informed, and intelligent that individual is judged to be. When individuals exhibit communicative behaviors that raise serious doubts about their competence, their competence ratings usually drop sharply.

TABLE 8.1

Credibility includes these three dimensions: competence, trustworthiness, and dynamism. How competent, trustworthy, and dynamic a communicator is judged to be will depend upon that individual's communication. Imagine that the twelve sets of terms are on twelve separate sets of bipolar scales. Begin by rating the communicator's credibility in the Initial Credibility column. Use a 7-point scale to rate the person, with a 7 to identify the term on the left side of the scale and a 1 to identify the term on the right side of the scale. For example, if you judge an individual to be extremely competent before communication begins, you would put a 7 in the first blank in the Initial Credibility column. If you cannot decide whether the person is competent or incompetent, you would put a 4 in the same blank. A person perceived as extremely incompetent would receive a rating of 1. Any value from 7 through 1 may be used.

Dimensions of Credibility	Initial Credibility	Terminal Credibility
Competence:		
(1) competent/incompetent		
(2) qualified/unqualified		
(3) well-informed/poorly informed		
(4) intelligent/unintelligent		
Trustworthiness:		
(1) honest/dishonest		
(2) straightforward/evasive		
(3) trustworthy/untrustworthy		
(4) sincere/insincere		
Dynamism:		
(1) assertive/unassertive		
(2) bold/timid		
(3) forceful/meek		
(4) active/inactive		
Communicator's Name _____		

Until recently, one's competence was thought to be affected almost solely by the manifest content of one's speech communication. The key questions were: (a) how much relevant and useful information does an individual have on a given subject?; (b) how familiar is the individual with that information?; and (c) does the individual use that information effectively to support carefully qualified generalizations? As we shall see, our nonverbal communication often exerts a dramatic influence on how competent we are perceived to be.

In the presidential campaign of 1968, Richard Nixon's advisors made unprecedented use of the potential of nonverbal cues to enhance Nixon's perceived competence. Nixon's advisors recognized that many Americans do not monitor the content of a politician's speech very closely, but they may be strongly affected by implicit messages communicated visually. Thus, Joe McGinniss wrote that the "words would be the same ones Nixon always used—the words of the acceptance speech. But they would all seem fresh and lively because a series of still pictures would flash on the screen while Nixon spoke. If it were done right, it would permit television to create a Nixon image that was entirely independent of the words . . . The flashing pictures would be carefully selected to create the impression that somehow Nixon represented competence, respect for tradition, serenity . . ." (McGinniss, 1969, p. 85).

Trustworthiness

A few months ago, a recent acquaintance invited me to go deep-sea fishing with him, in the Gulf of Mexico. I raised some questions about the safety, in a relatively small boat, of such a venture. He understood that my unstated question (Did I trust him enough to go deep-sea fishing with him?) was more important than my explicit questions about his competence as a seaman. I have not yet answered that question in my own mind. I do recognize, however, that my response will be determined by how trustworthy I judge him to be.

As a dimension of credibility, *trustworthiness* is a measure of our character as seen by those persons with whom we interact. Our presumed level of trustworthiness is based on an assessment of our personal qualities, intentions, and attitudes. The dominant sources of information that are used to determine how trustworthy we are judged to be may be nonverbal (McMahan, 1976). This is so because individuals will not usually tell you how honest or sincere they actually are. Their actions are usually more important than their words.

As Table 8.1 indicates, an individual's perceived level of trustworthiness may be assessed by rating that individual on a set of scales that reveal how honest, straightforward, trustworthy, and sincere that individual is judged to be. Successful communicators almost invariably receive high ratings on this dimension of credibility.

Dynamism

Dynamism is the third dimension of credibility. *Dynamism defines a person's credibility or image in terms of the level of confidence they are perceived to have.* The ability to project a feeling of confidence is important because it is apt to trigger a reciprocal feeling of confidence in us, by those with whom we communicate. Clearly, the more dynamic we are perceived to be, the more credible we are apt to be. According to one authority, the "shy, introverted, soft-spoken individual is generally perceived as less credible than the assertive, extroverted, and forceful individual. The great leaders in history have generally been dynamic people. They were assertive and dynamic people" (DeVito, 1980).

A communicator's level of dynamism may be accurately assessed by rating that individual on a set of scales that reflect how assertive, bold, forceful, and active he or she is judged to be. The timid and meek may ultimately inherit the earth, but for the moment, at least, they have a serious credibility problem. Political satirists, who had delighted in their caricature of the 1984 presidential candidate, Walter Mondale, as weak and indecisive, obviously recognized the importance of dynamism in shaping perceptions of credibility. Such a caricature had a humorous impact precisely because of the incongruous and implausible image conjured up by a presidential candidate so lacking in dynamism.

The development of a communicator's credibility requires that individual dimensions of credibility be assessed at two points in time: *Initial credibility* is the credibility the communicator possesses *before* communication begins. *Terminal credibility* is the credibility that the communicator is seen to possess *after* communication occurs in a given situation. Terminal credibility is the product of the communicator's initial credibility and the credibility that was *derived* as a result of the individual's communicative behaviors (DeVito, 1980).

To make an accurate evaluation of a person's credibility, the scales in Table 8.1 should be used. Write in the name of the communicator and rate the individual on the 12 scales used to measure level of competence, trustworthiness, and dynamism. The initial set of ratings should be in the Initial Credibility column. After the communication is completed, cover up the first column and rate the person again in the Terminal Credibility column. You should then have a before-and-after profile of the communicator's credibility.

Illustrating the Impact of Nonverbal Cues on Credibility

Presidential candidates engage in the type of personal selling that has generated widespread interest in this country. Millions of people study the candidates' efforts to sell themselves, and make their own judgments as to how the candidates' communication affected their credibility. Because of the high visibility of the candidates' communicative efforts, the presidential debates represent a useful vehicle for illustrating how nonverbal cues can affect credibility.

After the first televised presidential debate between Jimmy Carter and Gerald Ford, I was contacted by Rafshoon Advertising. Rafshoon was Carter's media advisor in this campaign. As the Rafshoon representative viewed the situation, Carter had a problem. All the public opinion polls showed Carter with a substantial lead over Ford *before* their first debate. Carter's advisors thought he had done well in the first debate, in terms of the traditional factors that are usually thought to affect credibility. He was well-informed on the major issues, he had good command of his information, and he took pains to qualify the generalizations he made.

In terms of his *speech communication* Carter appeared to have been at least the equal of Gerald Ford. Nonetheless, the polls showed that Carter had lost the first debate, and a loss in the second debate would be a serious and possibly catastrophic blow to Carter's chances. The request from the Rafshoon representative was simple. Would I do an analysis of Carter's nonverbal cues in the first debate, in order to develop a nonverbal profile that might be used to enhance Carter's credibility in the second debate?

The Selling of Presidential Candidates

Gerald Ford approached the first presidential debate with some serious image problems. Both friends and foes raised questions about his competence. Political satirists wondered aloud whether Ford was smart enough to think and chew gum at the same time. He was pictured on *Saturday Night Live* as an amiable but uncoordinated bumbler who, while trying to trim it, fell off a ladder, onto the White House Christmas tree. Few had forgotten the satisfaction Lyndon Johnson seemed to get from saying that Gerald Ford had played much too much football "without a helmet."

Ford's own actions seemed to suggest that he might have been competent enough to have been a United States Congressman from Michigan, but raised doubts about his competence as President. Newspaper photographs frequently showed Ford hitting his head on the door of the presidential helicopter when exiting, or showed him falling on the ski slopes of Colorado. And photos showed one of his golf balls bouncing off the head of a spectator after an errant tee shot. Ford made matters even worse by his propensity for appearing before a political rally in a state such as Nebraska and solemnly remarking how pleased he was to be in Kansas. Things go so bad at one point that Ford reportedly said that he really enjoyed "watching" something on radio (Schlenker, 1980).

As the candidates approached the first presidential debate, there seemed good reason to believe that Gerald Ford had a serious credibility problem. The media had frequently depicted Ford as marginally competent, at best. In contrast, his opponent, Jimmy Carter, was thought to possess a first-rate mind. Aside from an admission that he was occasionally overcome by "lustful" thoughts, Carter had done little to damage his personal credibility. His credibility had not been challenged as frequently or persistently as Ford's had. Although one of Carter's opponents in the presidential primaries had run a television spot which showed Carter talking out of both sides of his mouth, his trustworthness had not become an issue.

My careful analysis of the videotape of the first Ford–Carter debate resulted in some unanticipated conclusions (CBS Television, 1976). Gerald Ford projected an image of superior credibility. He did so by his skillful use of visual cues. In contrast, Jimmy Carter's nonverbal communication was so ineffective as to raise serious questions about his competence, trustworthiness, and dynamism. In my opinion, the candidates' eye behaviors, gestures, postures, and vocal cues were the nonverbal factors which most strongly affected the images they projected. As a result, my analysis of Ford's and Carter's nonverbal behaviors focused on these factors.

As I have already indicated in Chapter 2, eye behaviors are known to affect strongly the way we are perceived. The eye behaviors of the two candidates contrasted strikingly in the first debate. Carter almost always paused and looked down or away before answering a question. The characteristic direction of Carter's gaze was downcast when not speaking; instead of looking at Ford when he was speaking, Carter stared off into space or down at his notes. Carter also exhibited a high blink rate, and often appeared shifty-eyed. Ford, in contrast, sustained direct eye contact with the reporters when answering their questions, and looked at Carter when Carter was speaking.

In my recommendations to Carter's media advisors, I emphasized that Carter *must* stop looking down at the beginning of each answer; must sustain eye contact *with Ford* while Ford is speaking, and *must* avoid the "downcast eyes" in all situations, in the second presidential debate.

To look down before answering a question, and to exhibit shifty eyes while answering a question, is likely to negatively affect both perceived competence and trustworthiness (Burgoon & Saine, 1978). The unwillingness to establish or maintain eye contact with Ford quite clearly suggested a lack of assertiveness, and even timidity, which is associated with the nondynamic individual. Worst of all, Carter's characteristically downcast eyes connoted meanings inconsistent with the desired image of a man trying to sell himself as the nation's leader. For these reasons, I concluded that Ford's eye behaviors, when compared with Carter's, played an important role in the first debate, and helped Ford to project an image of superior competence, trustworthiness, and dynamism.

Ford and Carter exhibited gestures that differed noticeably, with regard to both number and kind. Many, but not all, of Ford's gestures seemed calculated to create the impression that he was a powerful person. His frequent hand gestures were so forceful that they resembled a subdued karate chop. Ford combined his forceful hand gestures with frequent head nodding and shoulder movement, to add emphasis and feeling to the points that he was making verbally. In short, Ford used illustrator gestures purposefully, to make him seem more dynamic.

In contrast, Carter used few gestures. The gestures he did use were weak and tentative, for the most part, and took the form of adaptor gestures. Carter's gentle hand gestures suggested a lack of confidence and an elevated level of anxiety. For example, Carter licked his lips, moved his hands in and out of his pockets, and sometimes put his hands together in a prayerful position. The aggregate effect was to depress Carter's perceived dynamism and make him appear to be anxious.

In my recommendations, I stressed that Carter should use many, and more forceful, hand gestures, to emphasize those points about which he felt deeply. At the same time, he must *eliminate* those gestures that suggested that he was hesitant, uncertain, or tentative about his answer. Ford's gestures gave him an additional advantage over Carter, although eye behaviors were more important than gestures in the candidates' efforts to sell themselves nonverbally.

Posture is very significant for individuals who wish to be perceived as credible leaders. This is so because one's posture is known to be a potent source of information for people who wish to make judgments about another person's power. In the Ford-Carter debate, Ford made skillful use of the image-building potential of certain types of postures. If you viewed the debate, you will have noticed that Ford's characteristic posture was that of standing with his feet and arms spread widely, gripping the opposite sides of the podium. He usually leaned forward as he began to answer a question, and increased the forward lean during the answer. Ford's widespread stance helped him to project an image of superior power; as he spoke, the forward lean communicated a sense of confidence and immediacy; and his fairly frequent postural shifts made him seem responsive to the reporter's questions. Although Ford's postures were somewhat exaggerated, they were synchronized with his gestures in such a manner as to suggest quite clearly that this was not a man who was apt to fall out of his helicopter or onto the family Christmas tree.

Carter, in contrast, rarely if ever spread his arms expansively in front of him or leaned forward. In fact his relative bodily rigidity, when combined with hands clasped in what appeared to be almost a prayerful pose, suggested a passivism that was not useful for a person trying to project the image of a dynamic leader and man of action. Leaders are usually viewed as active rather than passive.

In short, Ford exhibited many of the positive indicators of perceived power identified in Chapter 3, and Carter exhibited a distressing number of nonverbal cues which are known to be indicators of powerlessness. My recommendation to Carter was to accentuate the gestures and postures associated with perceptions of power, and to deemphasize those gestures and postures associated with powerlessness.

Neither candidate used the image-molding potential of vocal cues to good effect. Ford's voice lacks the orotund quality that would make it pleasing, and his tendency to give vocal emphasis to unimportant words, as opposed to thought units, hardly had the effect of accentuating his intellectual capacity. At the same time, Ford's substantial volume helped him communicate a sense of emotional intensity.

Carter's use of his voice was less than desirable for at least three reasons. His speaking rate was much too fast. At a number of points in the debate, Carter's speaking rate was in the range of 200 to 260 words per minute. A speaking rate of over 275 words per minute makes comprehension difficult, particularly if the communicator is using a regional dialect. When speaking at 200 to 260 words per minute, Carter had exceeded the range for conversational speech by around 100 words per minute. Such a rapid speaking rate also creates the impression that a person is anxious.

Secondly, Carter exhibited a very narrow pitch and volume range, and dropped his voice at the ends of sentences. Anything approaching monotone speech makes the communicator seem to be emotionally uninvolved, uninteresting, and nondynamic. The personality traits and personal qualities usually ascribed to a communicator who is vocally unexpressive are known to be primarily negative.

Finally, Carter paused frequently, filled a number of his pauses with nonfluencies, such as "ah," and repeated certain words. By exhibiting these vocal phenomena Carter reinforced the impression that he lacked confidence. To be persuasive, the communicator must *sound* confident. We know that the "ideal voice is smooth, free of hesitation, and clear, possess good tone and volume, and varies in speech rate. Public speaking experts and coaches agree that speakers who control loudness, pitch, fluency, resonance, and rate of speech are thought to be more active and dynamic, more persuasive" (Gray, 1982, pp. 85–86).

I recommended that Carter take the necessary actions to develop a more confident speaking voice in the second presidential debate with Gerald Ford. To communicate greater emotional involvement and commitment to the positions he was taking, Carter had to use greater variation in pitch and volume. To become more conversational, he would have to slow down his speaking rate. Finally, he would have to minimize nonfluencies because nonfluencies are usually perceived to be strong and reliable indicators of an elevated level of anxiety.

Although some of Carter's media advisors were concerned about the impact of his personal appearance in the debates, I do not believe the candidates' personal appearance strongly affected the images they projected. Personal appearance is particularly important in shaping the first impression an individual makes, but both candidates were already well known by the electorate.

Carter was subsequently briefed on the probable perceptual impact of specific kinds of communicative behaviors before his second debate with Gerald Ford. Polls show that Carter won the second debate, in the opinion of the American electorate. A Gallup poll conducted for *Newsweek* magazine indicated that 50 percent thought Carter had won, 27 percent thought Ford had won, and 23 percent were not sure. Those polled also felt that Carter was better informed than Ford, and would be more honest and open with the public about his foreign policy than Ford. In short, Carter was judged to be more credible on the important dimensions of competence and trustworthiness. Ken Cooper (1979) concluded that "the NVC information these two candidates transmitted in the debates explains the results of the poll, and ultimately the choice Americans made for President" (p. 185).

I certainly would not claim that Carter's nonverbal communication in the second debate with Ford was responsible for his victory in that debate. To watch the second debate, however, is to recognize that Carter controlled his eye behavior, and used gestures, postures, and vocal cues much more skillfully than he did in the first debate—for the purposes of selling himself nonverbally. His media advisors apparently also felt that nonverbal factors played an important role in the second debate. After Carter was elected, I got another call from a Rafshoon representative. He offered to contribute all of the television videotapes and radio audiotypes of commercials used in the primaries and the presidential campaign to me, and through me to the University of Georgia, as a gesture of appreciation for my analysis of the role nonverbal factors played in affecting Jimmy Carter's image in his debate(s) with Ford. I accepted this generous offer.

The Selling of the Corporate Sales Representative

Nonverbal factors quite clearly do play a central role in determining how successfully presidential candidates and others sell themselves nonverbally. Although most of you are not likely to be a presidential candidate, you may be in a situation where the selling of your abilities is important. Most of us attach importance to success in the job interview, where the ability to sell oneself is pitted against the abilities of competing job applicants. And many of you will undoubtedly accept a position which requires that you sell a product.

Modern corporations recognize that you must sell yourself to the potential customer before he or she will buy from you. The sales training manual of one corporation, Burst Inc., identifies "Sell Yourself First" as a principle of overriding importance in sales training. Sales trainees are reminded to sell themselves first, even though some "people think it's an old worn-out cliche, but it's not worn out. It's absolutely essential for success in selling or any other occupation."

My own experience in presenting sales and communication programs to corporate sales representatives has convinced me that nonverbal factors are vitally important in personal selling. The case of Omar Johnson helped to convince me. Omar is a sales representative for a pharmaceutical company. He has been reasonably successful because he works hard and has good product knowledge. He does not make a good first impression, however, primarily because he stutters, fills his frequent pauses with nonfluencies, and is unexpressive vocally.

Recently, a sales manager received a telephone call from a salesman who wanted to discuss an upcoming visit he was to make with a sales prospect. After talking to the salesman for five minutes, the sales manager realized that he did not know to whom he was talking, so he asked, "Who is this?" The caller replied in a carefully modulated voice, which was free of stutters or nonfluencies, "Why this is Omar Johnson. Don't you know who I am? I have worked for you for ten years." The sales manager was amazed, because Omar projected such a totally different image, by vocal means, that he was unrecognizable. "What have you done, Omar?" said the sales manager. "You have changed dramatically. You now seem to be confident and forceful." Omar explained, it "is the sales and communication program that I recently attended. I saw myself on the six-foot television screen for the first time, and I listened to myself. I looked and sounded like a fool. Since then, I've practiced my sales presentation on a tape recorder, and I'm a new man."

The sales manager subsequently accompanied Omar when he made a sales presentation to a prospect. Omar used his newly acquired communication skills to project an image of a much more competent, trustworthy, and dynamic salesperson. He persuaded the prospect to use a large quantity of the product that he was selling. Omar's sales manager was so impressed that he recommended that all of his company's salespeople be required to take a sales and communication training program. The sales manager's recommendation is currently being implemented by his company. The training program emphasizes the central role of nonverbal cues in developing the credibility of the corporate sales representative.

I have had the opportunity to observe and analyze the persuasive efforts of individuals who were selling products that ranged from wine to electrical appliances to fertilizer. Although product salespeople and politicians must both sell themselves first, the selling situations they encounter are different in important respects. Politicans who attempt to sell themselves on television via a persuasive speech have control over many situational variables. Their captive audiences have no opportunity to provide immediate feedback, therefore the politician need not make any on-the-spot adjustments in a preplanned message. The well-known politician need not be concerned with making a favorable first impression, because that impression has already been made. The politician need not be concerned about exercising the listening skills associated with effective communicative interaction, because no direct interaction with another individual occurs.

But corporate sales representatives engage in interpersonal rather than public communication. Because they interact directly with the prospective customer, they cannot adhere rigidly to a preplanned text. They frequently encounter sales resistance that is both unanticipated and unwelcome. They frequently encounter questions that directly challenge their credibility. To be successful, they must be able to adjust to the continually changing demands of distinctive kinds of communicative situations, over which they can exercise only partial control.

Because of the distinctive situational demands of successful product selling, the development and maintenance of a corporate salesperson's personal credibility is a particular challenge. To meet the constant threats to their credibility, less successful salespeople often communicate in ways that are either inappropriately aggressive or unassertive. The aggressive salesperson, for example, seems to delight in cultivating an image of irreverence, toughness, and insensitivity, which limits sales.

The development of a salesperson's credibility places a premium on the ability to communicate in an assertive, as opposed to an unassertive or aggressive manner. Judgments of a salesperson's level of assertiveness are strongly affected by the nature of his or her visual and vocal communication.

The Nonverbally Unassertive Salesperson.   Many corporate sales representatives are so unassertive visually and vocally that they damage their credibility. Visually unassertive salespeople rarely look at the prospect during the greeting or the close of a sale, and they fail to sustain eye contact during the sales presentation. They tend to reveal their anxiety by means of hand-to-face gestures and other extraneous movements, and they use few gestures to emphasize the selling points they do make. Their rigid bodily posture makes them seem unresponsive to what the customer is saying. *They frequently respond in inappropriate nonverbal ways when they encounter sales resistance or receive negative feedback from the customer.* When encountering sales resistance, I have observed many salespeople become defensive; they cross their arms over their chest, smile nervously, and laugh at inappropriate times.

The nonverbally unassertive salesperson usually does not sound convincing. I was dismayed when I heard one salesman ask a client, "Can I send out five cases of our product, then?" in such a timid and unassertive tone of voice as to almost assure noncompliance. If you do not sound convinced that you are selling a product with many tangible benefits, how can you expect the sales prospect to be convinced?

Vocally unassertive salespeople often try to let their product sell itself. They tend to read to the prospective customer from company literature, in an unexpressive voice that suggests a lack of enthusiasm about the product. Their speaking rate is too fast to allow purposeful pauses just before they make their most important selling points. Although they may not speak in a monotone voice, their pitch and volume range is narrow. Their anxiety is reflected not only in an excessive speaking rate but in the many nonfluencies they utter.

I made the following recommendations to one vocally unassertive salesperson, after listening to his sales presentation: "Avoid dropping the pitch of your voice at the ends of sentences, since this practice makes you seem less enthusiastic about the product you are selling—and indecisive. Your fast speaking rate and many filled pauses will have the effect of eroding your perceived competence. When you asked the customer whether you could 'send out five cases of our product?' you said it with a lack of conviction that might make it more likely that the customer would hesitate, or say no. Be sure to enunciate clearly and speak with vocal conviction. You must sound convinced that you are selling a superior product. Work for greater variation in pitch, rate, and volume. Practice your sales presentation with a tape recorder, in order to develop a persuasive voice."

The Nonverbally Aggressive Salesperson. Nonverbally aggressive salespeople have a different problem, which threatens their perceived trustworthiness. They act and sound aggressive. Their apparent confidence borders on arrogance. Their visual and vocal image is such that customers can hardly avoid the feeling that they are being coerced rather than persuaded.

The aggressive salesperson frequently fixes the prospect with an unremitting stare, assumes a beligerent posture, and shakes a finger in the prospect's face in order to emphasize a selling point. Exaggerated gestures and postures are often combined with manipulative questions and judgmental statements, such as: "Why ask me?"; "Don't you agree?"; "Isn't

that right?"; and "That's a false economy, son." *Unassertive salespeople become defensive when they encounter sales resistance, but the aggressive salesperson often becomes condescending.* The stare becomes more pronounced, the tone of voice becomes sarcastic, and volume becomes excessive. Nonverbal condenscension is reinforced by statements such as, "It would be a serious mistake not to use our product," or "Did you really buy that product?"

In their zeal to sell their product, aggressive salespeople appear to be insensitive to the needs and feelings of the prospect. They not only dominate the prospect visually, vocally, and verbally, but they are poor listeners. Unknowingly, they parody the hardsell image of the used-car salesperson, who is commonly believed to have a credibility problem of gigantic proportions.

After evaluating the unsuccessful sales presentation of one aggressive salesman, I made the following recommendations to him: "In your sales presentation you were so forceful that you ran the risk of being perceived as aggressive. Avoid putting the customer down, sounding argumentative when the customer raises objections, and pointing and shaking your finger at him. Note that at times your unremitting eye contact, your strident and condescending tone of voice, and your emotionally loaded gestures made you seem aggressive and less empathic than you actually are. The ring of conviction in your voice can be a real selling asset, but do not get carried away so that you sound like Mr. Hardsell. Given your ability to establish rapport with the customer, I am not sure why you lost this advantage by becoming aggressive. Rather than drawing the customer out and letting him do the talking, it seemed that you were determined to control the conversation from your frame of reference. In short, seek to be nonverbally assertive rather than aggressive."

Developing Personal Credibility

The foregoing examples were designed to illustrate the impact of nonverbal cues on credibility. A careful reading of the previous section should give you a rather good idea of what you should and should not do if you wish to sell yourself nonverbally. Nonetheless, you may find it helpful to have a specific set of guidelines to use for developing your own credibility. Figure 8.1 presents such a set of guidelines. The guidelines focus on the four classes of nonverbal cues that are known to have the strongest potential for affecting personal credibility. Study the guidelines carefully, for they represent the nonverbal profile of the credible communicator.

Eye behaviors are treated first because they play a central role in the development of personal credibility. We spend much more time monitoring the eye region of persons with whom we interact than any other part of their body, therefore eye behaviors strongly affect judgments of credibility.

In Chapter 2, I discussed in detail some of the reasons why our eye behaviors play such a central role in developing or damaging our personal credibility. Perhaps the most important reason is that our eye behaviors directly reflect the amount of self-confidence we are perceived to have. Jurich and Jurich (1974) found that failure to sustain eye contact correlated more highly with traditional measures of a communicator's level of anxiety than any other type of nonverbal cue. In short, *failure to sustain eye contact is the most damaging thing you can do nonverbally if you are particularly concerned about being perceived as confident.*

Eye behaviors are quite clearly important determinants of credibility (Beebe, 1974; Burgoon & Saine, 1978; Edinger & Patterson, 1983; Harper, Wiens, & Matarazzo, 1978; Hemsley & Doob, 1978; Kleinke, 1975). They are important because we are simply not believable unless we exhibit certain types of eye behaviors. Figure 8.1 specifies what eye behaviors should and should not be exhibited in developing one's personal credibility. Think again of Jimmy Carter's eye behaviors in his first debate with Gerald Ford, and how they affected his credibility, as you study Figure 8.1. Think also of the visually unassertive and aggressive salespeople who damaged their credibility by exhibiting too few positive eye behaviors and too many negative eye beheviors. Do you have any doubt that your own eye behaviors will have a major impact on your credibility?

Gestures and postures may also exert a powerful impact on our credi-

FIGURE 8.1 GUIDELINES FOR DEVELOPING YOUR CREDIBILITY
NONVERBALLY

Eye Behavior

Eye behaviors represent particularly important kinds of cues which are used to make judgments about how credible individuals are perceived to be. There is a well-developed cultural stereotype that specifies the kinds of eye behaviors that will raise and lower a communicator's credibility.

Positive Eye Behaviors: Sustained eye contact while talking to others; sustained eye contact while others talk to you; and the maintenance of direct eye contact with the individual(s) with whom you are communicating.

Negative Eye Behaviors: Looking down before responding to a question; exhibiting shifty eyes; looking away from the person with whom you are communicating; keeping your eyes downcast; excessive blinking; and eye flutter.

Gestures

Positive Gestures: Gestures should be used to add emphasis to the points that one is making; gestures should appear spontaneous, unrehearsed, and relaxed; gestures should be used to signal whether one wishes to continue talking or wishes another individual to begin talking; hand and elbows should be kept out and away from the body; and gestures should be used to communicate the intensity of one's feelings and emotions.

Negative Gestures: Gestures that suggest a communicator lacks confidence, is defensive, or is nervous should be avoided. Hand-to-face gestures, throat-clearing, fidgeting, tugging at clothing, visible perspiration on face or body, lip-licking, handwringing, finger-tapping, extraneous head movements, out-of-context smiling and grimacing, and weak and tentative gestures should be avoided, as they are apt to undermine a communicator's credibility.

Posture

Posture is particularly important in communicating an individual's status or power; how responsive the communicator is; and how strongly a communicator desires to establish a warm rapport with those with whom he or she is interacting.

Positive Postures: Communicators who wish to be perceived as powerful will spread their arms expansively in front of them, will assume an open and relaxed posture, and will walk confidently. Responsiveness is communicated by frequent and forceful postural shifts while one is communicating. Rapport is established in part by leaning forward and smiling (when appropriate) as one begins to answer a question.

Negative Postures: Communicators should avoid constricted postures that suggest that they are timid or lack assertiveness. Bodily rigidity, crossed arms and legs, arms and hands kept close to the body, and overall bodily tension are apt to impair a communicator's credibility.

FIGURE 8.1 (Cont.)

Voice

A communicator's vocal cues frequently play a major role in shaping his or her credibility. The personality characteristics a communicator is presumed to have are often determined by the sound of his or her voice. Vocal qualities shape impressions about an individual's credibility, status, and power.

Positive Vocal Cues: A communicator should strive for a conversational speaking style. Appropriate variation in pitch, rate, and volume is particularly important in projecting the image of a confident, competent, and dynamic person. Monotone delivery should be avoided. Sufficient volume has been found to be particularly important for individuals who wish to be perceived as competent and dynamic.

Negative Vocal Cues: Communicators should avoid speaking in such a way that their voices sound flat, tense, or nasal. Nasality is a particularly undesirable vocal quality. Communicators should also avoid speaking at an excessive rate, and should not use frequent pauses, which suggest a lack of confidence, and may suggest a lack of competence. The following nonfluencies have been shown to have a markedly negative impact on credibility: "ahs," repeating words, interruptions or pauses in mid-sentence, omitting parts of words, and stuttering. Persons who wish to enhance their credibility should strive to eliminate the use of such nonfluencies.

bility. Before considering Figure 8.2, you may want to return to Chapter 3. Think about the kinds of nonverbal cues that communicate liking versus disliking, assertiveness versus nonassertiveness, and power versus powerlessness. You will recognize that the development of your personal credibility depends to a considerable degree on how likable, assertive, and powerful others perceive you to be.

As you become actively engaged in developing your own credibility by nonverbal means, you must seek to eliminate those negative gestures and postures (see Figure 8.1) that you frequently use. At the same time, you must seek to use those gestures and postures that are known to have the potential to positively affect your perceived competence, trustworthiness, and dynamism.

Finally, vocal cues may be the single most important nonverbal determinant of credibility. As I indicated in Chapter 6, the sound of our voice strongly affects the personality traits and personal qualities we are presumed to have. Scherer, London, and Wolf (1973) emphasize that the "Confident Voice" exhibits considerable variation in pitch and volume, has high energy, and uses pauses of short duration infrequently. Communicators who use the Confident Voice are perceived as more competent, forceful, active, and enthusiastic than those who use the Doubtful

Voice. *The development of personal credibility requires the development of a confident voice.*

The "Doubtful Voice," that suggests a low level of self-confidence and a high level of anxiety must be eliminated (Cooper, 1979; Erickson, Lind, Johnson, & Barr, 1978; Miller, Beaber, & Valone, 1976). *Speech errors or nonfluencies in the form of stuttering, tongue slips, incoherent sounds, sentence changes, incompletions, and pauses filled with "ah," repetitions, and phrases such as "you know" are known to be strong and reliable indicators of anxiety.*

The individual who pauses and stutters before answering a question will probably be seen as less competent. The individual who pauses at length and uses many sentence fragments in trying to answer a question will probably be seen as untrustworthy; vocal cues such as these are frequently associated with evasiveness. Finally, the individual who exhibits many nonfluencies will probably be seen as less than dynamic. Nonfluencies correlate highly with how anxious the nonfluent communicator is perceived to be (Jurich & Jurich, 1974).

Senator Ted Kennedy's strikingly nonfluent responses to Roger Mudd's questions illustrate dramatically the powerfully negative impact that nonfluencies can have on a person's cerdibility. What did Kennedy say, when Roger Mudd asked him if he thought that anybody would ever really believe his explanation of Chappaquiddick? Kennedy replied: "Well there's the, the problem is, is from that night uh, I found, the, the the uh, conduct of behavior almost beyond belief myself. I mean that's why it's been uh (pause) uh, but I think that that's that's the way it was. That's that's, that happens to be the way it was. Now, uh, I find as I've stated it, that I've found that the conduct that uh, in that evenig and in, in the uh, as a result of the impact of the accident and the, the sense of loss, the sense of tragedy and the, the whole set of circ, circumstances the u, that the uh, behavior was inexplicable. So I find that those, uh, those types of questions as they apply to that are questions of my own, uh, could as well ut uh, that, that happens to be the way it was." ("CBS Reports: Teddy," 1979)

Figure 8.1 spells out in detail what you should and should not do if you are to use the full potential of your voice to develop your own credibility. As we have seen, the cultivation of the persuasive voice is a major responsibility of individuals who wish to develop their personal credibility.

Monitoring the Communicator's Nonverbal Cues

In order to make full use of the potential of nonverbal cues in developing their personal credibility, individuals must be able to monitor the nonverbal cues they exhibit in specific persuasive situations. Figure 8.2 should be used to make a record of the nonverbal cues you actually do exhibit.

The form provided in Figure 8.2 may be used to make a record of the nonverbal cues you exhibit in either a real or a simulated situation. You

FIGURE 8.2

Communicator_____ Evaluator_____

Please monitor the communicator's nonverbal cues very carefully to determine which cues had a positive and negative impact on credibility. The communicators should use these evaluations to make the adjustments in persuasive communication that are necessary to develop personal credibility.

EYE BEHAVIORS   Yes   No

  During the sales presentation, did the salesperson:
  + (1) Sustain eye contact with customer?   _____   _____
  + (2) Look directly at the customer?   _____   _____
  − (3) Look down or away before making a point?   _____   _____
  − (4) Exhibit shifty eyes?   _____   _____
  − (5) Blink excessively?   _____   _____

GESTURES

  + (1) Use hand and head gestures to emphasize points?   _____   _____
  + (2) Use gestures to signal a desire to continue talking? _____   _____
  + (3) Keep hands and elbows out and away from the
        body?   _____   _____
  + (4) Avoid using distracting hand-to-face gestures?   _____   _____
  − (5) Exhibit any weak and tentative gestures?   _____   _____
  − (6) Clear throat?   _____   _____
  − (7) Smile out of context?   _____   _____
  − (8) Fidget?   _____   _____
  − (9) Put hand in pockets or on objects in the room?   _____   _____

POSTURE

  + (1) Assume an open and relaxed posture?   _____   _____
  + (2) Use postural shifts to indicate interest?   _____   _____
  + (3) Lean forward while making a point?   _____   _____
  + (4) Face the customer directly?   _____   _____
  − (5) Exhibit bodily tension?   _____   _____
  − (6) Appear rigid?   _____   _____
  − (7) Communicate with crossed arms and/or legs?   _____   _____

VOCAL CUES

  + (1) Use a conversational speaking style?   _____   _____
  + (2) Emphasize important points with change in pitch
        and volume?   _____   _____
  + (3) Communicate with sufficient volume?   _____   _____
  + (4) Speak at an appropriate rate?   _____   _____
  − (5) Speak with a limited pitch rate?   _____   _____
  − (6) Sound flat, tense, or nasal?   _____   _____
  − (7) Pause at length before answering questions?   _____   _____
  − (8) Use nonfluencies such as "ah" and word repeti-
        tions?   _____   _____
  − (9) Interrupt the customer?   _____   _____

FIGURE 8.2 (Cont.)

Provide your written evaluation of the persuasive communication. Begin by reviewing the assessments you have made on page one. Then please identify each of the communicative cues that you felt had a positive or negative impact on credibility. Be sure to identify points not covered on the evaluation sheet.

DESIRABLE ASPECTS OF COMMUNICATION:

UNDESIRABLE ASPECTS OF COMMUNICATION:

SUGGESTIONS FOR IMPROVEMENT:

may try to sell a product to a potential customer in a real situation, where other individuals can unobtrusively observe your persuasive effort, or you may make a sales presentation in a role-playing situation. In either case, it is easy enough to ask a third party to make a record of your nonverbal cues. Or you may be able to have the session videotaped. In this case, either you or another person may make a record of your visual and auditory cues by placing check marks in the appropriate blanks while the videotape is being replayed.

Students and trainees who have used the monitoring and evaluation form provided in Figure 8.2 have found it to be valuable. The completed form provides a detailed profile of the nonverbal cues you actually have exhibited in a persuasive situation. The guidelines in Figure 8.1 identify the profile of nonverbal cues you should exhibit in order to be most credible. By comparing your actual profile with the desired profile, you should have a clear idea of the modifications you will have to make in your nonverbal communication if you wish to sell yourself more effectively.

Summary

Selling yourself is essential for successful persuasive communication. Selling yourself successfully requires the development of your personal credibility. Your credibility, in turn, is defined by how competent, trustworthy, and dynamic others judge you to be. Traditional treatments of credibility have been based on the assumption that our perceived competence, trustworthiness, and dynamism are controlled almost exclusively by the words we utter. This chapter provides information that challenges that assumption. In fact, we now know that nonverbal cues have the potential to exert a controlling influence on our personal credibility, in many instances.

The persuasive efforts of presidential candidates and corporate sales representatives which are analyzed in this chapter illustrate *how* and *why* specific kinds of nonverbal cues affect our credibility. Eye behaviors, gestures, postures, and vocal cues are highlighted as the most important determinants of credibility.

In order to make maximum use of the image-building potential of nonverbal cues, careful attention should be given to the guidelines in Figure 8.1. The nonverbal profile presented spells out in detail what one should and should not do to develop personal credibility. Figure 8.2 provides you with a systematic means of identifying the nonverbal profile you actually do exhibit. By carefully comparing the nonverbal cues you exhibit with the nonverbal cues you should exhibit, you can determine what changes must be made in your nonverbal communication in order to sell yourself successfully.

References

Baird, J. E., Jr. (1977). Some nonverbal elements of leadership emergence. *Southern Speech Communication Journal, 42,* 352–361.

Beebe, S. A. (1974). Eye contact: A nonverbal determinant of speaker credibility. *Communication Education, 23,* 21–25.

Brembeck, W. L., & Howell, W. S. (1976). *Persuasion: A means of social influence,* 2nd. ed. Englewood Cliffs, NJ: Prentice-Hall.

Burgoon, J. K., & Saine, T. (1978). *The unspoken dialogue: An introduction to nonverbal communication.* Boston: Houghton.

CBS Television (September 23, 1976), *The First Ford-Carter Presidential Debate.*

CBS Television (November 4, 1979), *CBS Reports: Teddy.*

Cooper, K. (1979). *Nonverbal communication for business success.* New York: AMACOM.

DeVito, J. A. (1980). *The interpersonal communication book,* 2nd ed. New York: Harper.

Edinger, J. A., & Patterson, M. L. (1983). Nonverbal involvement and social control. *Psychological Bulletin, 93,* 30–56.

Erickson, B., Lind, E. A., Johnson, B. C., & Barr, W. M. (1978). Speech style and impression formation in a court setting: The effects of "powerful" and "powerless" speech. *Journal of Experimental Social Psychology, 14,* 266–279.

Gitter, G., Black, H. & Fishman, J. E. (1975). Effect of race, sex and nonverbal communication on perceptions of leadership. *Sociology and Social Research, 60,* 46–57.

Gray, J., Jr. (1982). *The winning image,* New York: AMACOM.

Harper, R. G., Wiens, A. N., & Matarazzo, J. D. (1978). *Nonverbal communication: The state of the art.* New York: Wiley.

Hemsley, G. D., & Doob, A. N. (1978). The effect of looking behavior on perceptions of a communicator's credibility. *Journal of Applied Social Psychology, 8,* 136–144.

Jurich, A. P., & Jurich, J. A. (1974). Correlations among nonverbal expressions of anxiety. *Psychological Reports, 34,* 199–204.

Kleinke, C. L. (1975) *First impressions.* Englewood Cliffs, NJ: Prentice-Hall.

McGinniss, J. (1969). *The selling of the president, 1968.* New York: Trident.

McMahan, E. M. (1976). Nonverbal communication as a function of attribution in impression formation. *Communication Monographs, 43,* 287–294.

Miller, N., Beaber, R. J., & Valone, K. (1976). Speed of speech and persuasion. *Journal of Personality and Social Psychology, 34,* 615–624.

Schlenker, B. R. (1980). *Impression management.* Monterey, CA: Brooks/Cole.

Sherer, K. R., London, H., & Wolf, J. J. (1973) The voice of confidence: Paralinguistic cues and audience evaluation. *Journal of Research in Personality, 7,* 31–44.

CHAPTER NINE

Detecting Deception

Society has placed a premium on the detection of deception, from the beginning of recorded history. In part the fascination with deception may be attributed to the fact that it occurs so often in so many forms. Thus, "white lies, cover-ups, bluffing, euphemisms, masks, pretenses, tall-tales, put-ons, hoaxes, and other forms of falsehoods, fabrications, and simulations have coexisted with truthfulness and honesty in human communication for centuries" (Knapp & Comadena, 1979, p. 270).

Some of the ancient methods used to detect deception seem humorous today, but they reflect societal determination to ferret out the liar. In King Solomon's day, a rather unusual method was used to resolve a dispute between two women who both claimed to be the mother of the same child. An order was given to cut the child in two by a sword. The woman who cried out against the order was presumed to be telling the truth and the woman who remained silent was presumed to be lying. The ancient Chinese also used a rather novel method to detect deception. A suspected deceiver was required to chew on rice powder while being questioned. If, after spitting it out, the rice powder was dry, the person was judged to be deceptive. The theory was that the anxiety associated with lying would block off the salivary glands, resulting in a dry mouth. (Larson, 1969)

Law enforcement officials have of course been particularly concerned with refining methods and techniques for detecting deception. Their efforts have always been based on the same fundamental assumption: deceivers will experience an elevated level of anxiety at the moment of deception, which will be reflected in changes in one or more of the internal states of the body. The polygraph has been developed to monitor changes in heart rate, blood pressure, skin resistance, and other presumed physiological indicators of deception (Podlesny & Raskin, 1977). Israeli police

have recently begun using a device that measures palpitations of the stomach to detect deception of terrorist suspects whom they are interrogating. And a number of corporations now require that the Psychological Stress Evaluator be used when job prospects are being interviewed. This device is designed to pick up microtremors of the voice that indicate that deception is occuring (Goodwin, 1975).

In a more general sense, societal concern with deception has never been more evident. Our form of goverment requires that we trust our elected public officials to represent us in ways that are both straightforward and truthful. In the face of repeated acts of deception by governmental officials, it is not surprising that only 16 percent of a group of one thousand citizens surveyed in the San Francisco Bay area described their national government as "trustworthy" (Sniderman, 1981). Quite clearly, members of society must be able to determine if and when elected public officials are lying, if we are to have a defensible basis for trusting those officials who are not lying.

Most of us, however, are most immediately concerned about the deception of those individuals with whom we interact on a personal and face-to-face basis. In order to make accurate assessments of the attitudes, feelings, and motivations of friends, business associates, and intimates, we must develop the capability to detect deception when it occurs. As we shall see, familiarity with the nonverbal profiles of deceivers provides us with the potential to develop that capability.

Nonverbal Indicators of Deception

Deception in interpersonal communication is difficult to detect. In fact, we know that untrained individuals can detect the deception of strangers at, or just above, an accuracy level that would be expected by chance (Knapp, Hart, & Dennis, 1974). We also know that a person's speech communication is not apt to reveal, in a consistent and reliable way, whether that person is engaging in deception. As a result, analyses of communicators' verbal behavior for purposes of identifying indicators of deception is uncommon (Knapp & Comadena, 1979).

The potential of verbal messages as useful indicators of deception is limited. This is true because many deceivers can consciously control their verbal presentation of self. The skillful impression manager will presumably consciously control those verbal statements that might lead to an inference of deceit. In fact, the carefully formulated verbal message should minimize rather than maximize's the chances that deception will be detected.

Although deception is difficult to detect, the development of successful interpersonal relationships depends to a considerable extent on our ability to detect deception when it occurs. Rare indeed is the individual who would wish to develop a personal or business relationship that is not based upon interpersonal trust. Interpersonal trust is in turn based on the anticipation that the individuals with whom we interact will be honest and straightforward in their dealings with us. In order to have a defensible basis for assessing an individual's level of trustworthiness we must be able to determine whether and when that person chooses to be deceptive.

Those with whom we interact must also be concerned about their ability to determine whether we are engaging in deception. We must recognize that even when we are being completely truthful we may be perceived as being deceptive. This is true because there is a well-developed *deceiver stereotype* in our society which leads us to expect that deceivers will behave in certain ways. A recent survey suggests that the most striking feature of the deceiver stereotype is the belief that deceivers will exhibit *more* bodily movements than truthful communicators. Those surveyed believed that, on over two-thirds of the 45 behavioral indicators that were identified, deceivers will exhibit more movements than their truthful counterparts (Hocking & Leathers, 1980). The implication is clear: If you do not wish to be perceived as a deceiver, you must make sure that your nonverbal behaviors do not conform to the defining features of the deceiver stereotype.

There is of course no foolproof method for detecting deception. Even when time-tested machines such as the polygraph are used, the accuracy with which deception is detected may fall as low as 64 percent (Lykken, 1974). Furthermore, the use of machines (such as the polygraph or the Psychological Stress Evaluator) to detect deception is not feasible in the typical interpersonal communication situation.

Deception that occurs in interpersonal communication must be detected without the aid of machines. We can detect this sort of deception without the use of mechanical monitoring devices if we become thoroughly familiar with the nonverbal profiles that differentiate lying from truthful communicators. We now know that liars exhibit a number of identifiable nonverbal cues at the moment of deception, which are distinctively different from the nonverbal cues exhibited by truthful communicators. Recent research on deception clearly documents that the guilt, and the resultant anxiety associated with deception, are reflected not only in changes in such internal physiological factors as the deceiver's heart and breathing rate. Deceivers also behave differently nonverbally because of an elevated level of anxiety that markedly affects their nonverbal communication. These external nonverbal indicators of deception have proven to be very valuable to the human lie detector.

A recent review of the performance of trained judges in 16 deception studies (DePaulo, Zuckerman, & Rosenthal, 1980) indicated that the judges' accuracy level was significantly better than chance in all but three of the studies. Druckman, Rozelle, and Baxter (1982) report significant gains in the accuracy with which judges were able to differentiate between honest, evasive, and deceptive communication, after the judges were trained in the use of the nonverbal profile for each of these three types of communication. Finally, nearly two-thirds of a group of trained police interrogators report that their judgments of deception on the part of criminal suspects is "highly accurate" when they rely solely on the suspects' nonverbal cues to make their judgments (Leathers, 1982).

Nonverbal Profile of the Deceptive Communicator— Type I

The nonverbal behaviors of laboratory liars, who are asked to lie by an experimenter, have been examined in detail. Results from laboratory studies cannot of course be used to develop the nonverbal profile of all types of deceivers in the real world. These results are most useful in developing the nonverbal profile of the real-world deceiver, who is exposed to conditions fundamentally similar to conditions experienced by laboratory liars.

Consider the following examples of deception: You lie to the telephone caller about your real reason for not accepting a date. You lie to your boss's secretary, when you call in and say you are sick. You lie to your children about the depth of your religious convictions, in order to get them to attend Sunday School. You lie to a job interviewer, in order to pad your credentials. You lie about your business expenses to an IRS income tax auditor. Each of these lies might be labeled *Type I deception*. They represent the kind of lying that occurs frequently in the real world, as well as in the laboratory.

Type I deception may be identified by three defining features. From the perspective of the deceiver: (a) the level of anxiety experienced at the moment of deception is typically fairly low; (b) the consequences of being detected as a deceiver are not severe; and (c) deception occurs for a short period of time. As we shall see, Type I and Type II deception are quite different. In fact, Type II deceivers typically experience a high level of anxiety in their long-term efforts to deceive, because they recognize that the consequences of being detected may be catastrophic.

Type I deceivers can consciously control at least some of the nonverbal cues that serve as telltale signs of their deception. Because their level of anxiety is relatively low, they have the opportunity to concentrate on their presentation of self without being overly distracted by their guilt feelings. Zuckerman, DePaulo, and Rosenthal (1982) emphasize that "the extent to which deception fosters guilt, anxiety and/or duping delight varies according to the purposes of the deception, its social context and the characteristics of the deceiver" (p. 9).

In addition, Type I liars are not ordinarily faced with the prospect of the gas chamber or a long jail sentence if their deception is detected. They can concentrate on what they perceive to be credible actions as they engage in impression management. In short, they are impression managers who should not be distracted from their goal of monitoring those nonverbal cues which they believe may reveal their deception, or from taking the necessary actions to suppress those cues which might reveal deception.

Finally, the Type I liar is usually required by an experimenter to lie for only a short period of time. Conventional wisdom suggests that a deceiver may effectively control his or her presentation of self for limited periods of time, but lying convincingly for extended periods of time is much more difficult. The longer deception must be sustained, the greater the level of anxiety the deceiver is likely to experience. As we shall see, the nonverbal profiles for Type I and Type II deceivers do differ in some important respects. The differences may be attributed to the contrasting conditions experienced by the two types of deceivers.

To develop the nonverbal profile for the Type I deceiver, I have concentrated on those kinds of nonverbal cues that have most frequently and consistently been found to be indicative of deception. No single cue will always be exhibited at the moment of deception, however. Nonetheless, the patterns of cues exhibited by Type I deceivers are quite consistent.

To be successful in detecting deception, you must decide which type or class of nonverbal cue will receive your closest scrutiny. Vocal cues have proven to be a particularly rich source of deception cues. A number of studies have found that *deceivers exhibit more speech errors than honest communicators* (Druckman et al., 1982; Knapp et al., 1974; Mehrabian, 1971). Deceivers also consistently *hesitate* and *pause more frequently* and *for longer periods of time* than their truthful counterparts (Harrison, Hwalek, Raney, & Frtiz, 1978; Kraut, 1978). Speech errors or *nonfluencies* associated with deception take the form of *sentence changes, word repetition,* and *intruding sounds.* The *speaking rate* of deceivers has been found to be *both abornmally fast and slow,* with *overall vocal nervous-*

ness identified as a particularly reliable indicator of deception (Hocking & Leathers, 1980).

Gestures have also been found to be reliable indicators of Type I deception. To make optimal use of gestural cues you should *be alert for any abnormality in the rate or frequency with which certain kinds of gestures are exhibited* (DePaulo et al., 1980). *Self-adaptors*, in the form of hand-to-face gestures and hand shrugs, and *object adaptors*, in the form of touching or playing with objects in the room, are exhibited with abnormal frequency by deceivers (Ekman & Friesen, 1972, O'Hair, Cody, & McLaughlin, 1981; Cody & O'Hair, 1983). Because gestural adaptors are known to reflect anxiety, we should not be surprised that even Type I deceivers exhibit an abnormal number of adaptors. Type I deceivers exhibit much less anxiety than Type II deceivers, but they are more anxious when lying than when telling the truth. The deceiver's adaptor rate is understandably accelerated because of the increased anxiety level.

Although deceivers exhibit more gestural adaptors, they exhibit fewer gestural illustrators. A number of studies have found that deceivers reduce the number of head movements, foot movements, and leg movements. In short, deceivers may seem abnormally unexpressive because of their reduced illustrator rate (Ekman & Friesen, 1972; Hocking & Leathers, 1980; Mehrabian, 1971).

Postural indicators of deception are more limited in number. However, in a number of instances deceivers have exhibited a preference for more distant seating, with little trunk swiveling, and an indirect bodily orientation (Druckman et al., 1982). When the characteristic gestures and postures of Type I deceivers are considered together, the image projected is one of unusual *impassivity, immobility,* and *bodily rigidity.*

The eye behaviors of Type I liars have been found to be different in different studies (Matarazzo, Wiens, Jackson, & Manaugh, 1970; McClintock & Hunt, 1975). A number of studies have found, however, that *the eye contact of deceivers is more limited* than for truthful communicators (Exline, Thibaut, Hickey, & Gumpert, 1970; Hocking & Leathers, 1980), and that averted gazes and *substantial time spent looking away from the person with whom the deceiver is communicating* may be indicative of deception (Druckman et al., 1982).

Finally, facial expressions seem to be important primarily in a negative sense. For example, Ekman and Friesen (1969) theorize that facial expressions are apt to be less useful indicators of deception than bodily cues because facial cues are more susceptible to effective conscious control than bodily cues. Subsequent research by Ekman and Friesen (1974) did support the view that bodily cues are more accurate indicators of deception than facial expressions.

Hocking and Leathers (1980) also theorize that facial expressions are less reliable indicators of deception than bodily cues, although their theoretical perspective is based on different assumptions than the theory of Ekman and Friesen. In fact, recent evidence suggests that facial expressions of lying and honest communicators do not differ in ways that are consistently and reliably identifiable (Cody & O'Hair, 1983; Hocking & Leathers, 1980).

To the human lie detector, the face should be considered primarily as a source of noise. To concentrate on the suspected deceiver's facial expressions is to divert attention from nonverbal cues that are known to be much more useful indicators of deception. When considered in the aggregate, vocal cues and bodily cues are the most useful nonverbal indicators of Type I deception.

In order to use the nonverbal profile of the Type I deceiver to develop our capacity to detect deception, we must understand why these deceivers behave as they do. A colleague and I (Hocking & Leathers, 1980) developed a theoretical perspective designed to explain the distinctive behaviors of Type I deceivers. This perspective focuses exclusively on the behaviors of deceivers who are using prepared, as opposed to spontaneous, lies. At this point, we know relatively little about the behavioral profile of the spontaneous liar. Because the spontaneous lie will probably induce more anxiety than the prepared lie, however, individuals engaging in the two types of lying may manifest somewhat different nonverbal behaviors (O'Hair, et al., 1981).

The theoretical perspective is grounded in three explanatory propositions. The Type I deceiver is apt to: (a) attempt to exercise conscious control over those nonverbal behaviors that he or she believes to be important defining features of the cultural stereotype for deceivers; (b) exercise conscious control over those nonverbal behaviors that can be most directly and easily monitored at the moment of deception; and (c) exercise effective conscious control over those behaviors that are most susceptible to conscious control.

As already indicated, the cultural stereotype of the deceiver fosters the expectation that deceivers will exhibit more bodily movements than truthful communicators. For example, deceivers are expected to exhibit *more* defensiveness gestures, *more* extraneous movements suggestive of anxiety, and *greater* bodily nervousness. Clearly, skillful deceivers will not wish to be associated with the deceiver stereotype. Therefore, in order to avoid this sort of association, they will presumably attempt to suppress the number of bodily movements they exhibit.

In fact, the theoretical perspective developed by Hocking and I predicts that Type I deceivers will exhibit an abnormal lack of bodily movements. The perspective also provides a basis for understanding the facial expressions and vocal cues that Type I deceivers exhibit.

The perspective focuses on the three classes of nonverbal cues that have most frequently been examined as potentially useful indicators of deception—bodily movements, facial expressions, and vocal cues. Bodily cues in the form of head, foot, and leg movements can be easily monitored by the deceiver and are fairly difficult to control. Vocal cues are most difficult to monitor and, therefore, are difficult to control consciously.

Two recent studies provide support for the explanatory value of this theoretical perspective. In fact, these two studies produced detailed information that can be used to develop fully the nonverbal behavioral profile of the Type I deceiver. The first study (Hocking & Leathers, 1980) supports the conclusion that bodily movements and vocal cues are particularly useful indicators of deception and facial expressions are not. Results from the second study (Cody & O'Hair, 1983) "support the Hocking and Leathers perspective" and provide additional information about the nonverbal profile of the Type I deceiver.

If you wish to have the potential to increase the accuracy with which you can detect Type I deception, consider carefully the nonverbal indicators of deception identified in Table 9.1. Certain kinds of vocal cues are strongly indicative of deception. In contrast to truthful communicators, deceivers exhibit *more* hesitations, pauses, and longer pauses, word rep-

TABLE 9.1. Nonverbal Indicators of Deception: Type I

	Deceivers Exhibit	
	More	*Less*
Vocal Cues	Hesitations Pauses Lengthy pauses Sentence changes Word repetitions Intruding sounds Rapid speaking rate Overall vocal nervousness	Lengthy Answers
Gestures	Self-adaptors (touching face and body, and hand shrugs). Object-adaptors (touching or playing with objects in room) Overall bodily nervousness	Head movement Head nodding Foot movements Illustrators Leg movements
Posture	Distant spacing	Direct bodily orientation Trunk swiveling
Eye Behaviors	Time spent looking away Averted gazes	Eye contact duration
Facial Expressions	Facial expressions do *not* reliably differentiate deceitful from honest communicators	

Rather than concentrating on a single cue that might indicate deception, the lie detector should concentrate on classes of indicators. When trying to determine whether an individual is engaging in some sort of low-risk deception, vocal cues are probably the most useful indicators of deception, followed, in order of their potential value, by gestures, eye behaviors, postures, and facial expressions.

etitions, intruding sounds, and an accelerated speaking rate. Most importantly, deceivers are apt to *sound* nervous.

Bodily cues that may reveal deception require careful scrutiny. Type I deceivers have been found consistently to exhibit *fewer* of the kinds of bodily movements that they can consciously control than their truthful counterparts. Thus, deceivers when compared with nondeceivers exhibit *less* head movement, foot movement, leg movements, and illustrator activity. They also exhibit a less direct bodily orientation and do less trunk swiveling. By contrast, deceivers exhibit *more* self-adaptors and object-adaptors than truthful communicators. Most importantly, deceivers exhibit greater overall bodily nervousness.

Eye behaviors are less useful indicators of Type I deception. This may be true because some eye behaviors are susceptible to effective conscious control and others are not. We do know that deceivers seem to have *eye contact of relatively limited duration.* In addition, deceivers exhibit a propensity to avert their gaze and more frequently look away from individuals with whom they are communicating than honest communicators.

Finally, facial expressions of deceitful and honest communicators do not seem to differ consistently. For this reason, human lie detectors would be well-advised to pay little attention to a suspected deceiver's facial expressions and concentrate instead on vocal and bodily cues.

Nonverbal Profile of the Deceptive Communicator— Type II

The lying criminal suspect who is interviewed by the police interrogator is clearly a Type II deceiver. Most Type II deceivers do not of course experience a comparable level of stress. Nonetheless, the typical Type II deceiver is a highly anxious person. Type II deceivers experience a high level of anxiety for at least two reasons: The probable consequences of being detected as a deceiver are severe, and they must successfully sustain their deception for a considerable period of time.

A number of the government officials who were indicted in the Watergate scandal were Type II deceivers. They faced public disgrace, the loss of important positions, and jail sentences if their long-term efforts to deceive were detected. Additional examples of Type II deceivers abound. Consider the many married persons who have been cheating on their spouses; the athletes who have been surreptitiously using hard drugs; employees who have been stealing from their employers; or alcoholics who struggle to conceal their affliction from friends and associates. All of these individuals experience high levels of anxiety in their long-term efforts to deceive because the consequences of being detected are hardly trivial.

Do Type II deceivers exhibit an identifiable nonverbal behavioral profile which can be used as an aid in detecting their deception? There is now considerable evidence to suggest that they do. The evidence comes primarily from the reports of police interrogators who have interviewed lying criminal suspects. Because all Type II deceivers are apt to experience a high level of anxiety, and fear the cosequences of being detected as a deceiver, there seems good reason to believe that a number of different kinds of Type II deceivers will exhibit similar nonverbal behaviors at the time of deception.

Knowledge of the nonverbal behaviors of Type II deceivers comes primarily from law enforcement agencies. Law enforcement agencies continue to have extensive exposure to Type II deception. These agencies are of course committed to detecting criminal deception when and where it occurs. Investigators receive highly specialized training which is designed to detect deception, and trained interviewers have many opportunities to study the behaviors of criminal suspects, under the controlled conditions of the police interview.

The police interview is ideally suited to the study of Type II deception. If criminal suspects do exhibit identifiable nonverbal cues at the moment of deception, both the probability of occurrence and detection should be enhanced in this setting. In contrast to the low levels of guilt and anxiety typically experienced by the Type I deceiver, guilt and anxiety levels for the lying criminal suspect should both be exceptionally high.

As a result of my research on deception, I have established personal contact with interrogators who work for the Georgia Bureau of Investigation. The GBI, as well as other police agencies in various parts of the country, attaches much importance to the value of nonverbal cues as indicators of deception.

Mike Smith is one of the GBI's most experienced and respected interrogators. He is convinced that nonverbal cues are reliable indicators of deception. In a guest lecture to one of my classes in nonverbal communication, Smith revealed which nonverbal cues he uses to detect Type II deception, and why (Smith, 1979).

In Smith's view, the anxiety level of the Type II deceiver is so high that a substantial number of nonverbal cues are readily discernible to the trained observer. For example, during his many years as a police interrogator, Smith said that he observed suspects, who were undergoing interrogation do the following: (a) bite their lips until they bled; (b) foam at the mouth; (c) make clicking sounds while talking (because of a dry mouth); (d) bend their feet beneath their chair, at a painful angle; and (e) give a "weak, wet, and clammy" hand shake. (These particular suspects were proved to have been lying.) Smith emphasized, however, that he relies on no single cue in making an inference of deception; instead, he is alert for *sets of cues*, in the form of eye behaviors, gestures, and vocal cues, all of which seem to support a judgment that deception is taking place.

To determine whether police interrogators agree on the defining features of the nonverbal profile for Type II deceivers, a colleague and I recently conducted a survey of all active interrogators employed by the Georgia Bureau of Investigation. The survey was designed to accomplish two objectives. We wanted to determine to what extent police interviewers rely on a suspect's nonverbal cues to detect deception. We also wanted to identify the nonverbal cues which are viewed as the most important in the nonverbal profile for the lying suspect (Leathers & Hocking, 1983).

Results from the survey indicate that the nonverbal cues of the lying criminal suspect represent a major source of information used by police interrogators to make a judgment of deception or truthfulness. Of the 86 police interrogators interviewed, 76.7 percent indicated that they either relied *equally* on both verbal and nonverbal behaviors to detect deception, or that they relied *more heavily on nonverbal* than verbal behaviors to detect deception. When forced to rely solely on nonverbal cues, 64 percent of the agents indicated that their judgments would be proven "highly accurate."

Police interviewers in this study strongly endorsed the value of nonverbal cues as indicators of deception. They not only believe that nonverbal cues are a valuable and accurate source of information about Type II deception; they have a nonverbal behavioral profile of the deceiving criminal suspect, which is both detailed and internally consistent.

To begin, each GBI interrogator was asked to describe, in two or three words, each of the nonverbal behaviors that deceivers exhibit when lying in the police interview. Their responses were illuminating. Many of the nonverbal cues seem directly linked to the Type II deceiver's elevated level of anxiety (e.g., noticeable perspiration; fidgeting and twitching; pupil dilation; dry mouth, reflected in lip-licking; unusual breathing; and abnormal swallowing).

Police interviewers clearly believe that *eye behaviors* and *bodily movements* are the *two most important kids of indicators of deception.* Poor eye contact was identified as a distinctive and indentifiable behavior of lying criminal suspects, by a much higher percentage of police interviewers (82.6 percent) than the next most frequently identified variable, hand movement (50 percent). The importance of specific kinds of bodily movements as indicators of deception is reflected in part by the number of specific bodily movements identified. Of the 11 most frequently identified nonverbal cues, 15 involved a specific kind of bodily movement, e.g., hand movements, foot movements, fidgeting, posture shifts, and object-adaptors.

The nonverbal profile for the Type II deceivers that police interrogators encounter is presented in Table 9.2. Results were obtained by asking police interrogators to rate 20 variables (identified in previous deception research as potential indicators of deception) on a 10-point scale as to their *usefulness* as indicators of deception (a rating of *10* indicated high usefulness and a *1* indicated very little usefulness). Directional ratings, using a 5-point scale, indicate whether police interrogators believe lying criminal suspects exhibit *more* or *less* of a given nonverbal variable at the moment of deception. Thus, interrogators reported that Type II deceivers exhibit eye contact of more limited duration (Mean = .14) and more overall body nervousness (Mean = 1.33) than their truthful counterparts.

Results in Table 9.2 indicate that the eye behaviors and bodily move-

TABLE 9.2.   Nonverbal Indicators of Deception: Type II

Variable	Usefulness (0 to 10)			Direction (−2 to +2)		
	Mean	Standard Deviation	Mode	Mean	Standard Deviation	Mode
Eye contact duration	8.12	1.70	10.0	−.14	1.68	−2.0
Overall body nervousness	7.79	1.60	7.0	1.33	.70	1.0
Eye movement	7.44	2.07	7.0	1.31	.83	2.0
Defensiveness gestures	7.07	1.74	7.0	1.07	.66	1.0
Overall vocal nervousness	6.95	1.55	7.0	1.15	.52	1.0
Posture shift	6.94	1.86	8.0	1.08	.73	1.0
Overall facial nervousness	6.89	1.84	7.0	1.04	.70	1.0
Length of time pausing	6.82	2.09	7.0	.90	.36	1.0
Leg movement	6.75	1.93	7.0	1.01	.69	1.0
Hand movement	6.55	1.78	8.0	.92	.59	1.0
Number of pauses	6.54	2.04	5.0	.88	.77	1.0
Hand-to-face gestures	6.25	2.05	8.0	.81	.77	1.0
Foot movement	6.52	2.05	8.0	1.01	.72	1.0
Head movement	6.20	2.09	5.0	.77	.74	1.0
Number of "ahs"	6.19	2.15	5.0	.81	.64	1.0
Number of stutters	6.04	1.85	5.0	.69	.72	1.0
Speaking rate	5.90	1.82	5.0	.52	.85	1.0
Illustrating gestures	5.53	2.15	5.0	.65	.73	1.0
Facial pleasantness	5.09	2.20	5.0	.09	.84	0.0
Number of smiles	4.94	2.30	5.0	.10	.85	0.0

ments of Type II deceivers are the most useful kinds of specific nonverbal cues that indicate deception. Type II deceivers are thought to be identifiable in part by their *limited eye contact* and by their *shifty eyes*. In conversations with me, almost all interrogators reported that the *pupils* of Type II deceivers *dilate at the moment of deception.*

Type II deceivers interviewed by police interrogators clearly *exhibit an abnormal number of specific kinds of bodily movements.* Whereas Type II deceivers exhibit more bodily movements than truthful communicators, Type I deceivers exhibit fewer bodily movements than their truthful counterparts. The difference may be attributed to the fact that Type II deceivers cannot effectively suppress bodily movement at the time of deception because of the high level of anxiety they experience. In contrast, Type I deceivers do suppress the number of bodily movements they exhibit in their attempts to escape detection. They have the opportunity to consciously control a number of the bodily movements they exhibit because of the relatively low level of anxiety they experience.

As you study the nonverbal profile for the Type II deceiver, you should recognize that any single nonverbal cue that seems indicative of deception may be misleading. Police interrogators repeatedly emphasized that they relied on their overall impression of the suspects nonverbal behaviors rather than on a single cue. Thus, *overall body nervousness, overall vocal nervousness,* and *overall facial nervousness* were viewed as particularly useful indicators of deception.

The nonverbal profile presented in Table 9.2 may not of course apply to all Type II deceivers. In fact, this is a profile for one specific kind of deceiver. Opportunities for effective impressive management are minimal in the high-stress conditions of the police interview. At the same time, there seems good reason to believe that the factors that exert a controlling impact on the nonverbal behaviors of Type II deceivers, both within and outside the context of the police interview, are fundamentally similar. For this reason the nonverbal profile presented in Table 9.2 should cetainly be helpful to you as you seek to identify Type II deception when and where it occurs in the real world.

Summary

The development of successful interpersonal relationships requires that individuals develop the ability to detect deception. Successful interpersonal relationships are built upon mutual trust. In order to have a defensible basis for determining our level of trust for another person, we must be able to determine if and when that person chooses to be deceptive.

Nonverbal cues have proven to be useful indicators of deception in interpersonal communication. In order to make optimal use of the informational value of nonverbal indicators of deception, however, the human lie detector must be thoroughly familiar with the nonverbal profile for Type I and Type II deceivers. Type I and Type II deceivers differ with regard to the level of anxiety they experience, their fear of the consequences of being detected, and in the length of time they are required to sustain their deception.

Nonverbal cues characteristically exhibited by Type I deceivers seem to be controlled by three factors. Type I deceivers attempt to: (a) exercise conscious control over those nonverbal behaviors that he or she believes to be the defining features of the cultural stereotype for deceivers; (b) exercise conscious control over those nonverbal behaviors that can be most directly and easily monitored at the moment of deception; and (c) exercise effective conscious control over those behaviors that are susceptible to conscious control.

Type I deceivers characteristically exhibit greater overall vocal nervousness, more nonfluencies, more pauses, and speak faster than their truthful counterparts. They also exhibit *less* overall bodily nervousness, and they use fewer of the bodily movements that they can control, such as head, foot, and leg movements. However, they exhibit more self-adaptors and object-adaptors than their truthful counterparts; these kinds of bodily movements cannot be consciously controlled. Facial expressions do not provide a reliable basis for differentiating deceiving from truthful communicators.

Type II deceivers differ from Type I deceivers in that they exhibit many more bodily movements than truthful individuals. Bodily movements and eye behaviors of Type II deceivers are particularly useful cues to their deception. However, we, as human lie detectors, should concentrate on collective measues, such as overall bodily nervousness and overall vocal nervousness, in order to maximize our chances of detecting Type II deception.

References

Cody, M. J., & O'Hair, H. D. (1983). Nonverbal communication and deception: differences in deception cues due to gender and communicator dominance. *Communication Monographs, 50,* 175–192.

DePaulo B. M., Zuckerman, M., & Rosenthal, R. (1980). Humans as lie detectors. *Journal of Communication, 30,* 129–131.

Druckman, D., Rozelle, R. M., & Baxter, J. C. (1982). *Nonverbal communication: Survey, theory, and research.* Beverly Hills: Sage.

Ekman, P., & Friesen, W. (1969). Nonverbal leakage and clues to deception. *Psychiatry, 32,* 88–106.

Ekman, P., & Friesen, W. (1972). Hand movements. *Journal of Communication, 22,* 353–374.

Ekman, P., & Friesen, W. (1974). Detecting deception from the body and face. *Journal of Personality and Social Psychology, 29,* 288–298.

Exline, R. V., Thibaut, J., Hickey, C. B., & Gumpert, P. (1970). Visual interaction in relation to machiavellianism and an unethical act. In R. Christie & F. L. Geis (Eds.), *Studies in Machiavellianism,* (pp. 53–75). New York: Academic.

Goodwin, G. L. (1975). PSE: New security tool. *Burroughs Clearing House, 59,* 29.

Harrison, A. A., Hwalek, M., Raney, D. R., & Fritz, J. G. (1978). Cues to deception in an interview situation. *Social Psychology, 41,* 158–159.

Hocking, J. E., & Leathers, D. G. (1980). Nonverbal indicators of deception: A new theoretical perspective. *Communication Monographs, 47,* 119–131.

Knapp, M. L., & Comadena, M. E. (1979). Telling it like it isn't: A review of theory and research on deceptive communications. *Human Communication Research, 5,* 270–285.

Knapp, M. L., Hart, R. P., & Dennis, H. S. (1974). An exploration of deception as a communication construct. *Human Communication Research, 1,* 15–29.

Kraut, R. E. (1978). Verbal and nonverbal cues in the perception of lying. *Journal of Personality and Social Psychology, 36,* 380–391.

Larson, J. A. (1969). *Lying and its detection.* Montclair, NJ: Patterson Smith.

Leathers, D. G. (1982, November). An examination of police interviewers' beliefs about the utility and nature of nonverbal indicators of deception. Paper presented at the annual convention of the Speech Communication Association, Louisville, KY.

Leathers, D. G., & Hocking, J. E. (1983). *An examination of police interviewers' beliefs about the utility and nature of nonverbal indicators of deception.* Unpublished manuscript.

Lykken, D. T. (1974). Psychology and the lie detector industry. *American Psychologist, 29,* 725–727.

Matarazzo, J. D., Wiens, A. N., Jackson, R. H., & Manaugh, T. S. (1970). Interviewer speech behavior under conditions of endogenously-present and exogenously-induced motivational states. *Journal of Clinical Psychology, 26,* 148.

McClintock, C. C., & Hunt, R. G. (1975) Nonverbal indicators of affect and deception in an interview setting. *Journal of Applied Social Psychology, 5,* 62–66.

Mehrabian, A. (1971). Nonverbal betrayal of feelings. *Journal of Experimental Research in Personality, 5,* 64–75.

O'Hair, D., Cody, M. J. & McLaughlin, M. L. (1981). Prepared lies, spontaneous lies, Machiavellianism, and nonverbal communication. *Human Communication Research, 7,* 325–339.

Podlesny, J. A., & Raskin, D. C. (1977). Physiological measures and detection of deception. *Psychological Bulletin, 84,* 784–785.

Smith, M. (1979, May). Nonverbal indicators of deception: The lying suspect. Lecture given at University of Georgia, Athens, GA.

Sniderman, P. M. (1981). *A question of loyalty.* Berkeley: University of California Press.

Zuckerman, M., DePaulo, B. M., & Rosenthal, R. (1982). Verbal and nonverbal communication of deception. In L. Berkowitz (Ed.), *Advances in experimental social psychology,* Vol 14. New York: Academic.

CHAPTER TEN

Communicating Consistently

Interpersonal communication frequently features inconsistent messages that represent serious problems for both the message sender and receiver. Message senders who communicate inconsistently invite the inference that they are inept communicators. The message sender who uses inconsistent messages is also apt to be perceived as less sincere, honest, straightforward, genuine, and credible than one who does not. When inconsistent messages are used repeatedly in interpersonal communication, they virtually assure that a relationship of mutual trust will not develop.

Inconsistent messages also represent serious problems for the receiver or decoder. Decoders find it unpleasant to respond to messages that contain inconsistent or mutually contradictory meanings. They must decide which of the contradictory meanings is most believable, and why. Individuals who must cope frequently with inconsistent messages find that they become anxious. Individuals who are frequently the target of inconsistent messages in a specific context, such as in husband-wife communication, have been known to develop mental illness.

With the exception of the sadists or masochists in our midst, individuals rarely make a conscious attempt to communicate inconsistently. When we do use inconsistent messages, we usually do so unintentionally. We often communicate inconsistently when we experience one emotion but feel, at least subconsciously, that it is socially appropriate to convey a different emotion.

Consider, for example, the times when someone has called you on the telephone and asked you for a date. Did you respond by saying, "I will not go because I find you to be physically unattractive?" You probably did not, because it seems to be an insensitive way to respond. You may have said, "There is nothing I would rather do, but I have a previous commitment."

If you really did not wish to accept the date, it is likely that your words and vocal cues communicated inconsistent messages. Your spoken words probably suggested that the date would have been a highly pleasurable experience, but your unenthusiastic tone of voice probably suggested your conviction that such a date would be anything but a pleasurable experience.

Inconsistent messges are particularly dysfunctional when they create or reinforce an impression quite different from the impression the message sender intended to make. For example, Mehrabian (1981) cites the example of the department head who is welcoming a new employee to his job. The department head wants to make clear that both department heads and members of the department are treated as equals in his firm, and that all employees are encouraged to express their feelings openly to their department heads.

> When the department head actually speaks with the new employee, however, his posture, facial expressions, and vocal expressions convey his awareness of his dominant relationship relative to the new member of his department, who comes away from this pep talk with the feeling that the boss is a bit of a phony, that he is trying to be a nice guy, but that he doesn't really mean what he says. In other words, the new man feels that he will be wise not to be critical of anything the boss says or does. (p. 81)

This chapter examines the nature of multichannel messages that communicate inconsistent meanings, as well as the attitudinal, perceptual, and behavioral impact of such messages on decoders, those who must assume the unwelcome burden of coping with inconsistent messages. It becomes clear that multichannel messages that communicate inconsistent or contradictory meanings are a formidable barrier to successful communication, therefore a set of guidelines are provided. These can be used by communicators to help assure that they communicate consistently.

The Nature of Inconsistent Messages

The study of inconsistent communication is based to a large extent on the double-bind theory of interpersonal communication. Not surprisingly, this theory evolved from a study of schizophrenic patients. Schizophrenic patients frequently express themselves in inconsistent ways. Indeed, "where double-binding has become the predominant pattern of communication, and where the diagnostic attention is limited to the overtly most disturbed individual, the behavior of this individual will be found to satisfy the diagnostic criteria of schizophrenia" (Watzlawick, Beavin, & Jackson, 1967, pp. 214–215).

A double bind is a situation where: (a) two or more ego-involved individuals are attempting to communicate on matters of substantial physical or psychological value for them (parent–child, husband–wife interactions are examples); (b) a message is transmitted that (1) asserts something; (2) asserts something about its own assertion; and (3) these two assertions are mutually exclusive (the meaning of the messages appears to be undecidable in the traditional sense); and (c) the recipient is often so tied to his own frame of reference that he or she is unwilling to seek, or is incapable of obtaining, clarification as to the *intended* meaning of the message. Therefore, even though the message may be mildly contradictory, at best, or logically meaningless, at worst, it is communicational reality.

Paradoxical messages illustrate why the decoder may experience a double-bind. Consider the popular paradoxical injunction, *"Be spontaneous!"* Or the road sign that reads, *"Ignore This Sign."* Both messages are paradoxical because they require contradictory responses. To respond to the first command—to be spontaneous—requires a deliberative effort, which is by definition nonspontaneous. To respond to the second command—to ignore the sign—requires obedience within a perceptual framework which assures disobedience.

Paradoxical expressions represent an extreme type of inconsistent message. Such expressions force addressees to respond with behaviors that are incompatible. When employed repeatedly, paradoxical messages may threaten the sanity of the individuals to whom they are addressed. Thus, Watzlawick et al. emphasize that "there is something in the nature of paradox that is of immediate pragmatic and even existential import for all of us; paradox not only can invade interaction and affect our behavior and our sanity but it challenges our belief in the ultimate soundness of our universe" (p. 187).

The double-bind message and response are both forms of maladaptive behavior. As such, they have assumed major importance in the diagnosis and treatment of mental illness. Another type of inconsistent message is much more important to the reasonably well-adjusted individual, however. The object of increasing attention at present is the multichannel message which conveys conflicting meanings through the verbal and nonverbal channels.

Mehrabian (1981) maintains that the messages we communicate exhibit varying degrees of *pleasure–displeasure, arousal–nonarousal, dominance–submissiveness,* and *like–dislike. Our messages are inconsistent when our words and nonverbal cues communicate different degrees of pleasure, arousal, dominance, and liking.* For example, the individual who encounters a business associate who is held in low esteem may express pleasure in a verbal greeting but displeasure through such nonverbal cues as averted eyes, frowning, and unenthusiastic tone of voice. The fast-talking tour guide may communicate high arousal with his or her speaking rate but low arousal with a bored facial expression. The department head welcoming the new employee stressed verbally that the department head and all employees were equals, but contradicted this message with his high-power visual cues. Finally, the wife may express verbally her unqualified affection for her husband while displaying nonverbal indicators of unhappiness or even contempt.

In practice, our inconsistent messages may be either negatively inconsistent or positively inconsistent. A message is *negatively inconsistent* when the nonverbal channel(s) communicates meanings with a negative connotation while the verbal channel communicates a positive connotation. Consider the person with a contemptuous look on his or her face, who says, "That was a very perceptive statement." In contrast, a message is *positively inconsistent* when the nonverbal channel(s) communicates meanings with a positive connotation while the verbal channel communicates a negative connotation (e.g., a person nods his or her head, as if to signify understanding, while saying, "Now you've got me totally confused.").

When we express ourselves inconsistently, there is frequently a strong predisposition to use negatively inconsistent messages. This is so because most communicators are reluctant to express negative emotions and attitudes verbally. As a result, we are inclined to say relatively positive things about individuals with whom we interact, even though our true feelings about that person, or at least about their actions, are rather negative. Consider the scene depicted in Figure 10.1. Few women are apt to find the spilling of coffee on their plush carpet a pleasurable experience, but their spoken words probably will not express their true degree of displeasure, and may not express any overt displeasure. When our words express an emotion quite different from the one we are actually experiencing, we run a high risk of communicating an inconsistent message. In a high proportion of cases, the type of inconsistent message we do communicate is negatively inconsistent.

"IT'S PERFECTLY ALRIGHT, I KNOW MY FUTURE SON-IN-LAW WOULD NEVER DO THAT ON PURPOSE!"

Decoding Inconsistent Messages

Because inconsistent messages contain meanings that are ambiguous or contradictory, it is not surprising that such messages are a formidable barrier to successful communicaton. We know, for example, that parents of disturbed children are more likely to use inconsistent messages that the parents of normal children (Bugental, Love, Kaswan, & April, 1971). Relatedly, the children of parents who communicate inconsistently seem to be less pleasant and more anxious than children of parents who communicate consistently (Hall & Levin, 1979).

Counselors who use inconsistent messages are perceived as less attractive, sincere, and genuine than those who do not (Graves & Robinson, 1976). Both quality of communication and quality of outcomes in negotiating sessions may be negatively affected when negotiators communicate inconsistently (Johnson, McCarthy, & Allen, 1976). The fact that inconsistent messages can represent a serious threat to our personal credibility is illustrated by a study that shows that teachers who communicate inconsistently raise serious doubts in their students' minds about the authenticity and truthfulness of their verbal statements (Feldman, 1976).

Finally, we now know that laboratory researchers may introduce experimenter bias into their own experiments by the use of multichannel messages that are inconsistent (Duncan, Rosenberg, & Finkelstein, 1969). Rosenthal (1966) found that experimenters who introduced bias into their experiments were perceived by subjects as less honest than experimenters who did not introduce bias, because of the telltale information provided by their vocal cues.

In short, the impact of the use of inconsistent messages on a communicator's image is usually highly negative. Successful communication reinforces the perception that we are trustworthy, sincere, honest, empathic, and caring individuals. By contrast, the habitual use of inconsistent messages results in the attribution of undesirable image traits that are apt to damage our personal credibility.

Decoders have repeatedly reported an aversion to coping with inconsistent messages. Decoders find inconsistent messages to be anxiety-producing. They frequently force the decoder to make negative inferences about the person who uses them, and it is difficult to respond to inconsistent messages in socially acceptable ways. When decoders are forced to respond to inconsistent messages, they prefer to do so in informal as opposed to formal situations (Mehrabian, 1970). Formal situations presumably invite closer scrutiny of the way(s) decoders actually respond to inconsistent messages.

When decoders are asked to resolve the apparent contradictions in the meanings of multichannel messages that are inconsistent, they must decide which communication channel is the most reliable source of information. Decoders typically rely much more heavily on nonverbal, as opposed to verbal, cues to determine the dominant meaning of an inconsistent message (Argyle, Salter, Nicholson, Williams, & Burgess, 1970). Mehrabian (1981) emphasizes that the nonverbal portion of inconsistent messages exert a disproportionate impact on the decoder when determining the meaning(s) of such messages. Mehrabian writes that, when non-verbal communication "contradicts speech, it is more likely to determine the total impact of the message. In other words, touching, positions (distance, forward lean, or eye contact), postures, gestures, as well as facial and vocal expressions, can all outweigh words and determine the feelings conveyed by a message" (p. 78).

Research has shown that visual communication in the form of facial expressions, gestures, and postures is the dominant source of emotional meaning (Fujimoto, 1972). When a communicator's words and visual cues convey contradictory information about the emotions the communicator is experiencing, the decoder typically relies on the visual cues as the accurate source of information. Empirical research also supports the formula Mehrabian (1981) has developed, i.e., to show the relative importance that decoders attach to words, facial expressions, and vocal cues when they are trying to determine the meaning of inconsistent messages. Of the "total feeling" communicated by a message, decoders attribute 7 percent to words, 38 percent to voice, and 55 percent to facial expressions.

DePaulo and Rosenthal (1979) have conducted some fascinating research that further clarifies the weight that decoders attach to different communication channels as sources of information when messages are discrepant or inconsistent. They find that decoders rely much more heavily on nonverbal as opposed to verbal cues in decoding inconsistent messages. In addition, they find that the face is the primary nonverbal source of information in inconsistent messages, and bodily movements and vocal cues much less important. When the amount of information conveyed by each of these channels was measured, the face was assigned a value of *4*, the body a value of *2*, and the voice a value of *1*. In short, the face communicates twice as much information as the body, and the body communicates twice as much information as the voice.

Decoders who took the Nonverbal Discrepancy Test (DePaulo & Rosenthal, 1979) quite clearly established the primacy of the video channel as the source of information they used to resolve contradictions of meaning in inconsistent messages. *Decoders place particular reliance on visual cues when they are trying to determine whether the message sender is experiencing a positive or a negative emotion. However, decoders are more likely to rely on vocal, as opposed to visual, cues in determining the message sender's level of assertiveness.* This finding may be attributed in part to the fact that facial expressions are a particularly effective medium for conveying emotions, and the loudness (volume) with which we speak is known to be a particularly effective way of communicating degrees of dominance or submissiveness.

When messages become *highly* inconsistent, however, visual cues become less important and vocal cues more important as sources of information. In cases where the face communicates a highly pleasant emotion and the voice communicates an unpleasant emotion, for example, decoders tend to discount the reliability of the face as a source of information. Decoders may recognize intuitively that facial expressions are more easily controlled for purposes of deception than vocal cues. "When a communication becomes more and more discrepant, the overall message may begin to seem more and more like a deceptive one, and subjects may begin to weight the audio information relatively more heavily" (DePaulo & Rosenthal, 1979, p. 222).

In fact, Bugental (1974) contends that the weight a decoder attaches to information provided by a given communication channel when messages are inconsistent depends on the credibility of the information. If the information provided by each communication channel is equally credible, the decoder will place primary emphasis on visual cues, with decreasing degrees of emphasis given to vocal cues and to the verbal content of the message. *If the decoder has reason to believe that the information provided by one communication channel lacks credibility, however, a discounting process occurs wherein less weight is attached to the information provided by that channel.*

In contrasting the informational value of verbal and vocal cues in inconsistent messages, Bugental (1974) stresses that *the verbal content is disregarded if the vocal cues seem believable.* She emphasizes that, what "appears to be occurring is a channel-discounting process; that is, if the intonation is convincing, the content is disregarded. If, on the other hand, the speaker has a slow, deliberate, polished delivery (which was found here to be associated with noncongruence between facial expression and voice), the approval or disapproval with the voice fails to have any significant direct effects on the interpretation of the message" (p. 131).

This same channel-discounting process may help explain why vocal cues become more important and facial expressions less important when messages are highly inconsistent. Decoders clearly attach the greatest importance to visual cues as the source of information which is to be used in determining the dominant meaning of an inconsistent message. Their commitment to visual cues is qualified, however. If decoders have reason to believe that visual cues are providing counterfeit or deceptive information, they tend to discount this information and place a higher priority on information that can be obtained from other communication channels.

Research cited to this point reveals the priorities that decoders attach to different communication channels as sources of information that can be used to interpret inconsistent messages. What this research does not reveal, however, is what communicative behaviors decoders exhibit in responding to inconsistent messages. I addressed this subject in a study designed to determine the impact of inconsistent messages on verbal and nonverbal decoding behaviors (Leathers, 1979).

In this study, subjects were assigned to twenty separate problem-solving groups. Each group was asked to discuss what, if anything, should be done to promote better relations between black and white students at the University of Georgia. Subjects in ten of the groups had to respond to inconsistent messages introduced by a Confederate, who was a member of these groups; subjects in the other ten groups had to respond to consistent messages by a Confederate.

Both negatively and positively inconsistent messages were introduced into the discussions of the experimental groups. For example, a Confederate introduced a *negatively inconsistent message* when he or she addressed another discussant, with a look of contempt, while saying, "That was a very perceptive statement." A Confederate introduced a *positively inconsistent message* when he or she responded to another discussant, while leaning forward (as if to signify interest) and saying, "I find that to be a very uninteresting statement." Discussants in this experiment were required to respond to four types of negatively inconsistent, and four types of positively inconsistent, messages.

Detailed analyses of the verbal and nonverbal behaviors that discussants used to respond to inconsistent messages lends support to the following conclusions: (a) discussants decoded consistent messages with ease, but inconsistent messages had a highly disruptive impact on their decoding behaviors; (b) discussants responded to inconsistent messages in a way that is seemingly inconsistent; and (c) discussants responded to positively inconsistent messages in a much more guarded and negative manner than to negatively inconsistent messages.

The highly disruptive impact of inconsistent messages is reflected in the fact that decoders responding to inconsistent, as opposed to consistent, messages were more *uncertain, withdrawn, confused, displeased,* and *hostile.* However, they were also more *deliberative, analytical, responsive,* and *interested* than decoders responding to consistent messages. One wonders how a decoder could be *withdrawn* and *interested* at the same time, or exhibit both *deliberative* behavior and *hostility.*

In fact, the videotapes of the discussions reveal that the behavioral response to inconsistent messages appears to be defined characteristically by a sequence made up of three phases. In *Phase I,* the receiver exhibits *confusion* and *uncertainty* about how to decode the inconsistent message. In *Phase II,* the receiver's *level of concentration seems to increase* markedly as he or she becomes more *deliberative* and *interested* in the inconsistent message; the receiver frequently stares thoughtfully at the Confederate, as if searching for additional clues which would clarify the meaning of the inconsistent message. In *Phase III,* the receiver seems to move from expressions of *displeasure* and *hostility,* directed to the message sender, then to outright withdrawal.

To illustrate the sequential nature of the decoder's behavioral response to inconsistent messages, a representative response from the experiment is provided here:

Inconsistent Message

(Contempt) Ron, that was a very perceptive statement.

Response

Verbal Channel: *(Pause)* Huh? What are you referring to?

Nonverbal Channel: Ron's eyebrows move up, his mouth drops open, and he gets a quizzical and confused expression on his face. Ron bites his lower lip with his teeth, jabs nervously at his belt with his left hand, and turns away from the confederate to the other discussants, with his palms upturned, as if seeking their help in dealing with the inconsistent message. [Phase I decoding behavior signals confusion and uncertainty.] Ron then turns back toward the confederate, leans forward, rubs his forehead with the middle fingers of his right hand, as if deep in thought, and stares intently at the confederate. [Phase II decoding behavior signals a high degree of deliberation and interest in the message just transmitted.] At this point, Ron scowls at the confederate and, after brief thought, his scowl changes to a sneer. Finally, Ron completely abandons his attempt to interpret the meaning of the inconsistent message and stares down into his notes. [Phrase III decoding behavior has moved from expressions of displeasure and hostility to withdrawal from the discussion.]

Decoders who were forced to respond to positively inconsistent, as opposed to negatively inconsistent, messages became quite uncertain and tentative in their actions, although they expressed displeasure, both facially and bodily. The obvious question is, Why did decoders find it more difficult and more unpleasant to cope with positively inconsistent than negatively inconsistent messages? There maybe a number of reasons, but two seem particularly important. Because decoders encounter negatively inconsistent messages much more frequently than positively inconsistent messages, they may be more accustomed to dealing with this type of message. Secondly, decoders may prefer sarcastic messages (e.g., a compliment accompanied by a look of contempt) to insincere messages (e.g., a verbal expression of disinterest accompanied by a nonverbal expression of interest.)

Finally, results of this study support the double-bind theory, which predicts that individuals will respond to inconsistent messages in one of the following ways: (a) they will attempt, unsuccessfully, to determine the literal meaning of the inconsistent message; (b) they will increase their level of concentration as they search diligently for what they believe to be overlooked clues that will clarify the meaning of the message; and (c) they will withdraw from further involvement with the message sender. The results of this study support the conclusion that decoders responding to inconsistent messages employ not one but all three of these behavioral alternatives.

Guidelines for Communicating Consistently

Inconsistent messages represent a major deterrent to successful communication. They deter communication for several reasons: In the first place, they reflect negatively on the communicator's skills. They suggest that the communicator is unwilling to, or does not have the capacity to, communicate clearly. Multichannel messages that communicate inconsistent or contradictory meanings are by definition unclear. As a result, they place an unwelcome burden on the individuals who must decode them. In contrast, results from a number of studies have clearly demonstrated "that when nonverbal cues convey consistent meanings, the availability of greater numbers of these cues facilitates communicational accuracy" (DePaulo & Rosenthal, 1979).

Inconsistent messages are undesirable because they also deprive the communicator of the valuable opportunity of exercising effective conscious control over his or her communicative behaviors—for instance, to project a particularly desirable image. The perceptual impact of inconsistent messages on the image we project is almost always undesirable. The primary reason for this is because the defining features of the image we wish to project are not accepted by the decoder as believable. The desirable features of our image are often discounted or rejected, because the inconsistent messages invite inferences about our personal qualities and image traits which are far from flattering.

While I maintain that the impact of inconsistent messages is usually undesirable, I do recognize the growing number of theorists who argue that the purposely or strategically ambiguous message can serve many useful functions. In his stimulating article on ambiguity as strategy in organizational communication Eisenberg (1984) stresses that *"clarity is only a measure of communicative competence if the individual has as his or her goal to be clear."* (p. 230)

Successful communication does usually place a premium on the ability to communicate consistently. We must, therefore, make a special effort to assure that the communication channels we use do in fact communicate similar, or at least mutually compatible, meanings. When our words, facial expressions, and vocal cues all function to provide the same kinds of information, there is a minimal probability that our message will be misinterpreted. In contrast, the communication of inconsistent messages via two or more of the human communication channels invites unflattering inferences—about our communication skills and about the kind of person we are perceived to be.

To communicate consistently, we must carefully monitor our communicative cues to make sure they are communicating essentially the same kinds of meaning(s). If they are not, we must make adjustments in the messages communicated by one or more of the channels we are using. The following guidelines should be useful in helping to assure that we do communicate consistently.

Guideline #1: Because our facial expressions are the major medium for the expression of our emotions, we must make a special effort to display genuine facial emotions that are compatible with the type and intensity of emotions that we express verbally.

Guideline #2: The level of attentiveness, interest, and arousal communicated via our eye behaviors must be consistent with the level of attentiveness, interest, and arousal communicated through other communication channels.

Guideline #3: Because of the importance of gestures and postures as indicators of liking, assertiveness, and power, we should strive to communicate similar degrees of liking, assertiveness, and power via our spoken words and bodily cues.

Guideline #4: The distance we maintain when communicating with another person should suggest a level of interpersonal involvement that is comparable to the level of involvement we communicate by other nonverbal as well as verbal behaviors.

Guideline #5: In order to project an image that emphasizes a set of personality traits and personal qualities that are mutually reinforcing, we must carefully consider the decisions we make with regard to clothing and other items that define our personal appearance.

Guideline #6: We must carefully monitor our vocal cues to help assure that the personality traits that are inferred from such cues are consistent with the personality traits that are inferred from the words that we utter.

Guideline #7: The level of intimacy, reassurance, and/or emotional support we seek to communicate via our touching behaviors must not deviate markedly from the level of intimacy, reassurance, and/or emotional support we communicate by means of other nonverbal and verbal behaviors.

Guideline #8: To avoid the inference that we are being deceptive, our verbal, vocal, and visual cues must communicate similar levels of self-confidence, self-assurance, and immediacy.

Summary

Multichannel messages that are inconsistent may take one of two forms. A message is *negatively inconsistent* when the nonverbal channel(s) communicates meanings with a negative connotation while the verbal channel communicates a positive connotation. In contrast, a message is *positively inconsistent* when the nonverbal channel(s) communicates meanings with a positive connotation while the verbal channel communicates a negative connotation. Both types of inconsistent messages represent formidable barriers to successful communication to the message sender as well as to the message receiver.

Decoders typically rely much more heavily on visual cues than on other types of nonverbal or verbal cues in resolving the meaning of inconsistent messages. Visual cues are a particularly important type of cue, when the inconsistent message communicates contradictory information about the type of emotion the message sender is experiencing. Vocal cues are given greater weight when different degrees of assertivensss are communicated by nonverbal and verbal means. Ultimately, the importance attached to information provided by different communication channels (when the message(s) is inconsistent) depends upon the believability of the information provided by a given communication channel.

The use of inconsistent messages is highly undesirable. To use inconsistent messages repeatedly is to invite unflattering characterization of one's communication skills, and undesirable attributions about one's personality traits and personal qualities. The communicator who is to be successful must attach the highest priority to the goal of communicating consistently. To help assure that we do communicate consistently, the guidelines presented at the end of this chaper should be carefully considered.

References

Argyle, M., Salter, V., Nicholson, H., Williams, M., & Burgess, P. (1970). The communication of inferior and superior attitudes by verbal and nonverbal signals. *British Journal of Social and Clinical Psychology, 9,* 230.

Bugental, D. E. (1974). Interpretations of naturally occurring discrepancies between words and intonation: Modes of inconsistency resolution. *Journal of Personality and Social Psychology, 30,* 125–133.

Bugental, D. E., Love, L. R., Kaswan, J. W., and April, C. (1971). Verbal-nonverbal conflict in parental messages to normal and disturbed children. *Journal of Abnormal Psychology, 77,* 9.

DePaulo, B. M., & Rosenthal, R. (1979). Ambivalence, discrepancy, and deception in nonverbal communication. R. Rosenthal, editor. *Skill in Nonverbal Communication: Individual Differences.* Cambridge, MA: Oelgeschalager.

Duncan, S. D., Rosenberg, M. J., & Finkelstein, J. (1969). The paralanguage of experimenter bias. *Sociometry, 32,* 217.

Eisenberg, E. M. (1984). Ambiguity as a strategy in organizational communication. *Communication Monographs, 51,* 227–242.

Feldman, R. S. (1967). Nonverbal disclosure of teacher deception and interpersonal affect. *Journal of Educational Psychology, 68,* 807–816.

Fujimoto, E. K. (1972). The comparative communicative power of verbal and nonverbal symbols. *Dissertation Abstracts International, 32,* 7A. Ohio State University, Columbus, Ohio.

Graves, J. R., & Robinson, J. D., II (1976). Proxemic behavior as a function of inconsistent verbal and nonverbal messages. *Journal of Counseling Psychology, 23,* 336–337.

Hall, J. A., & Levin, S. (1979). Affect and verbal-nonverbal discrepancy in schizophrenic and normal family communication. Unpublished manuscript.

Johnson, D. M., McCarthy, K., & Allen, T. (1976). Congruent and contradictory verbal and nonverbal communication of cooperativeness and competitiveness in negotiations. *Communication Research, 3,* 288–289.

Leathers, D. G. (1979). The impact of multichannel message inconsistency on verbal and nonverbal decoding behaviors. *Communication Monographs, 46,* 88–100.

Mehrabian, A. (1970). When are feelings communicated inconsistently? *Journal of Experimental Research in Personality, 4,* 206–211.

Mehrabian, A. (1981). *Silent messages,* 2nd ed. Belmont, CA: Wadsworth.

Rosenthal, R. (1966). *Experimenter effects in behavioral research.* New York: Appleton.

Watzlawick, P., Beavin, J. H., & Jackson, D. D. (1967). *Pragmatics of human communication: A study of interactional patterns, pathologies, and paradoxes.* New York: Norton.

CHAPTER ELEVEN

Impression Formation and Management

Study the drawing of the defendant on the witness stand on p. 198. He has been accused of making sexual advances to two boys who are under eight years of age. What sort of impression does this defendant make? As you study him, do any defining features of the image he projects stand out? Place a check mark by any of the following traits you associate with this defendant:

dominant	submissive
assertive	unassertive
hard	soft
natural	prissy
masculine	feminine
strong	weak
dominant	submissive
athletic	sedentary
hot-tempered	gentle-tempered
enthusiastic	placid
rough	gentle
unaffected	affected

If most of your check marks are in the right-hand column, you probably view the defendant as effeminate. His visual image quite clearly conforms to the defining features of the effeminate stereotype. What effect will the defendant's effeminate appearance probably have on the jury members? Would the defendant's chances for acquittal be better if he projected an image with different defining features?

Within the past year, I was contacted by a criminal attorney regarding

a client who was accused of making sexual advances to two young boys. The attorney's overriding concern was the undesirable image he felt his client was apt to project to the jury. In the attorney's opinion, his client was a decent, hard-working person, who was not guilty of the charge. The problem, he said, was that the man "looks and sounds effeminate. To a jury in a small town in southern Georgia he will be seen as queer as a three-dollar bill." The attorney was concerned that the negative impact of his client's visual and vocal image would be greater than the positive impact of the exonerating evidence he would introduce to the court. To deal with his client's problem, the attorney proposed that I work as a trial consultant with the defense team. My proposed task was to use my knowledge of impression management to make the necessary changes in the image the defendant projected.

The importance of managing impressions in the courtroom has been apparent to attorneys for some time. As a result, the legal profession has led the way in the use of image consultants for purposes of trying to control, consciously, the impressions made by a legal team and their client when facing a jury. Organizations (such as the Association of Trial Behavior Consultants) have been formed to meet attorneys' rapidly expanding need for specialized advice on the nature of impression formation and management.

People who have been notably successful in their chosen careers have often been known for their skill as impression managers. Skillful impression managers exercise conscious control over many of the defining features of the image they project. Consider the case of General George Patton. Schlenker (1980) notes that:

> *Patton recognized the importance of controlling nonverbal activities to create the impressions he desired . . . He developed hypotheses about what attributes soldiers would most respect in their commander and acted accordingly. For example, he was careful about when he went to and departed from the front lines. (p. 235)*

Patton liked to be seen driving toward the front lines during the day but preferred to return from the front lines at twilight or even after dark—sometimes in a small liaison airplane. He believed that a commander should be highly visible when going to the front but not conspicuous when returning.

Until age and paranoia began to affect his cunning shrewdness, J. Edgar Hoover was a master of the art of cultivating a public image that captivated his admirers and intimidated his detractors. In *Witness to Power: The Nixon Years* (1982), John Ehrlichman provides a fascinating account of the carefully contrived steps Hoover took to make the desired impression.

When Ehrlichman arrived at Hoover's office for a visit, he encountered a staggering array of television monitors, electronic gear, and FBI agents, all of whom had short haircuts, narrow lapels, quiet ties, and shined shoes. As he entered the anteroom to Hoover's office, he noted that every available inch of wall space was used for plaques, framed citations, mounted trophies, medals, and certificates. Many of the awards featured torches, eagles, flags, and gavels. Later, in Hoover's private office, he tried in vain to identify a wavering purplish light that came from behind a segment of the soffit, because he was convinced that television cameras were recording his every move.

Ehrlichman goes on to describe Hoover's private office, which "was about twelve or thirteen feet square and dominated by Hoover himself; he was seated in a large leather desk chair behind a wooden desk in the center of the room. When he stood, it became obvious that he and his desk were on a dais about six inches high. I was invited to sit on a low, purplish leather couch to his right. J. Edgar Hoover looked down on me and began to talk" (Ehrlichman, 1982, p. 158).

Can you understand why Hoover was able to intimidate Presidents and Senators for many decades, as you consider the image he projected? Can you imagine yourself challenging the competence of a "legend," whose walls are lined with trophies, medals, and certificates? Can you imagine challenging the authority of a man who controlled the nation's most sophisticated surveillance techniques, and who had immediate access to your classified files? Can you believe that a man not vitally concerned

with impression management would sit at an elevated desk and seat you below him, to his right?

The Importance of Nonverbal Cues in Interpersonal Perception

The kind of person you are judged to be is much more heavily influenced by nonverbal than verbal cues. Argyle, Salter, Nicholson, Williams, and Burgess (1970) found that nonverbal cues have 4.3 times the impact on the impressions we make than do verbal cues. Walker (1977) found that, to express confidence, nonverbal cues were ten times more important than verbal cues.

Schlenker (1980) puts it succinctly:

A picture is worth a thousand words. When face-to-face we get the complete moving picture. We see the look in their eyes, the expression on their faces, the way their bodies lean, how closely they are willing to approach, the way they sit, the tenseness or relaxedness of their gestures. We hear the tones of their voices and the speed of their speech. We may not even be conscious at the time of the impact this information has on our overall impressions, but there is no doubt that it plays a major role in shaping our views of others. The other person's "style" comes through to form images that can mean more than the specific words he or she speaks. (p. 235)

We not only rely heavily on nonverbal cues in attributing personal traits and qualities to others; we now know that *nonverbal cues do provide accurate information about personal traits* (Paunonen & Jackson, 1979). We rely heavily on nonverbal cues in forming our impressions of other individuals because we recognize, intuitively, that a person's words provide information about their actions but their nonverbal cues provide information about themselves as individuals.

The impression we make on others is of course heavily influenced by our credibility. As demonstrated in Chapter 8, our credibility, or believability, is frequently a major determinant of our success, or lack of it, as persuaders. Although a communicator's image is defined in part by credibility, there is more to our image than our credibility. Our likableness, level of self-confidence, personality traits, attitudes, and characteristic emotional states—as perceived by others—all interact to shape the image we project.

Factors that Affect Interpersonal Perceptions

Interpersonal perception is the complex process by which individuals select, organize, and interpret stimuli, or sensory stimulation, into a meaningful view of the world (Sereno & Bodaken, 1975). If every perceiver attended to the same stimuli, organized the stimuli from the same perspective, and interpreted the stimuli in the same way, interpersonal perception would be a simple and completely predictable matter. In practice, however, interpersonal perception is a subjective matter. *We frequently rely on subjective impressions of people and events to try to explain what kind of people they are and why they behaved as they did.* When we try to explain why individuals behaved as they did, we must make *attributions.* Shaver recognizes that the attributions we make are often subject to error because we "are not dispassionate observers of human behavior, watching without evaluation. On the contrary, we try to understand behavior, to explain it, to determine what it means for us, and to make value judgments about it" (Shaver, 1975, p.v).

When we make judgments about a person's past behavior, or predict their future behavior, we make attributions about the reasons for their behavior. We make either *situational* or *dispositional* attributions. To illustrate the point, consider the case of Congressman Jeremy Funkhouser (a hypothetical Congressman), who was apprehended in the Abscam investigation and convicted of taking one million dollars in bribe money from FBI agents posing as Arab Oil Sheiks. The situational attribution would be that Funkhouser took the money because of the pressures of his family situation—his terminally ill wife was running up huge medical bills. The dispositional attribution would be that Funkhouser took the money because of the kind of person he really is—unethical, weak, unprincipled, sneaky, and exploitative.

The *perceptual judgments* we make about other people and their actions are *made more difficult by the fact that our perceptual judgments may be unduly influenced by the following: (a) stereotypes; (b) the primacy effect (first impressions); (c) selective perceptions; and (d) the recency effect (last impressions).* Because these factors all play a central role in shaping the impressions others have of us, it is easy to understand why nonverbal cues are so important in impression formation and management.

Stereotypes. The impressions other people have of us are often controlled to a startling degree by stereotypes. An individual who belongs to a particular group is expected to exhibit certain personal characteristics and attitudes, and to act in certain ways.

Particularly when someone meets you for the first time, he or she may stereotype you, primarily on the basis of how you look and sound. If you are shifty-eyed, appear nervous, engage in frequent postural shifts, and exhibit many nonfluencies during a police interrogation, for example, you will fit the *liar stereotype.* Regardless of whether convicted hijackers actually confirm the accuracy of the hijacker profile, your own chances of being stopped by security personnel at an airport certainly increase when your appearance and behavior differ markedly from the typical, middle-class American.

The physical-attractiveness stereotype and vocal stereotype both exert a profound impact on interpersonal perception. Adams and Crossman (1978), in *Physical Attractiveness: A Cultural Imperative,* emphasize that there exists in our culture a well-developed physical-attractiveness stereotype which has a perceptual impact matched by few, if any other, stereotypes. They write that physical attributes "are the most salient characteristics individuals have in presenting themselves. Although you can put on different masks or self-images for different situations, it is difficult to alter physical attributes . . . However, since we can't change our physical characteristics from moment to moment, our body image messages are likely to be relatively constant over a variety of social situations" (p. 3).

Individuals who deviate from the normative profile for the physically attractive person suffer severe perceptual penalties. Consider the impact of a female's bust size on the personal traits attributed to her, for example. Kleinke and Staneski (1980) found that females with medium, as opposed to small or large, busts were perceived as more likable, and as having greater personal appeal. In addition, big-busted women were judged to be relatively less intelligent, competent, moral, and modest, but small-busted women were viewed as most intelligent, competent, and moral. In short, the big-busted woman who wishes to be perceived as highly intelligent, and moral, must take action to cope with the unflattering portion of her physical stereotype. As we have already seen, the endomorphic male with excessive body weight must also deal with the negative connotations associated with his stereotype.

The unfavorable stereotype of the big-busted woman may be a singularly American stereotype, however. Members of the Latino, South American, and Mediterranean cultures, in particular, seem to value highly the amply built, big-busted woman. In contrast, these cultures tend to have a negative view of the flat-chested, hipless, bony fashion models—who can command staggering fees in America. In fact, the flat-chested woman seems to be viewed, in a number of cultures, as uninteresting, and lacking in desirable womanly qualities.

Body weight is another important aspect of the physical-attractiveness stereotype. In our culture, we consistently attribute very unflattering characteristics to individuals who are seriously overweight; we stigmatize the obese. Worsley (1981) recently conducted a study where subjects were asked to look at silhouette figures of four 18-year-old persons: a slim young woman (SYW), a slim young man (SYM), a fat young woman (FYW), and a fat young man (FYM). After looking at the silhouettes, the subjects were asked to identify the personality characteristics they associated with SYW, SYM, FYW, and FYM.

Because physical attractiveness and body image is more important for women than for men (Adams & Crossman, 1978), it is not surprising that the fat young woman was viewed more negatively than the fat young man. Both FYW and FYM were perceived to have personality characteristics that would be a decided handicap in almost any social situation, however. The *fat young woman* was viewed as *lacking confidence, sad, bored, tense, submissive, weak-willed, easily embarrassed,* and a *poor social mixer.* Several of the same (but not as many) negative personality characteristics were attributed to the Fat Young Male. The stereotypical description for the FYM was less complete than for the female, although he was dismissed by subjects as an uninteresting person—*slothful, lazy,* and *lacking in physical agility* (Worsley, 1981).

The physical attractiveness we are judged to possess quite clearly affects in striking ways the dispositional attributions made by the perceiver. Thus, subjects who viewed photographs of physically attractive boys with whom they had never interacted, believed that the boys would be more popular, have a more pleasant personality, and would be more active in extracurricular activities than their less physically attractive counterparts (Tompkins & Boor, 1980). Perceivers anticipated that physically unattractive students would behave more aggressively than their physically attractive peers (Langlois & Downs, 1979). The attributional power of the physical-attractiveness stereotype even extends to the predicted performance of classroom instructors. Subjects who viewed physically attractive and unattractive instructors predicted that the former would be better instructors, in part, because they would be more sensitive and have greater communication skills (Lombardo & Tocci, 1979).

Adams and Crossman have provided detailed empirical support for their claim that the physical-attractiveness stereotype has a significant impact on the personal qualities attributed to the interactants, in almost every conceivable sort of social situation. In *Physical Attractiveness: A Cultural Imperative* (1978), they write that the "numerous studies completed by social scientists across the country suggest that attractiveness is influential in almost *every* social setting in which it has been investigated (the exception perhaps being those studies conducted in absolute darkness)" (p. 4). They add that the contexts in which physical attractiveness strongly affects the images projected by the interactants include the school classroom, the home, hetereosexual dating situations, performance appraisal, and clinical settings. We should not be surprised, therefore, that an individual's appearance affects not only our perceptions of what kind of a person he or she is, but also our perceptions of the quality of that individual's performance as a member of organizations (Ross & Ferris, 1981).

The vocal stereotype also strongly affects the perceptual judgments we make. Few would deny that Walter Cronkite's vocal image helped to make him the world's most popular and trusted newscaster (Gray, 1982). Franklin Roosevelt's vocal image was one of his major assets, which perhaps helped him to become our only four-term president. Because they sounded the way competent, trustworthy, and confident individuals are supposed to sound, Cronkite and Roosevelt were placed in a preferred perceptual category.

The vocal stereotype is important because notions of who we are and how we are likely to behave are based heavily on the sound of our voices. We use the sound of a person's voice to make judgments about his or her sex, age, race, occupation, and socioeconomic state. Above all, *we rely heavily on the sound of a person's voice to develop the personality profile we attribute to them.*

Vocal cues are also a major source of information in making predictions about how individuals have behaved and will behave in the future. When the truthfulness of one's current statements is at issue, the *anxious voice* may raise questions about the propriety of both past and future actions. If you doubt that vocal cues can serve such important impression-formation functions, think again about the perceptual impact of Senator Kennedy's stammering responses to Roger Mudd's questions about the state of his marriage, and about Chappaquiddick.

First Impression.   Our image in the eyes of others is strongly affected by the primacy effect, or first impression. In simple terms, the *primacy effect* is the impact of first impressions on interpersonal perception. The first impressions people form may affect all subsequent perceptions; these first impressions are resistant to change. First impressions creat a "cognitive category" in the mind of the perceiver. Attitudes and evaluative judgments formed during the creation of such categories are extremely difficult to change later (Shaver, 1975).

First impressions account for a disproportionate amount of the information used in the formation of all impressions, and nonverbal cues exert a controlling influence on the development of first impressions. When we meet someone for the first time, we know that "conversation is not a very good source of initial information. When we are first introduced to someone, talk is frequently limited to social amenities and topics such as the weather. We have to rely heavily on nonverbal cues" (Burgoon & Saine, 1978, p. 145). We must rely on a limited amount of information to make the evaluative judgments that form first impressions; initial impressions are formed by treating others as objects, with an emphasis on how they look and sound; and our first impressions are strongly affected by the stereotypic expectations we bring to a social encounter.

Because of the imporance of the physical appearance and the vocal stereotypes in interpersonal perception, it is not surprising that our appearance and our vocal cues are the two most important nonverbal determinants of first impressions. Remember that, during the critically important seconds when we first meet someone, their guarded speech communication is unlikely to reveal very much about their personal qualities. Thus, *a person's visual and vocal cues assume the dominant perceptual role in the formation of first impressions.*

Selective Perception. Selective perception is the tendency to attend to and interpret only those stimuli or perceptual cues that are consistent with our past experiences and concerns. To put it another way, individuals frequently see and hear only what their own beliefs and values will let them see and hear. Therefore, because our perceptions are filtered through our beliefs and values, it is not surprising that most of us are highly susceptible to selection perception.

When we wish to project a favorable image, it is particularly important that we be aware of the perils of selective perception. If the person with whom we are communicating likes us, we need not be overly concerned that we avoid exhibiting eye behaviors, gestures, and postures that might ordinarily damage our credibility. The person who likes us will probably de-emphasize those cues that could provide negative information about our personal qualities, and emphasize those cues that would provide positive information. When dealing with an unfriendly person, or with one who does not like us, however, selective perception works in reverse. The unfriendly person is predisposed to single out and emphasize those nonverbal cues that are least flattering to us.

Last Impressions. The *recency effect,* or the last impression a person makes, can also be extremely important in impression formation. Perceptual distortion often seems to result from the disproportionate influence of an individual's most recent actions, or from our last contact with that individual. General George Patton obviously recognized the importance of last impressions. He took pains to make sure that the last impression he left with his soldiers and the public, before a military battle, was the impression that Patton was moving aggressively to the front rather than retreating hastily to the rear.

If you were aloof, unfriendly, and stolid the last time you saw Person

X, Person *X* is likely to remember you as an aloof, unfriendly, and stolid person. The recency effect has proven to be a strong force in shaping perceptions of top Soviet leaders, for example. We have been conditioned to expect that the most recent Soviet leader will exhibit the same sort of personality characteristics as his immediate predecessors. Leonid Brezhnev and Yuri Andropov were recent general secretaries of the Communist Party. Whether fairly or not, both men were characterized by the media as conservative, dull, phlegmatic, and too cautious to "make waves." Not surprisingly, the widespread expectation was that Konstantin U. Cherenko, Andropov's successor, also would be conservative, dull, phlegmatic, and too cautious to "make waves." This expectation was nurtured by the recency effect, even before Cherenko had officially assumed his duties as leader of the Soviet Union.

The Role of Nonverbal Cues in Impression Formation and Management

Nonverbal Impression Management

Up to this point, we have demonstrated that nonverbal cues can, and frequently do, have a major impact on interpersonal perception. The impact of nonverbal cues is particularly strong on the impressions people form of each other. There can be little doubt that our nonverbal cues strongly affect our image, but how can we consciously control the image we project?

Impression Management Defined. Edinger and Patterson (1983) maintain that "impression management may be seen as an actor's behavioral strategy designed to create some beneficial image or presentation for the individual" (p. 43). In emphasizing strategy, these researchers draw attention to the fact that successful impression managers attempt conscious control of all nonverbal cues that have perceptual significance, in order to project an image that will be useful in attaining goals which are part of a general plan.

Impression management may be so defined: *an individual's conscious attempt to exercise conscious control over communicative cues—particularly nonverbal cues—for purposes of projecting a winning image.* You have projected a winning image when that image assumes a central role in helping you achieve your specific goals as a communicator.

The Association Principle. To project a winning image, impression managers must carefully consider which impressions are consistent with their current reputation, known abilities, and attitudes. In short, the impression manager must consider not only what kinds of impressions can be emphasized and de-emphasized, but what impressions will be believable.

In seeking to project a winning image by the conscious control of nonverbal cues, the communicator should be guided by the *association principle*: *We must, through our communication, seek to associate ourselves with desirable image traits, while disclaiming association with undesirable image traits.* (Schlenker, 1980).

The *principle of association* can be illustrated by the actions of successful magicians. Successful magicians are by definition extremely skillful impression managers. They are masters of the art of misdirection; they draw our attention to movements that have no relevance to the performance of a certain trick while diverting our attention from those movements that are absolutely necessary to perform the trick. Magicians practice "magic by misdirection," through the use of simulation, dissimulation, ruse, disguise, and maneuver (Fitzkee, 1975).

Harlan Tarbell, a legendary magician, understands that the Principle of Association must be used to focus an audience's attention on those details of a presentation that will make an individual look good, and divert an audience's attention from details of a presentation that will make an individual look bad. Thus, Tarbell (1953) wrote, *"Do not look at your hands. Watch your hands in the mirror. Never look at them directly. If you watch your hands when performing, your audience will not get your effect"* (p. 50). In short, magicians attempt to present an image of mystification by diverting attention from the sometimes simple movements essential to perform the trick, to flashy hand movements, which serve only to distract and impress.

Principles That Control the Attribution of Personal Traits

We have already established that individuals will rarely provide a voluntary verbal description of their personal traits and qualities. In those rare instances when they do provide such a description, the description may be incomplete and contain inaccuracies. A man who specializes in conducting selection interviews for a large department store recently told me that applicants' resumes represented a notably inaccurate source of information. "Everyone lies about themselves to some extent on such resumes," he said.

As impression managers, our goal certainly should not be to mislead others intentionally with regard to the sort of person we are. Our obligation as an impression manager is to try to influence the attributions made about us in such a way that our desirable traits are emphasized and our undesirable traits are de-emphasized.

Hamachek (1982) has identified a set of principles of attribution that should prove particularly useful to the nonverbal impression manager. Among the most important principles identified are the following: (a) we tend to give more weight to negative information about others than to positive information; (b) in view of the resilience of stereotypes, we must work to identify ourselves with the more desirable personal qualities and behaviors associated with the stereotype; (c) we tend to be influenced by those stimuli that are most obvious; (d) we tend to judge others on the assumption that most people are like us.

The first principle is an important one. Because people seem to be inclined to look for negative information about others, we must take pains to consciously control those nonverbal cues that reflect negatively on the judgments others make about our self-confidence, self-esteem, likability, power or status, and certainly, our credibility. We know, for example, that the *anxious voice* is strongly associated with the attribution of a low level of self-confidence. We know also that individuals who exhibit closed and defensive postures are perceived to have less status and power than individuals who exhibit open and confident postures.

Stereotyping represents a special problem for the impression manager. This is true because the individual communicator can do little to change the way they have been stereotyped. Let us assume, for example, that you are perceived as lazy because you are a member of a given ethnic group. Even though you may in fact be a diligent, hardworking person, many individuals who observe your behavior may engage in *discounting.* They would discount, or minimize, the importance of your being a hard worker, even if they had *seen* you working hard, in order to avoid contradicting their stereotyping you as lazy.

Because stereotypes are difficult to change, successful impression managers must make stereotyping work to their advantage. They must accentuate the positive aspects of their stereotype. For example, the physical-attractiveness and vocal stereotypes associate a wide array of undesirable personal qualities with the person who does *not* "look right" or "sound right." Impression managers should, therefore, concentrate on necessary changes in their personal appearance and vocal cues if they wish to be identified with the desirable aspects of their stereotype.

Clearly, people do tend to be influenced by that aspect of our communication which is most obvious. In the case of Edward Kennedy, in his interview with Roger Mudd, the most obvious part of his nonverbal presentation of self was his stammering, nonfluent response to questions. So obvious was this deviation from what is desirable vocal communication that the importance of his speech communication was diminished. Impression managers must identify the most strikingly positive and negative features of their own communication, because these are the features the perceiver is likely to remember. The *principle of association* dictates that the most strikingly positive features should be highlighted, and the negative features should be eliminated, or attention directed *away* from them.

Finally, perceivers tend to judge others on the assumption that most people are like them. When our nonverbal communicative behaviors are different from the nonverbal communicative behaviors of those with whom we interact, our behaviors are seen as less socially desirable. Fiorello LaGuardia is frequently considered to have been a skillful impression manager. While he was mayor of New York City, he visited its various ethnic sections, and he not only spoke the languages of the people there, but used the kinds of gestures that were distinctively associated with the ethnic group he was addressing. In short, successful impression managers will not confine their efforts to establishing a common ground, or to making statements that stress their similarities in interest and background. They will also take pains to suppress those nonverbal communication cues that make them seem discernibly different from those with whom they interact.

The Management of First Impressions

Successful impression managers pay particular attention to first impressions. They do this because first impressions create images in the mind of the perceiver that are highly resistant to change. First impressions assume a central role in interpersonal perception because they tend to be lasting impressions. First impressions are critically important in defining your personal qualities and traits in the eyes of others.

The impression manager who wishes to make a favorable first impression must recognize at least two facts: (a) nonverbal cues are the major determinants of the kind of first impression that we make; and (b) the most important nonverbal factors that affect first impressions are personal appearance and vocal cues. By exercising conscious control over our visual and vocal images, we greatly enhance our chances of making a favorable first impression.

When considering the way you would like to look and sound, remember the importance of the physical-attractiveness stereotype and the vocal stereotype. These stereotypes dictate that individuals who look and sound unappealing will pay a stiff perceptual penalty. These stereotypes provide a rather detailed picture of the look and the sound that is widely viewed as desirable in our culture. And because we also know that perceivers give more weight to negative rather than to positive information, the impression manager begins with an advantage. The message is clear: We should be less concerned with cultivating idealized visual and vocal images and more concerned with eliminating those undesirable features of our image that perceivers use to make unflattering attributions about us.

Clothing Guidelines

Most communicators may of course exercise a number of options to modify, conceal, or eliminate negative features of their personal appearance. The obese individual can diet; the individual with a physical deformity can undergo plastic surgery; the individual with acne can use medicinal ointments; and the individual with crooked teeth can seek orthodontal treatment. In practice, however, these options may not be feasible, because they are both time-consuming and costly, or because they will not correct the physical deformity.

Clothing choice represents the most effective and efficient means of controlling your personal appearance if you want to make a favorable first impression. When you consider the implications of the association principle, you will realize that you must dress so as to concentrate attention on the most flattering features of your personal appearance, while diverting attention from those features that might be used to make negative attributions about your personal qualities.

There is, of course, no set of clothing guidelines that will serve the impression-management goals of all people in all situations all of the time. Nevertheless, there are basic guidelines which have proven to be particularly valuable to individuals who wish to emphasize or de-emphasize appearance features that are consistently associated with specific personal traits, attitudes, and personal beliefs.

Clothing guidelines are detailed in John T. Molloy, *Dress for Success* (Warner Books); John T. Molloy, *The Woman's Dress for Success Book* (Warner Books); and James Gray, Jr., *The Winning Image* (AMACOM).

These clothing guidelines are perhaps most useful in combatting or neutralizing those features of one's personal appearance that are associated in a negative way with some aspects of the physical-attractiveness stereotype. For example, what are the implications of these clothing guidelines for the big-busted woman with an endormorphic body type, who is overweight? If she chooses to wear bright colors, she accentuates those physical features that have been linked perceptually with low self-confidence, and with below-average intelligence and competence, and submissiveness. Such a perceptual penalty may be avoided or minimized by the choice of neutral colors which divert attention from bust size, body weight, and body type.

Consider also the importance of making clothing choices that minimize the possibility that the perceiver will obtain other kinds of negative information from your personal appearance. Why should the salesperson who is a graduate of Southeastern Institute of Technology not wear a class ring when making a sales call? The reason is obvious. The sales prospect might be a graduate of another university, and he or she may have negative feelings aout SIT. Also, the skillful impression manager should avoid wearing deeply tinted contact lenses or glasses. To hide or obscure your eyes is to perpetuate that part of the eye-behavior stereotype which suggests that untrustworthy individuals wear dark eyeglasses.

Vocal Guidelines

As we have already demonstrated, vocal cues play a central role in shaping the first impression that you make. In Chapter 8, we emphasized that the vocal cues of a communicator have been found to affect all three dimensions of credibility—competence, trustworthiness, and dynamism. Perhaps more importantly, we know that vocal cues are a major source of information which perceivers use to make attributions about an individual's personality traits. For example, we know that vocal cues are major determinants of how socially attractive, likable, and confident we are judged to be.

To make a favorable first impression, one must pay particular attention to accentuating those vocal cues associated with the attribution of desirable personal traits, and to de-emphasizing those vocal cues associated with the attribution of undesirable personal traits.

FIGURE 11.1 VOCAL GUIDELINES

Desirable Vocal Cues

1. Strive for a conversational speaking style of 125–150 words per minute. Individuals who use a conversational speaking style are viewed as more pleasant, likable, and friendly than those who do not.

2. Emphasize the most important points you are making with appropriate changes in volume and pitch—the monotone voice has been found to be very damaging to credibility.

3. The voice that is judged most credible is fluent, low-pitched, varied, moderately paced, and General American in dialect.

4. Individuals with a narrow pitch range are viewed as unassertive, uninteresting, and lacking in confidence.

5. Speaking with appropriate variation in rate and pitch will make you appear more dynamic, animated, and extroverted.

6. Faulty or sloppy articulation and improper pronunciation are apt to have a highly negative impact on your perceived competence.

7. Inconsistent messages have a particularly damaging impact on the first impresssion you make. If you tell someone that you like them or their ideas, be sure to use your voice to reinforce the point you are making so that it sounds believable.

8. Deliberate pauses before the most important points you are making will make you seem more competent and will increase the likelihood that the point you are making will be remembered.

Undesirable Vocal Cues

1. To make a favorable first impression, try to eliminate nonfluencies such as "ah," incomplete words, and incomplete sentences. The nonfluent individual is usually perceived as lacking in self-confidence, anxious, and less competent.

2. Avoid lengthy pauses before responding to a question, because such pauses raise questions about your competence and make you seem indecisive.

3. The excessively loud voice is associated with unseemly aggressiveness.

4. Seek to eliminate or minimize flatness, nasality, and tenseness in your voice. These vocal qualities reinforce perceptions that an individual is nondynamic, uninteresting, and withdrawn.

5. Do not speak at a rate of over two hundred words a minute, because an accelerated speaking rate is associated with an unacceptable level of anxiety.

6. Avoid interruptions, because they help to create the impression that you are socially insensitive.

Figure 11.1 provides specific guidelines, grounded in empirical research, which can be used by the impression manager to cultivate a vocal image that will help make a favorable first impression (Burgoon & Saine, 1978; Cooper, 1979; Leathers, 1976). By carefully considering the nature of desirable vocal cues, you increase the probability that others will attribute a flattering personality profile to you. As the guidelines suggest, positive personality traits and personal qualities are associated with a conversational speaking style that features substantial but appropriate variations in rate, pitch, and volume. Your perceived competence can be dramatically affected by your vocal cues, therefore it is particularly important that you sound competent. If you speak with a General American dialect (Burgoon & Saine, 1978), use proper articulation and pronounciation, and pause deliberatively before making important points, you are likely to enhance your perceived competence.

Because perceivers attach more weight to negative rather than to positive information about a person, you should take pains to minimize, or eliminate, the use of undesirable vocal cues. Undesirable vocal cues are known to have a particularly strong impact on the first impression you make. If you place a high value on being perceived as confident, you must take pains to avoid nonfluencies and an excessive speaking rate. Both kinds of vocal cues have repeatedly been found to create the impression that the communicator has an unacceptably low level of self-confidence and an unacceptably high level of anxiety.

The guidelines in Figure 11.1 should help you to use your voice in such a way that you associate yourself with the flattering features of the vocal stereotype and dissociate yourself from the unflattering features. When combined with the information contained in Chapter 6, these guidelines give you the potential to control the sound of your voice in ways advantageous to you.

The Management of Your Image

The last section in this chapter concentrated on ways of consciously controlling your visual and vocal image in order to make a favorable first impression. Although clothing choice and vocal cues are particularly important nonverbal determinants of the first impression you make, there are of course many other kinds of nonverbal cues that affect the first impression you make. The impact of facial expressions, eye behaviors, gestures, posture, spatial behaviors, and touching have already been treated in detail in this book. The impression manager who is particularly concerned about the specific ways that such nonverbal cues can affect interpersonal perception would be well-advised to recheck relevant sections of this book.

Although most of us are undoubtedly concerned about the first impression we make, we may be more concerned about a more enduring image in the eyes of those with whom we interact. In order to have a complete and objective description of our image, from the perspective of those with whom we interact, the image inventory provided in Figure 11.2 should be used.

Ken Cooper writes perceptively, in *Nonverbal Communication for Business Success* (1979), that the "first step in building a successful image is to determine what your current image is. You may not be aware of your image or you may think others don't have an image of you. You are wrong! . . . The challenge is to develop an accurate picture of yourself as others perceive you" (p. 195).

The personality traits and personal qualities that others attribute to you may be called *image traits*. Image traits identified in Figure 11.3 should be useful to the impression manager, for at least two reasons. First, each of these traits has been repeatedly identified in empirical research as image traits that perceivers frequently used in forming their impressions of others. Second, specific kinds of nonverbal cues have been shown to be strongly linked, perceptually, to each of these image traits.

To obtain a complete description of your own image, ask individuals with whom you frequently interact in social and/or business situations to use Figure 11.2. They should place a check mark by each trait that they

FIGURE 11.2 IMAGE TRAITS

confident–anxious	honest–deceitful
friendly–unfriendly	expressive–unexpressive
sensitive–insensitive	mature–immature
spontaneous–unspontaneous	direct–evasive
active–passive	powerful–weak
forceful–tentative	relaxed–tense
wise–foolish	flexible–rigid
feminine–masculine	honest–dishonest
dominant–submissive	interesting–uninteresting
extroverted–introverted	uninhibited–inhibited
strong-willed–weak-willed	intelligent–unintelligent
happy–sad	patient–impatient
likable–unlikable	tactful–tactless
strong–weak	unaffected–affected
assertive–unassertive	comfortable–uncomfortable
considerate–inconsiderate	artistic–inartistic
sociable–unsociable	warm–cold
poised–flustered	agile–awkward
opinionated–unopinionated	competent–incompetent
modest–immodest	pleasant–unpleasant
vigorous–lazy	energetic–sluggish
tolerant–intolerant	sophisticated–naïve
emotional–unemotional	gregarious–withdrawn
conventional–unconventional	selfish–unselfish
dependable–undependable	perceptive–dull

feel is clearly a defining feature of your image. Pay particular attention to the five positive and five negative image traits which are checked most frequently. By simply tabulating the check marks, you will know what the dominant positive and negative features of your image actually are.

Now that you have a detailed description of your own image, you are in a position to take action as an impression manager. If there are certain traits you view as highly desirable and which are not part of your image, you may wish to accentuate those nonverbal cues in your own nonverbal behavior—those known to be associated with attributions of those particular traits. More importantly, you are now in a position to modify those nonverbal behaviors that may, in the perceiver's mind, have been associated with a number of undesirable image traits.

Let us assume, for example, that you are viewed as an anxious, unemotional, uninteresting, unpleasant, and withdrawn individual. Many factors may of course account for the fact that these image traits have been attributed to you. We know, however, that vocal cues alone can account for such attributions. As a result, you should take particular pains to eliminate nonfluencies, minimize a nasal vocal quality, and speak with appropriate variation in pitch, volume, and rate. If you were judged to be unlikable, unassertive, and weak, you should consider the informational potential of specific kinds of gestures. As indicated in Chapter 3, gestures are powerful indicators of liking, assertiveness, and power.

Summary

This chapter examines the important role of nonverbal cues in interpersonal perception. Nonverbal cues are vitally important in interpersonal perception because they are the primary source of information used to attribute personality traits and personal qualities to individuals. In making judgments about a person's level of self-confidence, we rely much more heavily on their nonverbal than on their verbal cues.

The *impressions we form* of others are strongly affected by *stereotypes, first impressions, selective perception,* and *last impressions.* Each of these factors is strongly affected by a communicator's nonverbal cues. Impression managers recognize the perceptual importance of nonverbal cues. They attempt to execise conscious control over their own communicative cues for purposes of projecting a winning image.

Because of the importance of the physical-attractiveness and vocal stereotypes, clothing and vocal cues are the major determinants of first impressions. Impression managers can make use of the specific clothing and vocal guidelines presented in this chapter in order to make favorable first impressions. In using these guidelines, you should consider four major principles that can exert a controlling influence on the attribution of personal traits.

Before we can function effectively as impression managers, we must know what our current image is. In order to obtain a complete description of your own image by those with whom you interact, you should use the image inventory provided in Figure 11.2. Once you have a detailed description of your image, you are in a position to take action as an impression manager. You can begin to exercise conscious control over those nonverbal cues that will help you lay claim to a flattering image.

References

Adams, G. R., & Crossman, S. M. (1978). *Physical attractiveness: A cultural imperative.* Roslyn Heights, New York: Libra.

Argyle, M., Salter, V., Nicholson, H., Williams, M., & Burgess, P. (1970). The communication of inferior and superior attitudes by verbal and nonverbal signals. *British Journal of Social and Clinical Psychology, 9,* 222–231.

Burgoon, J. K., & Saine, T. (1978). *The unspoken dialogue: An introduction to nonverbal communication.* Boston: Houghton.

Cooper, K. (1979). *Nonverbal communication for business success.* New York: AMACOM.

Edinger, J. A., & Patterson, M. L. (1983). Nonverbal involvement and social control. *Psychological Bulletin, 93,* 30–56.

Ehrlichman, J. (1982). *Witness to power: The Nixon years.* New York: Simon & Schuster.

Fitzkee, D. (1975). *Magic by misdirection.* Oakland, CA: Magic Limited.

Gray, J., Jr. (1982). *The winning image.* New York: AMACOM.

Hamachek, D. E. (1982). *Encounters with others: Interpersonal relationships and you.* New York: Holt.

Kleinke, C. L., & Staneski, R. A. (1980). First impressions of female bust size. *Journal of Social Psychology, 110,* 123–134.

Langlois, J. H., & Downs, A. C. (1979). Peer relations as a function of physical attractiveness: The eye of the beholder of behavioral reality. *Child Development, 50,* 409–418.

Leathers, D. G. (1976) *Nonverbal communication systems.* Newton, MA: Allyn.

Lombardo, J. P., & Tocci, M. E. (1979). Attribution of positive and negative characteristics of instructors as a function of attractiveness and sex of instructor and sex of subject. *Perceptual and Motor Skills, 48,* 491–494.

Molloy, J. T. (1975). *Dress for success.* New York: Warner Books.

Molloy, J. T. (1978). *The woman's dress for success book.* New York: Warner Books.

Paunonen, S. V., & Jackson, D. N. (1979). Nonverbal trait inference. *Journal of Personality and Social Psychology, 37,* 1645–1659.

Ross, J., & Ferris, K. R. (1981). Interpersonal attraction and organizational outcomes: A field examination. *Administrative Science Quarterly, 26,* 617–632.

Schlenker, B. R. (1980). *Impression management.* Monterey, CA: Brooks/Cole.

Sereno, K. K., & Bodaken, E. M. (1975). *Trans per understanding human communication.* Boston: Houghton.

Shaver, K. G. (1975). *An introduction to attribution processes.* Cambridge, MA: Winthrop.

Tarbell, H. (1953). *The Tarbell course in magic.* New York: Louis Tannen.

Tompkins, R. C., & Boor, M. (1980). Effects of students' physical attractiveness and name popularity on student teachers' perceptions of social and academic attributes. *Journal of Psychology, 106,* 37–42.

Walker, M. B. (1977). The relative importance of verbal and nonverbal cues in the expression of confidence. *Australian Journal of Psychology, 29,* 45–57.

Worsley, A. (1981). In the eye of the beholder: Social and personal characteristics of teenagers and their impressions of themselves and fat and slim people. *British Journal of Medical Psychology, 54,* 231–242.

PART THREE

Successful Communication in Applied Settings

CHAPTER TWELVE

Nonverbal Determinants of Successful Interviews

Much like death and taxes, interviews are unavoidable. Because interviews play such a central role in our professional and personal lives, we attach a high priority to the successful interview. Rare indeed is the job applicant who does not prefer to approach a selection interview with a feeling of confidence and the anticipation of success. The married couple who bring the accumulated problems of a troubled marriage to a counseling interview can, or should, have a desire to resolve their problems.

In spite of the high aspirations we may bring to an interview, this kind of communication is often associated with a high level of anxiety. Such high anxiety may be attributed to at least two factors. Interviews have the potential to reveal much highly personal information about our self-definition, self-esteem, and self-confidence. Interviews are also a high-risk endeavor; unsuccessful interviews may have consequences that are both immediate and unpleasant.

Consider the case of Mark Harrington, job applicant. Harrington is about to have a selection interview. He is being interviewed for a position as a sales representative for a major firm which manufacturers and sells electrical appliances. As he contemplates the interview, he realizes that recent Equal Employment Opportunity legislation provides him with a measure of protection. He can no longer be asked certain types of questions that might reflect negatively on the impression he creates. For example, he cannot legally be asked to provide a picture of himself, to describe what kind of discharge he received from service, to reveal whether he is married or is living with someone, or to indicate what fraternity he belonged to in college (Stewart & Cash, 1982).

At the same time, Harrington realizes that he faces a paradoxical situation as a communicator. He recognizes that professional interviewers

have traditionally attached much importance to the interviewee's ability to communicate effectively. He must communicate in an assertive, self-confident, enthusiastic, and pleasant manner, one which serves to enhance the interviewer's perceptions of his intelligence, leadership potential, and sociability. He also recognizes that the pressures of the job interview are such as to minimize the probability that he will communicate in such a manner. In fact, he fears that the interview may prove to be disastrous, in view of the fact that he stutters, is forty pounds overweight, and has never been able to sustain direct eye contact. If you were Mark Harrington, what would you do to improve your chances for a successful interview?

Harrington would be well-advised to familiarize himself with the nonverbal profile of successful job interviewees. There is now a substantial body of research to support the view that an interviewee's nonverbal cues frequently function as major determinants of success in the job interview. In Harrington's case, most of the communicative cues that he can effectively control in his upcoming job interview will probably be nonverbal in nature.

Harrington's communicative liabilities are most likely more numerous and severe than yours. Nonetheless, the example may help focus attention on the *critically important role that nonverbal cues frequently assume, in not only shaping an interviewer's perceptions, but in affecting a decision to hire.*

Nonverbal communication assumes added importance in the context of the interview because nonverbal cues can provide the kinds of highly personal information frequently sought by interviewers. Stewart and Cash (1982) recognize the functional importance of nonverbal communication in the job interview when they write the "intimate and personal nature of the interview (the parties are often a mere arm's length apart and are directly involved in the topic and outcome of the interview) tends to magnify the importance of nonverbal communication" (p. 33).

There are many kinds of interviews in addition to selection and counseling interviews, of course. Exit interviews, informational interviews, performance-appraisal interviews, and sales interviews are all important in our society. This chapter will concentrate on two types of interviews, however. Successful communication in the selection and the counseling interviews is probably important to the largest number of people because of the frequency with which these kinds of interviews occur in our lives.

The central objective of this chapter is to specify the kinds of nonverbal cues that are consistently associated with both successful and unsuccessful communication in selection and counseling interviews. By providing detailed nonverbal profiles of the successful job interviewee and the successful counselor, we do not mean to de-emphasie the importance of more traditional kinds of performance criteria. The following remain important: (a) ability to express yourself verbally, in a clear and logical manner; (b) adapt to the interests and concerns of the interviewer; and (c) demonstrate your mastery of relevant information. As the following sections will demonstrate, however, the cultivation of the foregoing is necessary, but these abilities may not be sufficient to insure success in an interview.

The Job Interview

Success in a job interview may be defined in various ways. Interviewees may consider an interview successful simply because they acquired interviewing experience, or because they met or exceeded their own performance standards. They may even consider the interview successful if they resisted the temptation of accepting a position with dubious merits. The interviewer, on the other hand, may consider an interview successful if it elicited the information necessary to make a defensible decision.

Critical Interviewer Decisions

The most critical decision made by a selection interviewer is whether to accept or reject the job applicant; the interviewer may also place the interviewee in a "reserved" category, pending follow-up interviews. In addition, the interviewer must make critical decisions with regard to ratings of the applicant's qualifications, relative acceptability for a given position, and, perhaps, starting salary.

These critical decisions are in turn affected by the interviewer's judgments about the effectiveness of the interviewee's performance in the job interview. McGovern and Tinsley (1978) maintain that the following factors are critical in affecting a job interviewer's judgments about the interviewee: (a) ability to communicate; (b) aggressiveness and initiative; (c) self-confidence; (d) enthusiasm and motivation; (e) intelligence; (f) leadership potential; (g) maturity; (h) persuasiveness; (i) pleasant personality and sociability; and (j) positive attitude. Because most of these abilities and personal qualities are difficult to measure by objective means, interviewers must rely heavily on their own perceptions.

The prospective job interviewee would be justified in asking at least two questions, at this point. First, are the interviewee's nonverbal cues likely to exert a major influence on the judgments the interviewer makes about specific abilities and personal characteristics, such as ability to communicate, self-confidence, and sociability? Second, does the available evidence suggest that *accept* and *reject* decisons are affected in consistent and predictable ways by the nonverbal cues exhibited by the interviewee? As we shall see, the answers to both questions seem to be *yes*.

Nonverbal Profile of Successful Interviewees

McGovern and Tinsley (1978) provide solid support for the claim that interviewee's nonverbal cues can be important determinants of success in the job interview. In their research, two groups of interviewees were labeled, respectively, *"high nonverbal interviewees"* and *"low nonverbal interviewees,"* on the basis of the distinctive kinds of nonverbal cues they exhibited in a videotaped interview. The "high nonverbal interviewees" maintained steady eye contact, used varied voice modulation to express appropriate affect, demonstrated appropriately high energy level by hand gestures, smiling, and general body movement, and responded to interviewer questions with fluidity and little hesitation. By contrast, the "low nonverbal interviewees" avoided eye contact, displayed little or no affect, had a low energy level, and spoke in a broken, nonfluent manner.

Fifty-two professional interviewers from business and industry rated the two groups of subjects on the ten interviewee characteristics previously identified as particulary important to professional interviewers—ability to communicate, aggressiveness and initiative, self-confidence, and so on. They also classified interviewees on the basis of which ones they would invite for a second interview.

The results provide strong endorsement for the importance of nonverbal cues as determinants of successful interviews. Thus, the professional interviewers gave significantly higher ratings to the "high" as opposed to the "low" nonverbal interviewees on 39 of 40 ratings they made of factors such as enthusiasm/motivation, confidence in self, persuasiveness, and pleasant personality. Moreover, the ratings of the interviewees' effectiveness were made after each of four 4-minute excerpts from the interview. The strong positive impact of the desirable nonverbal cues on the interviewers' perceptions remained constant during the full 16 minutes of the interview.

Finally, the nonverbal behaviors of the two groups of interviewees had a dramatic impact on the interviewers' decisions to invite interviewees for a second interview. Fully 89 percent of the interviewers who saw the "high nonverbal interviewees" would have invited them back for a second interview, but 100 percent of those who saw the "low nonverbal interviewees" would *not* have invited them for a second interview. The researchers note that it would be hard to overstate the impact of nonverbal communication on the degree of success experienced in the job interview. They conclude that "it would be safe to say that the candidate who avoids eye contact, stutters and stammers, and is generally unemotional and flat will match a common stereotype of a 'reject' candidate" (p. 171).

A second study (Forbes & Jackson, 1980) is perhaps even more illuminating, in two respects. It focused on *real* as opposed to *simulated* job interviews, and examined the impact of desirable and undesirable interviewer nonverbal profiles on the *reject* and *accept* decisions of professional interviewers. In this instance, 101 recent engineering graduates were interviewed for real jobs, by professional interviewers with extensive education and experience in engineering. The authors hypothesized that favorable decisions to employ would be associated with the interviewees who exhibited positive nonverbal styles, and reject decisions would be associated with the job candidates who exhibited unfavorable nonverbal styles.

The hypothesis was strongly supported. Eye behavior seemed to be the most reliable nonverbal indicator of success or failure in these job interviews. Thus, direct eye contact occurred significantly more often in the *accept* interview than in the *reserve* or *reject* group—interviewees were either accepted or rejected for available jobs, or placed in a reserve category, where follow-up interviews were possible. Gaze-avoidance and "eye wandering" occurred much less frequently in the accept than in the reserve or reject group.

Although body position did not differentiate reliably between the three groups of interviewees, both smiling and frowning were important. Interviewees who were accepted for jobs smiled much more frequently than those who were placed on reserve or were rejected; and those who were rejected frowned more than those who were accepted.

Finally, interviewees who were accepted exhibited more head movement (in the form of affirmative nodding) and less frequently held their head in a static position than interviewees who were either rejected or placed on reserve. In short, eye behaviors, facial expressions, and head movements—both individually and collectively—proved to be good predictors of success or failure in the "real job" interview situation.

Eye behaviors, high-immediacy behaviors, and vocal cues have all been repeatedly identified as important determinants of success in the job interview. Physical attractiveness, in contrast, has not at this point been found to exert a strong and uniformly positive impact on the perceptions of job interviewers.

Eye behaviors clearly play a central role in the job interview. They are known to exert a significant impact on the perceived effectiveness of both the interviewee and the interviewer. Interviewees who sustain eye contact for the shortest amount of time have consistently been viewed as lowest in self-confidence (Tessler & Sushelsky, 1978). Similarly, interviewers who have received particularly unfavorable ratings from interviewees have been found to exhibit minimum amounts of eye contact (Kleinke, Staneski, & Berger, 1975).

Exhibiting high-immediacy behaviors is also extremely important in the job interview. Interviewees who communicate *high-immediacy* (via sustained eye contact, smiling, attentive posture, direct body orientation, illustrator gestures, and relatively close physical proximity to the interviewer) as opposed to low-immediacy, seem to markedly increase their chances of being hired. Imada and Hakel (1977) found that 86 percent of the interviewees who exhibited high-immediacy behaviors were recommended by the interviewers for the jobs for which they applied, but only 19 percent of the interviewees who exhibited low-immediacy behaviors received a similar recommendation.

Although nonverbal cues are frequently powerful determinants of success in the job interview, their relative importance has rarely been compared directly with the impact of verbal behaviors. Hollandsworth, Kazelskis, Stevens, and Dressel (1979) did conduct a study designed to yield estimates of the relative contributions of verbal and nonverbal behaviors to employment decisions. They found that verbal behaviors were the most important determinant of success in a job interview, and fluency of speech also contributed strongly to the employment decision. The most important verbal behaviors were: (a) ability to express oneself concisely; (b) answer questions fully; (c) state personal opinions when relevant; and (d) keep to the subject at hand.

The ability to speak fluently was clearly the most important nonverbal determinant of success in the job interview. Indeed, the use of nonfluencies proved so damaging to the job applicants that the researchers advocate the use of training designed to decrease speech disturbances and to improve speech fluency. Composure, as communicated via nonverbal cues, was also very important. Other less important nonverbal factors contributing to employment decisions (listed here in the order of their importance) were eye contact, body posture, loudness of voice, and personal appearance.

Physical attractiveness seems to be a less important determinant of success in the job interview than other kinds of nonverbal variables. In one study (Greenwald, 1981) social performance, previous experience, and qualifications were all found to be influential in affecting the interviewer's accept or reject decisions in a job interview. However, the study found no significant effect for the physical attractiveness of the interviewee. Results from this study should be interpreted with caution, however, because of the way physical attractiveness was manipulated—posed photographs from college yearbooks were used.

Heilman and Saruwatari (1979) found that *the impact of physical at-*

tractiveness in the job interview depends upon the sex of the applicant and the nature of the job he or she seeks. Although physical attractiveness was advantageous for male applicants seeking white-collar organizational positions, it was useful for female applicants only when the position they sought was a nonmanagerial one.

On the basis of the job interview, the physically attractive woman who applied for a managerial position was less likely to be hired than the physically unattractive woman. This finding has serious implications with

TABLE 12.1. Nonverbal Profile of Successful Job Interviewees

Should Exhibit	*Should Not Exhibit*
High-Immediacy Behaviors: sustained eye contact; smiling; attentive posture; direct body orientation; illustrator gestures; close physical proximity	*Low-Immediacy Behaviors:* intermittent eye contact; frowning; inattentive posture; indirect body orientation; adaptor gestures; distant seating
Vocal Cues	
Voice modulation to express appropriate affect: suitable variation in pitch, rate and volume	Monotone voice
Fluency	Nonfluencies: hesitation, stuttering word repetition, sentence fragments, and filled pauses (e.g., "ah")
Substantial Volume	
No hesitation in responding to interviewer questions	Soft voice—inadequate volume
Eye Behaviors	
Steady eye contact	Gaze-avoidance
Sustained eye contact	Wandering eyes
Substantial amount of eye contact	Limited amount of eye contact
	Eye contact of short duration
Bodily Cues	
Affirmative head nodding	Immobile head
Hand gestures communicating high energy levels	Hand gestures communicating low energy levels, or anxiety
Responsive postural shifts	Rigid posture
Confidence gestures	Nervousness gestures
Open posture	Closed and defensive posture
	Hand-to-face gestures
	Extraneous bodily movements

regard to the consequences of sex-role stereotyping for the female interviewee. Heilman and Saruwatari (1979) describe the problem graphically when they write that this finding "implies that women should strive to appear as unattractive and masculine as possible if they are to succeed in advancing their careers by moving into powerful organizational positions. Surely giving up one's womanhood should not be a prerequisite for organizational success" (p. 371).

The nonverbal profile for job applicants, which is associated with success and failure in the selection interview, is presented in Table 12.1. This profile is based entirely on results from empirical research. In view of the demonstrated importance of the interviewee's nonverbal cues as determinants of success in the job interview, this profile should be studied carefully by prospective job applicants.

The Counseling Interview

The counseling interview places a premium on the communicative skills of the interactants. This is so because counseling interviews are designed to solve problems. The problems addressed are not usually susceptible to resolution unless clients modify their attitudes and behaviors as a result of the confidence and trust they place in the counselor. In short, effective counselors must be able to promote self-disclosure and active problem-solving involvement on the part of the client. To achieve this objective, counselors must be perceived to be unusually sensitive individuals who are highly credible, empathic, and trustworthy.

Counseling takes many forms. People seek counseling in order to deal with problems of emotional instability, physical health, marriage, morals, work performance, alcoholism, and child abuse, for example. Contrary to popular belief, many counseling interviews are conducted by individuals who are not professionally trained as counselors. Many counselors—doctors, teachers, supervisors, fellow workers, students, friends, and family members—may be "professionals" but most are not professionally trained counselors (Stewart & Cash, 1982).

The acquisition of effective counseling skills is important, because all of us will, at some time, assume the role of counselor, whether as a parent, a friend, or a co-worker. And it is very likely that we may find ourselves in the role of client in a counseling interview. In either case, we are apt to put a premium on achieving success in the counseling interview. The degree of success achieved is often determined, to a striking degree, by the nonverbal behaviors exhibited by the counselor.

Critical Objectives

The success of a counseling interview is much more difficult to measure than the success of a job interview. From the perspective of the job applicant, the success or failure of the employment interview can be assessed directly and immediately. Job applicants are either accepted or rejected for the position for which they apply, but the success of the counseling interview must be assessed in terms of both short-range and long-range objectives. In most cases, the overriding short-term objective of the counselor is to inspire sufficient trust on the part of the client so that he or she will become actively involved in the problem-solving process. The long-range objective usually focuses upon the attempt to solve problems regarding alcoholism, drug abuse, marital discord, or sexual incompatibility, for example. Because successful resolution of such problems may take months or even years, much of the research on counseling interviews has focused on how successfully the counselor attains short-range objectives.

The short-term goals of the counselor are to exhibit interpersonal skills and to develop sufficient credibility in the eyes of the client so as to inspire trust in the counselor's therapeutic actions and methods. To inspire this trust, counselors must be perceived as *empathic, warm,* and *genuine* (Sherer & Rogers, 1980). You cannot persuade a client to modify the attitudes and behaviors that are causing a specific problem unless the client finds you to be a believable and caring person, one who will address your problems in a sensitive manner.

Imagine for a moment that you are about to have your initial counseling session with a psychiatrist. You suffer from depression. You have been so depressed for the last six months that you cannot sleep, you suffer from extreme fatigue, and you are convinced that you have a life-threatening heart disorder. As you enter the office of I. M. Cold, psychiatrist, you notice that he is talking on the telephone, with his back turned to you and his feet on the desk. He motions you to take a seat on the other side of the room and resumes his phone call. When, ten minutes later, he finally finishes his telephone conversation, he scowls, leans back in his chair and thumbs casually through your medical records. He then says to you, "I am positive that your symptoms can be easily treated. You are a hypochondriac who feels sorry for yourself. I have already written you a prescription for antidepressant pills. Take the pills for two months and call my secretary in the unlikely event that you still think you are depressed."

How would you react to such a counseling interview? In view of the fact that your psychiatrist is nationally recognized as an expert in the treatment of depression, does it really matter that you did not like him because he lacked empathy and warmth? Do you believe that his effectiveness as a psychiatrist will be measurably affected by the communicative behaviors he exhibited?

Nonverbal Profile of Successful Counselors

The level of expertness or competence attributed to the counselor by the *client* is perhaps the most important perceptual determinant of the counselor's effectiveness. Interestingly, a recent study (Siegel, 1980) found that a client's perception of the counselor's level of expertise was determined *both* by objective evidence of expertise and by the counselor's nonverbal behaviors. Counselors who displayed objective evidence of expertness (in the form of diplomas on the office wall) were judged as significantly more credible than those who did not. Less obvious but perhaps equally important is the finding that counselors who exhibited desirable nonverbal behaviors were judged more "expert" than counselors who did not exhibit such behaviors.

Counselors' nonverbal behaviors have been found to have a strong impact not only on their perceived competence but on their perceived trustworthiness. A study by Fretz, Corn, Tuemmler, and Bellet (1979) focused on three types of counselor nonverbal behaviors. One group of counselors maintained high levels of eye contact with the client, used a direct bodily orientation, and leaned forward while conversing. The other group of counselors exhibited an opposite set of nonverbal behaviors. Counselors in the first group were judged to be significantly more effective than those in the second group. They were judged by the clients to be superior, with regard to both *level of regard for the clients* and *empathy.*

This study clearly showed, in addition, that the display of just three types of desirable nonverbal behaviors by the counselors significantly enhanced their perceived competence and trustworthiness. Thus, the *counselors who exhibited the desirable nonverbal behaviors* were rated by clients as significantly *more poised, friendly, trusting, warm, attentive, intelligent, patient, capable, considerate, concerned, and expressive;* and significantly *less critical, cold, and aloof* than the other group of counselors.

The two kinds of nonverbal behaviors that seem to have the most positive impact on the counselor's perceived credibility and effectiveness are *immediacy* and *responsiveness* behaviors. Sherer and Rogers (1980) found that counselors who exhibited high-immediacy behaviors (i.e., sat within 36 inches of the client, maintained eye contact, and oriented the head toward the client 90 percent of the time) were rated much more effective than counselors who exhibited low-immediacy behaviors. The group of effective counselors were not only better liked but they were viewed as more empathic, warm, and genuine. Sherer and Rogers conclude that:

> *The present results strongly supported the prediction that a therapist who uses high-immediacy nonverbal cues, which communicate liking and acceptance, would be rated as possessing superior therapist interpersonal skills and as being a more effective therapist . . . Because people are more likely to approach and become involved with someone, who likes and accepts them, the use of immediacy cues may produce a variety of beneficial therapeutic outcomes (including continuation in therapy so that the therapist will have the opportunity to work on symptomatic complaints, disruptive behaviors, etc.) These results clearly support the assumption that the use of appropriate nonverbal cues may facilitate therapy. (p. 699).*

The counselor's nonverbal responsivity is also very important. Counselors who exhibit appropriate bodily movements are viewed as more responsive, warmer, and more empathic than those who do not. Arms crossed over the chest and crossed legs, with one leg resting on the other ankle, have been viewed by clients as particularly unresponsive forms of counselor behavior, with the result that the counselor is typically viewed as cold and nonempathic (Smith-Hanen, 1977). In contrast, appropriate client touching by the counselor is viewed as a desirable form of responsive behavior (Alagna, Whitcher, Fisher, & Wicas, 1979). In short, counselors who exhibit responsive nonverbal cues are viewed as more expert, trustworthy, and attractive than those who do not (Claiborn, 1979).

Finally, counselors who wish to be perceived as effective must take pains to make sure that their messages are consistent. The counselor who tells the client how interested he or she is in the client's problems while exhibiting low-immediacy behaviors, for example, runs the risk of alienating the client. Clients have a much lower level of regard for counselors who use inconsistent as opposed to consistent messages, and see them as less effective (Reade & Smouse, 1980).

The nonverbal profile associated with successful and unsuccessful counselors is presented in Table 12.2. This profile is also based on results

TABLE 12.2.   Nonverbal Profile of Successful Counseling Interviewers

Should Exhibit	*Should Not Exhibit*
High-Immediacy Behaviors: a high level of eye contact; close physical proximity (sit within three feet of the client); orient head and body toward the client	*Low-Immediacy Behaviors:* a low level of eye contact; distant seating; orient head and body away from the client
Responsive Behaviors: open posture and gestures; head nodding; postural shifts; illustrator gestures; appropriate touching of the client	*Unresponsive Behaviors:* closed and defensive postures; gestures with arms crossed over the chest and legs crossed at the ankles; immobile head and body; lack of touching
Consistent Messages: vocal cues, gestures, postures, close distancing, and appropriate touching should be used to reinforce the meaning(s) of verbal messages that communicate *liking, acceptance, empathy, warmth,* and a *genuine regard* for the client's feelings, concerns and problems	*Inconsistent Messages:* vocal cues, gestures, postures, physical separation, and inappropriate touching, which contradict the meaning(s) of verbal messages, with the result that a lack of *liking, acceptance, empathy, warmth,* and an *inauthentic regard* for the client's feelings, concerns, and problems is communicated
Sets of nonverbal behaviors which enhance the counselor's perceived competence and trustworthiness	Sets of nonverbal behaviors which lower the counselor's perceived competence and trustworthiness

from empirical research. Counselors who wish to increase their effectiveness must, quite clearly, exhibit both high-immediacy and responsive behaviors, and they must exercise special care to assure that their multichannel messages are consistent.

Summary

Nonverbal cues frequently are major determinants of success or failure in job and counseling interviews. The critically important role of nonverbal cues in the job interview has been clearly established. The interviewee's nonverbal cues are known to affect not only the interviewer's perceptions of the quality of the interviewee's performance, but also the critically important decision to accept or reject the interviewee for a job.

In the counseling interview, counselors must not only be perceived as credible but as empathic, if they are to be effective. The client's perceptions of the counselor's credibility and empathy are influenced to a striking degree by the nonverbal behaviors exhibited by the counselor.

The nonverbal profile for job applicants, which is associated with success and failure in the selection interview, is presented in Table 12.1. Successful job interviewees typically exhibit high-immediacy behaviors, use voice modulation to express appropriate affect, maintain a high level of sustained eye contact, and use affirmative head nodding, accompanied by responsive gestures and postures. In contrast, unsuccessful job interviewees frequently exhibit low-immediacy behaviors, speak in a broken and nonfluent manner, avoid eye contact, and are easily identifiable because of lack of head movements, rigid and defensive postures, and nervousness gestures.

Table 12.2 provides the nonverbal profile of successful counseling interviewers. Successful counselors consistently exhibit specific kinds of high-immediacy and responsive behaviors while communicating consistent messages. Counselors who wish to enhance their perceived credibility and cultivate their interpersonal communication skills should study the nonverbal profile of successful counseling interviewers.

References

Alagna, F. J., Whitcher, S. J., Fisher, J. D., & Wicas, E. W. (1979). Evaluative reaction to interpersonal touch in a counseling interview. *Journal of Counseling Psychology, 26,* 465–472.

Claiborn, D. D. (1979). Counselor verbal intervention, nonverbal behavior, and social power. *Journal of Counseling Psychology, 26,* 378–383.

Forbes, R. J., & Jackson, P. R. (1980). Non-verbal behaviour and the outcome of selection interviews. *Journal of Occupational Psychology, 53,* 65–72.

Fretz, B. R., Corn, R., Tuemmler, J. M., & Bellet, W. (1979). Counselor nonverbal behaviors and client evaluations. *Journal of Counseling Psychology, 26*, 304–311.

Greenwald, M. A. (1981). The effects of physical attractiveness, experience, and social performance on employer decision-making in job interviews. *Behavioral Counseling Quarterly, 1*, 275–287.

Heilman, M. E., & Saruwatari, L. R. (1979). When beauty is beastly: The effects of appearance and sex on evaluations of job applicants for managerial and non-managerial jobs. *Organizational behavior and human performance, 23*, 360–372.

Hollandsworth, J. G., Jr., Kazelskis, R., Stevens, J., & Dressel, M. E. (1979). Relative contributions of verbal, articulative, and nonverbal communication to employment decisions in the job interview setting. *Personnel Psychology, 32*, 359–367.

Imada, A. S., & Hakel, M. D. (1977). Influence of nonverbal communication and rater proximity on impressions and decision in simulated employment interviews. *Journal of Applied Psychology, 62*, 295–300.

Kleinke, C. L., Staneski, R. A., & Berger, D. E. (1975). Evaluations of an interviewer as a function of interviewer gaze, reinforcement of subject gaze, and interviewer's attractiveness. *Journal of Personality and Social Psychology, 31*, 115–122.

McGovern, T. V., & Tinsley, H. W. Interviewer evaluations of interviewee nonverbal behavior. *Journal of Vocational Behavior, 13*, 163–171.

Reade, M. N., & Smouse, A. D. (1980). Effect of inconsistent verbal-nonverbal communication and counselor response mode on client estimate of counselor regard and effectiveness. *Journal of Counseling Psychology, 27*, 546–553.

Sherer, M., & Rogers, R. W. (1980). Effects of therapist's nonverbal communication on rated skill and effectiveness. *Journal of Clinical Psychology, 36*, 696–700.

Siegel, J. C. (1980). Effects of objective evidence of expertness, nonverbal behavior, and subject sex on client-perceived expertness. *Journal of Counseling Psychology, 27*, 117–121.

Smith-Hanen, S. S. (1977). Effects of nonverbal behaviors on judged levels of counselor warmth and empathy. *Journal of Counseling Psychology, 24*, 87–91.

Stewart, C. J., Cash, Jr., W. B. (1982). *Interviewing principles and practices*, 3rd. ed. Dubuque, IA: Wm. C. Brown.

Tessler, R., & Sushelsky, L. (1978). Effects of eye contact and social status on the perception of a job applicant in an employment interview situation. *Journal of Vocational Behavior, 13*, 338–347.

CHAPTER THIRTEEN

Female–Male Interaction

T he communicative styles of men and women are distinctively different in our society. Our stereotypic conceptions of men and women are clearly and consistently reflected in their contrasting communicative styles. Men are stereotyped as active, dominant, aggressive, and insensitive persons, who dominate communicative interaction by virtue of their superior status. By contrast women, are perceived stereotypically to be passive, submissive, supportive persons, who are dominated as a result of their desire to adapt to men's needs, and to be accommodating. To a considerable degree, the stereotypes mirror the dominant characteristics of female–male interaction.

Sex-linked stereotypes are strongly reinforced by the use of sexist or exclusionary language which relegates women to narrowly defined and dependent roles (Thorne & Henley, 1975). The basic differences in male and female communication styles are revealed in implicit nonverbal messages rather than through the use of language, however. Men rarely communicate their desire to dominate women by the words they utter. Similarly, women do not generally use verbal communication to make clear their desire to be interpersonally accommodating. Such messages are communicated most frequently and forcefully by nonverbal cues.

Sex-Role Stereotyping

Strong and enduring sex-role stereotypes have developed in our society. Men are expected to assume the *proactive* role. The cultural norm dictates that the proactive person will be active, independent, self-confident, and decisive. Individuals who assume the proactive role place a high priority on accomplishing the task at hand. Women are expected to assume the *reactive* role. Reactive individuals respond to the contributions made by others rather than initiating contributions; they are emotionally expressive and sensitive to the emotional needs of the initiator, and they are interpersonally supportive and accommodating (LaFrance & Mayo, 1978).

The sex-role stereotypes reflected in these roles are quite detailed. The stereotype for women is more detailed than for men, although it is less socially desirable. The following descriptive labels are typically used to identify the more negative portion of the female stereotype: *submissive, dependent, touchy, moody, temperamental, excitable, frivolous, talkative,* and *timid.* The more positive portion of the female stereotype is identified by these descriptive labels: *affectionate, considerate, cooperative, supportive,* and *sensitive.*

Males are stereotyped in positive terms, such as *task-oriented, rational,* and *active.* More specifically, males are stereotyped by these positive adjectives: *logical, industrious, sharp-witted, shrewd, confident, forceful,* and *dominant.* Descriptive labels typically used to identify the negative portion of the male stereotype are *boastful, stubborn, arrogant, conceited, hardheaded,* and *opportunistic* (Eakins & Eakins, 1978; Heilbrum, 1976).

As we shall see, men and women frequently do behave in ways that are quite consistent with their stereotype. The obvious question is, why? Biological differences seem to have a relatively limited impact on the contrasting communicative styles of women and men. Some biological differences may of course affect communication. Women are usually physically smaller than men, and this difference may account, in part, for the fact that they *claim* less personal space than men. Because they are smaller than men, their vocal cords tend to be shorter, and their shorter vocal folds may help explain why women's modal pitch is significantly higher than men's. However, Thorne and Henley (1975) maintain that the female's characteristically higher pitch is more a function of social learning than of anatomical differences.

The greatest difference between male and female communicative behaviors seems to be attributable to gender differences as opposed to biologically determined sex differences. *Gender* is defined as the culturally established correlates of sex (Gofmann, 1979). The fact that women and men do behave differently, then, may be largely a result of cultural norms which specify appropriate behavior. The characteristic domination of females by males is a socially learned behavior, reinforced by a man's gender rather than by his sex. A man's primary sexual characteristics do not usually dictate that he behave in a particular way, but his gender is associated with well-developed social norms that specify how he should behave.

Goffman (1979) argues that the contrasting images of men and women have been strongly influenced by gender displays. *Gender displays* are conventionalized portrayals of those behaviors that society has defined as prototypically "masculine" and "feminine." The media have proven to be the strongest force in legitimizing and defining the gender displays that have become associated in the popular mind with "feminine" and "masculine" behavior.

Umiker-Sebeok (1981) has done the most detailed study of the ways gender displays are used to depict men and women in visual advertisements. She finds that the image of women which is portrayed in magazine advertisements is one of "weak, childish, dependent, completely domestic, irrational, subordinate creatures, the producers of children and little else compared with men" (p. 211). More specifically, she maintains that body size and clothing style are used in magazine advertisements to associate females with smallness, and subordination. Members of athletic teams are ordinarily portrayed as male, but females are pictured as primarily concerned with clothing, cosmetics, jewelry, hair products, and fragrances that can be used to enhance physical appearance.

In magazine advertisements, a young woman's high social status is frequently linked to her father's success, but a young man's success results from his own efforts; women are dependent and men are independent. The physical domination and subordination of the female is also frequently communicated clearly by the gender displays of the male. In the case of young lovers, it is the male who exhibits such stereotypic gestures as the "shoulder hold" and the "armlock"; it is the man who grasps the woman's upper arms, and it is the male who grasps the women's hand, rather than vice versa.

Umiker-Sebeok (1981) indicates quite clearly that the advertising industry consistently portrays the male in the proactive role and the female in the reactive role. In the marriage ceremony, for example, the bride is "given away" and "carried over the threshold" of the couple's new home. Middle-aged women are pictured as "plump" and "passive," but the middle-aged man assumes positions of even greater authority, status, and power. Although Umiker-Sebeok's description of male and female gender displays in visual advertisements may be somewhat selective, it makes the point that the stereotypical images of women and men are deeply embedded in cultural values.

Differences in Nonverbal Communication of Women and Men

There are many distinctive differences in the nonverbal communication of men and women. In order to communicate more successfully with each other, men and women must become fully aware of the nature of these differences. They must also understand which nonverbal behaviors must be modified, and why they must be modified, if more successful communication is to result. Gender differences in nonverbal communication are manifested most clearly in contrasting communicative styles, and in contrasting levels of encoding and decoding skills.

Nonverbal Profile of Female and Male Communicators

The vocalic communication of women and men is different in important respects. Contrary to the stereotype of women as *talkative,* men talk more than women. Men's vocal dominance of women is not confined to the amount of talking they do, however. Men tend to dominate opposite-sex interactions because of the following: (a) the average duration of their talk-turns is longer; (b) the number and rate of their filled pauses is greater; and (c) they interrupt more frequently than women.

Males' dominance of women in conversations is achieved in part by interruptions. The "interruption privilege" is one that men exercise frequently. LaFrance and Mayo (1979) emphasize that in same-sex conversations, interruptions, overlaps, and silences are almost evenly distributed between speakers. In male–female interaction, however, the following occurs: (a) women are frequently interrupted by men; (b) are often silent for long periods after being interrupted; (c) are often prevented from interrupting men by the exaggerated length of mens' "ums" and "hmms"; and (d) it is unusual for a woman to protest being interrupted by a male.

In contrast to men, women use reactive intonation patterns that may make them seem to be more emotionally expressive. Thus women, when surprised, characteristically use the "high–low down-glide," as in "Oh, how awful!," and women often answer questions with declarative statements that end with a rising inflection. The rising inflections which women use so frequently may make them seem more emotional than men, but also more uncertain and indecisive. Finally, it is important to note that women laugh significantly more than men, both when speaking and listening; the total time spent laughing is almost twice that of men. Excessive laughter or out-of-context laughter is frequently interpreted in our society as a sign that a person lacks self-confidence (Frances, 1979; LaFrance & Mayo, 1979).

The visual communication of men and women also differs in important respects. Oscar Wilde reportedly said, "A man's face is his autobiography; a woman's face is her work of fiction." There is limited evidence to support the view that women are more likely than men to control, consciously, their facial expressions in order to avoid displeasing the person with whom they are communicating.

The fact that women smile almost twice as much as men, and that they smile more frequently when listening, seems to support the inference that female smiles are not always completely genuine. Women maintain eye contact with their partners for longer periods of time when listening than when speaking; and low-status females sustain eye contact for significantly longer periods of time when listening than do high-status females (Ellyson, Dovidio, Corson, & Vinicur, 1980). Women appear to suffer severe perceptual penalties because of their excessive smiling and visual attentiveness. They not only reinforce their stereotypic image as status inferiors, but they raise doubts about the genuineness of the emotions they appear to be experiencing.

In general, men exhibit more bodily movements, they are more open, and they appear to be more relaxed than women. Women exhibit a disproportionate number of the gestures and postures that were identified in Chapter 2 as cues to nonassertiveness and powerlessness. Eakins and Eakins (1978) highlight fundamental differences in the bodily communication of males and females when they write that "communicators in general are more relaxed with females than with males. They show less body tension, more relaxed posture, and more backward lean. By their somewhat tenser postures, women are said to convey submissive attitudes. Their general bodily demeanor and bearing is more restrained and restricted than men's" (p. 161).

Men also use space as a means of asserting their dominance over women, as in the following: (a) they claim more personal space than women; (b) they more actively defend violations of their territories—which are usually much larger than the territories of women; (c) under conditions of high density, they become more aggressive in their attempts to regain a desired measure of privacy; and (d) men more frequently walk in front of their female partner than vice versa.

The characteristic differences of men and women in their tactile behavior has already been treated in detail in Chapter 7. In general, the male is the toucher and the female the touched. Males use the "touching privilege" to touch females much more frequently than they are touched by them. Women touch others more frequently than men only when they are interacting with children. This is not surprising, considering the stereotypical view that men are emotionally unexpressive individuals, who have difficulty in providing comfort and reassurance, but that women excel in this familiar familial role.

Most of the research done to date has attempted to classify the kinds of nonverbal behaviors that are characteristically exhibited by men in contrast to women. Little attention has been given to how these characteristically "male" or "female" behaviors may be modified as a result of the reaction of the person with whom we are interacting. Weitz (1976) maintains that the sex of the message receiver, as well as the sex of the message sender, affects communicative behaviors in opposite-sex interactions.

Women, but not men, seem to adapt their nonverbal behaviors to make them compatible with the personality traits and attitudes of their opposite-sex partners. Men tend to remain inflexibly committed to a proactive communicative style, but women do modify their nonverbal communicative behaviors. They adapt to meet their male partner's perceived needs, rather than to meet the distinctive requirements of a particular kind of communicative situation, however.

Weitz (1976) found that women are nonverbally adaptive when interacting with men. For example, women are nonverbally more submissive when interacting with a dominant male partner, during the first phase of female–male interaction. Similarly, women exhibit less nonverbal warmth when interacting with a male partner who shows strong affiliative tendencies. In short, women interacting with men seem to adjust their nonverbal behaviors in such a way as to "create an equilibrium in the interaction which would result in maximum interpersonal comfort (especially for the male) in the interaction" (p. 179). In contrast, women who are interacting with other women (in the early stages of interpersonal interaction) do not seem to adapt their nonverbal behaviors in order to be compatible with the dominant personality traits of the female partner.

A similar pattern emerges in male–female interaction, as they spend more time together. Women modify their nonverbal behaviors when interacting with a male partner, to make their behaviors more compatible with the male's personality characteristics, but men do not make a complementary effort—they do not modify their nonverbal behaviors in order to make their female partner more comfortable. Women's greater willingness to be accommodating to males may be attributable in part to the finding that individuals in general experience significantly more anxiety when interacting with a male than with a female.

Whether they are motivated by a desire to relieve their anxieties or by a desire to be accommodating, women do seem to adjust their nonverbal behaviors when they interact with a male. Females exhibit a higher focus of attention on their male partner, and show significantly more sexual interest in him than vice versa. Moreover, career-oriented women communicate significantly more nonverbal warmth when interacting with a male than do family-oriented women. This adjustment in nonverbal behavior may involve an attempt to counteract the stereotypic conception that career-oriented women are colder and less emotionally expressive than their family-oriented counterparts.

Weitz (1976), therefore, emphasizes that a woman's nonverbal communication is affected not only by sex-role stereotyping but also by a desire to be supportive and interpersonally accommodating. She emphasizes that the "finding of a possible female monitoring mechanism shown by the complementary relationship between female nonverbal style and male personality traits reinforces this idea of greater female responsiveness to the other person in the interaction. Of course, one can see this as a positive quality as well, except if this responsiveness is done at the expense of the assertion of the women's point of view, which it perhaps might be" (p. 183).

Gender Differences in Nonverbal Skills

We know very little about the relative ability of women and men to encode nonverbal messages. There is, however, some evidence to suggest that women communicate the basic emotions more clearly via their facial expressions than do men. Whereas women seem to be better at encoding negative emotions, such as dislike, men are better at communicating positive emotions, such as happiness. These differences in encoding performance may be related to the fact that women smile so much more than men.

Negative emotions are conveyed by facial expressions that are in striking contrast to the smile so often found on the face of a woman (LaFrance & Mayo, 1979). When men and women communicate more specialized kinds of emotional meaning, it appears that they exhibit comparable levels of encoding skill (Leathers & Emigh, 1980).

Women's decoding skills have consistently proven to be superior to men's, however. An exhaustive review of studies that compared the accuracy with which women and men decode nonverbal messages indicates quite clearly that women are superior decoders. Women's advantage in decoding nonverbal cues is greater when the message contains both visual and auditory cues than visual cues alone (Hall, 1981). The superiority of women over men as decoders has also proven to be greater when they were decoding visual messages rather than vocal messages. Because women spend so much more time looking at men than vice versa, it is not surprising that they decode visual cues with particular skill. In fact, these decoding data support the view that women use the visual channel as their primary nonverbal source of information about others.

Women's decoding superiority is most pronounced when they are decoding messages that have been intentionally communicated by the message sender. Women are very good at determining the meanings of messages they believe are intended for them. However, women seem reluctant, or unwilling, to determine the implicit meanings of messages that are not intended for them.

Rosenthal and DePaulo (1979) examined the comparative ability of women and men to decode messages that were communicated through channels that varied with regard to their "leakiness" (i.e., the probability that meanings were being communicated unintentionally). From the least to the most leaky, the channels used were facial expressions, bodily cues, tone of voice, and inconsistent messages (visual–auditory channels combined). Results indicated that women decoders lost their superiority over men when they were asked to decode messages transmitted over increasingly leaky channels. The diminution in decoding performance may be traced to a conscious decision on the part of women not to decode the meanings of messages transmitted through the leakier channels rather than to a relative lack of ability to decode such messages.

Subsequent research suggests that women recognize that it is not in their best interests to be too good at decoding the leaky, or unintended, nonverbal cues. They may simply not wish to know, or to acknowledge, that their male partner is deceiving them or is becoming unbearably anxious. Women may recognize intuitively that if they are to be supportive and interpersonally accommodating, they should refrain from decoding the meanings of messages that were not intended for them. In our society, the more accommodating a woman is nonverbally the more likely she is to experience satisfactory interpersonal outcomes (Blanck, Rosenthal, Snodgrass, DePaulo & Zuckerman, 1981).

In short, women's nonverbal skills are superior to men's in a number of important aspects. When decoding messages sent with a high level of awareness and intentionality by the message sender, women's superiority over men as decoders is quite striking. The fact that women exhibit no greater accuracy than men in decoding the meanings communicated through leaky channels should not be interpreted as evidence that women *cannot* decode messages communicated through leaky channels, and at high levels of accuracy. The plausible explanation seems to be that women choose not to decode certain unintended messages because they are difficult to cope with in ways which are socially appropriate. In these cases, the desire to be polite and accommodating seems to override the desire to utilize effectively their superior decoding skills.

Dysfunctional Male and Female Nonverbal Behaviors

A careful inspection of the nonverbal communicative behaviors that characterize male–female interaction reveals that many of these behaviors are dysfunctional. These behaviors are dysfunctional for the following reasons: (a) many link females and males directly to some of the most negative features of their respective stereotypes; (b) they are not consciously modified to meet the varying requirements for successful communication in different contexts; and (c) they often serve as barriers to satisfying interpersonal outcomes.

Men's nonverbal communicative behaviors seem to change little from one type of communication situation to another. Whether a man is trying to sell himself, to conduct an interview, or to run a business meeting, he exhibits a propensity to cultivate the proactive role. As we have seen, males talk more and for longer periods of time than females, and they inhibit immediate feedback by using long, filled pauses. By their visual inattentiveness, their exercise of the touching privilege, their familiar forms of address, and their bodily relaxation, men also indicate that they perceive themselves as status superiors who can legitimately exercise the right to dominate heterosexual interaction. Even though men may not be aware of the implications of their nonverbal communication, their characteristic nonverbal behaviors serve to legitimate the gender-related image traits that are attributed to them (i.e., *forcefulness, dominance, confidence, status, power, insensitivity*, and *inflexibility*).

Women, in contrast to men, are nonverbally adaptive and supportive. Their adaptive and supportive behaviors are frequently dysfunctional, however, because they are misdirected. Rather than adapting their nonverbal behaviors to meet the distinctive requirements of specific communication contexts, women adapt to meet the perceived needs of their male partner. In their self-deprecating efforts to please, appease, and placate their male partner, they frequently lend credibility to the stereotypic terms that are used to describe their actions (i.e., *reactive, submissive, dependent*, and *inferior*).

The nonverbal behavioral profile of males is dysfunctional for three more specific reasons: (a) males become inflexibly committed to a single, unchanging communicative style; (b) males come to accept their unexpressive, nondisclosing, and insensitive communication as the norm; and (c) males cultivate a self-directed intrapersonal orientation which is incompatible with successful female–male interaction.

In one sense, the unchanging "male" style of nonverbal communication seems to have some desirable features in business situations. In a business world dominated by males, the unyielding attachment to the proactive role might seem to be desirable. This seems particularly true for leaders and those who aspire to leadership. Individuals who initiate most of the contributions, control communicative interactions, and enhance perceptions of dominance and status by their nonverbal cues might be thought to have the edge. However, this is also an age that values *participative management* and *quality circles,* which put a premium on a communicative style that encourages flexibility and interaction; which minimizes status differences and accents the uniqueness and intrinsic value of each individual. In this new business climate, the male who remains inflexibly committed to a single, domineering communicative style is at a severe disadvantage.

This is also an age that values the ability to openly express one's emotions, and to read and respond with sensitivity to the feelings of those with whom we communicate. Although "women have been socialized to display their emotions, their thoughts, and ideas" (Thorne & Henley, 1975, p. 209), men continue to be nonverbally unexpressive, nondisclosing, and insensitive. Men's lack of expressiveness frequently means that their true feelings and emotions remain a mystery in female–male interaction. Their insensitivity is reflected, in part, in their inattentiveness to their female partner. This inattentiveness seems to be linked directly to the fact that men are much less skillful decoders of nonverbal messages than women. Men cannot respond to women in ways that are emotionally responsive until they have developed the capacity to determine more precisely the nature of their female partner's emotional needs.

Finally, men's characteristic nonverbal communicative behaviors are dysfunctional because they perpetuate a preoccupation with self. Whereas women communicate their concern for others nonverbally, men exhibit a primary concern with self-assertion and self-protection. Men's nonverbal behaviors focus upon a set of goals that are frequently important only to the man, but women's nonverbal behaviors focus upon a woman's desire to facilitate interpersonal outcomes that are satisfying to *both* the male and female interactant. Until men become less preoccupied with the importance of their own talk, and work actively to solicit the feedback of their opposite-sex partner, men's dysfunctional intrapersonal orientation will continue to be a barrier to successful female–male interaction.

In one sense, the nonverbal communicative behaviors that seem to be prototypically female are desirable. In a family setting, the emotionally sensitive and supportive woman has no peer in providing the comfort and emotional support that is so essential to the development of the cohesive family unit. The intrapersonally oriented father, in contrast, may be as likely to brood about his own concerns as to be concerned about the emotional needs of family members.

In contemporary society, however, women must function effectively in many contexts outside of the home. When they do so, their nonverbal behavioral profile can be dysfunctional because: (a) females frequently display nonverbal behaviors that invite the attribution of unflattering image traits; (b) females display adaptive nonverbal behaviors that raise questions about their motivations; and (c) females do not fully utilize their impressive nonverbal communication skills.

Skillful impression managers try to associate themselves with favorable images and dissociate themselves from unfavorable images. Women seem to associate themselves with unfavorable images, because of some of the nonverbal behaviors they most frequently display. The fact that women smile and laugh twice as much as men clearly implies that their anxiety is high and their self-confidence is low. Women's polite forms of address, the small amount of personal space they claim as theirs, their visual attentiveness to men, the disproportionate amount of touching they receive, and their constricted and tense bodily postuers almost assure that they will be perceived as persons of inferior status and power (Henley, 1977).

Women's repeated efforts to be emotionally supportive, and to adapt their behaviors to meet men's need to be made comfortable, may seem desirable, in one sense. But a woman's efforts to be interpersonally adaptive and supportive may raise questions about her motivations. How likely is it that a man will interpret a woman's smile as being genuine, when it is displayed so frequently? What motivation is a man likely to attribute to a woman who becomes noticeably submissive when interacting with a dominant male? Excessive smiling, laughter, and eye contact seem to invite inferences that a person is insincere, manipulative, and deceptive. Because these nonverbal behaviors are such prominent features of the nonverbal profile for women, it is not surprising that they sometimes reinforce doubts about the wholesomeness of women's motivations in female–male interactions.

Finally, women do not fully and effectively exercise their ability to decode nonverbal messages. In order to be polite, supportive, and accommodating, women apparently choose not to decode the meanings of messages they believe their male partners did not wish to send. In view of the great informational potential of unintentional messages, women's disregard of such messages represents a sacrifice of major proportions.

Guidelines for Successful Female–Male Interaction

The messages communicated nonverbally through female and male gender displays are both powerful and resistant to change. These messages frequently serve as barriers to successful communicative interaction between males and females, therefore the need for change is apparent. But the extent to which the dysfunctional features of female–male communication can be modified is a debatable question.

Potential for Modifying Nonverbal Cues

In their penetrating essay on the potential of nonverbal communication as an agent for modifying the dysfunctional features of gender displays, Mayo and Henley (1981) argue that gender-defining nonverbal cues are resistant to change for these reasons: (a) nonverbal behaviors that are out of awareness obviously will not be changed; (b) nonverbal behaviors characteristic of gender displays are reinforced by powerful social forces, such as the media; (c) nonverbal behavior that is gender-deviant is frequently punished.

These arguments clearly have merit. Neither males nor females can modify their undesirable nonverbal communication behaviors unless they know that these behaviors *are* undesirable. At the same time, we must recognize that individuals can be trained to become aware of nonverbal behaviors that are demonstrably dysfunctional or undesirable. In fact, some sensitivity training is based on the proposition that individuals learn to communicate more effectively by increasing sensitivity to their own behaviors.

Clearly, many of the nonverbal behaviors we have come to accept as characteristic of each sex are learned behaviors. Sex-role stereotypes reflect deeply embedded cultural values which are reinforced by powerful communicative forces, such as the media. Comprehensive changes in the nonverbal profile for males and females must be preceded by major changes in cultural values. Dysfunctional gender-related behaviors are learned, therefore they can become unlearned. The force of cultural norms is not so strong at present that dysfunctional "male" and "female" nonverbal behaviors cannot be modified. Individuals will attempt such modification, however, only when they become convinced that the advantages of change outweigh the disadvantages of inflexible attachment to fixed communication styles.

Gender-deviant behavior by a woman involves some degree of risk. Such behavior may be punished. Porter and Geis (1981) recognize the double-bind dilemma that a woman may encounter when interacting with a male who assumes the traditional proactive role. They write that, if "a woman is ignored when she presents ordinary, moderate demand signals which are effective for men, she may attempt to secure recognition by increasing the intensity of the signal, and end up being recognized, not for achievement, but as overly emotional, arrogant and abrasive. Indeed, from the perceiver's point of view, the strong demand is uncalled for" (pp. 55–56). Punishment and negative reinforcement are far from inevitable, however, when males recognize that such reactions on their part are counterproductive.

Although nonverbal behaviors characteristic of gender displays cannot be changed easily, there is an increasing amount of evidence that the most dysfunctional of these behaviors can be changed in specific situations. For example, the psychologically androgynous person has consistently exhibited the ability to add selective opposite-sex behaviors and eliminate the least desirable behaviors associated with his or her own sex (Mayo & Henley, 1981). Androgynous individuals are not inflexibly committed to perpetuating the defining traits of their sex-role stereotypes. In contrast to traditional males and females, androgynous persons show a blend of both masculine and feminine behaviors which are appropriate for specific situations.

Androgynous persons have a communicative flexibility not possessed by the person who conforms to the behavioral norms associated with traditional sex-role stereotypes. They have demonstrated the valuable ability of emphasizing or de-emphasizing the male and female traits they display, depending upon the specific requirements of the communication situation. This ability may account for the fact that androgynous individuals may experience more satisfying interpersonal outcomes than proactive males and reactive females (LaFrance & Carmen, 1980).

Sensitizing Communicators to Dysfunctional Gender Cues

The first step in modifying, and ultimately eliminating, dysfunctional nonverbal cues which are characteristic of gender displays is making the communicators *aware* of these cues. The success of conventional sensitivity training suggests that individuals can be made aware of behaviors that are dysfunctional. Individuals typically seek to change their own behaviors when they become fully aware that these behaviors serve neither their own ends nor the ends of successful interpersonal communication.

Nonverbal sensitivity training currently takes a variety of forms. For example, a colleague and I conduct a sales and communication training program which is designed to sensitize salespeople to their communicative behaviors which serve as barriers to effective persuasive communication. In order to make the salespeople aware of their most dysfunctional behaviors, they are videotaped in both simulated and real sales situations. Their dysfunctional behaviors are then identified by their peers and by the trainers, during a videotape replay. Similar formats are being used by others to train police officers, politicians, and labor-management negotiators. The objective is to make the trainees fully aware of which of their communicative behaviors are dysfunctional, and why they should be changed.

I believe that similar procedures should be used to sensitize interacting males and females to the nonverbal communicative behaviors which can and should be modified. The rapid growth of assertiveness workshops and seminars suggests that communicators realize that they must become aware of their problems before they can solve them. Women attend assertiveness workshops in disproportionate numbers. This fact may reflect the rapidly growing awareness of a number of women that their relative nonassertiveness is a gender-related problem.

Modifying Gender-Stereotypic Nonverbal Behaviors

Male and females, by virtue of their gender, tend to adopt inflexible communicative styles that limit their potential for successful communication. As I have indicated, these communicative styles cannot be easily modified. The reasons for trying to modify them are compelling, however. Helpful guidelines that can be used to modify stereotypic male and female dysfunctional nonverbal communicative behaviors have begun to appear (Cannie, 1979; Eakins & Eakins, 1978; Thorne & Henley, 1975).

The following guidelines are not comprehensive, because our current level of knowledge about the nature of female–male interaction is still incomplete. There is, nonetheless, a basis for a beginning.

Both men and women should begin by examining their own styles of nonverbal communication for sex-stereotypical cues that are dysfunctional. They should recognize that they will probably have to modify some of their gender-related behaviors in order to have a marked impact on the image traits that are attributed to them. Porter and Geis (1981) found, for example, that a woman who sits at the head of a discussion table does not increase her chances of being perceived as the group's leader. The implication is that women must modify more than one nonverbal behavior if they are to enhance their prospects of being perceived as leaders. For a man to become a successful leader in a group that prefers democratic leadership, he must seek to suppress a number of the dominating and autocratic behaviors associated with the traditional male style of communication.

Men in particular must begin by developing a style of communication that features an interpersonal rather than an intrapersonal orientation. Through a modified communication style, men must demonstrate quite clearly that their attention is focused on the needs, concerns, and opinions of their opposite-sex partner. Men must become more physically and psychologically attentive. As Cannie (1979) puts it, attending "is the basic nonverbal skill for valuing others. It is a process of showing people you are interested in them, you are listening, and what they say is important to you. This meets their self-esteem need and returns trust to you. Attending can be physical and it can be psychological" (p. 11).

In order to become a more flexible, sensitive, and attentive communicator, the male should do the following: (a) minimize the use of dominance and power cues which characterize him as an insensitive and condescending person, one who relegates females to the demeaning and defensive posture of an inferior; (b) develop his capacity to express clearly, and interpret accurately, a wide range of emotions, in the interest of facilitating emotionally appropriate and satisfying interpersonal communication; and (c) provide his opposite-sex partner with clear and complete feedback which can be used by the female to assess fully the nature of his communicative reactions.

Women should be guided by a different set of guidelines, including the following: (a) suppress those nonverbal communicative behaviors that associate them with such undesirable image traits as weakness, submissiveness, nonassertiveness, and powerlessness; (b) de-emphasize the display of nonverbal gender cues, such as excessive smiling and laughing, which reinforce the impression that they are insincere, manipulative, and dishonest; and (c) fully exercise their impressive decoding skills, rather than interpreting only those male messages they believe are intended for them.

These guidelines, when used by both sexes, should help promote successful female–male interaction, which should result in mutually satisfying outcomes. Men and women must be able to adapt their communication styles, not only to help satisfy mutual needs, but to make them more responsive to the requirements of various communication situations. The time is past when the Tarzan–Jane model of communication can be anything but a cruel and demeaning caricature of male–female interaction.

Summary

Sex-role stereotyping has had a pervasive impact on female–male interaction in our culture. Men have been stereotyped as confident, dominant, and forceful individuals who, at the same time, are stubborn, arrogant, and inflexibly committed to the accomplishment of specific tasks. By contrast, women are viewed stereotypically as affectionate, supportive, and sensitive persons who are submissive, excitable, dependent, and timid. To a considerable degree, the communicative behaviors of men and women confirm the accuracy of their respective stereotypes.

Nonverbal cues seem to be the most powerful medium for the communication of gender displays that feature prototypically "feminine" and "masculine" behaviors. The distinctive differences in the nonverbal communication of women and men are, in turn, manifested most clearly in their contrasting nonverbal communicative styles, and in the contrasting levels of their encoding and decoding skills.

The most dysfunctional features of the nonverbal communication styles of men and women are examined in detail in this chapter. Men's characteristic nonverbal communication style is dysfunctional because it is inflexible. It is emotionally nondisclosing and insensitive, and it reflects a preoccupation with self. In contrast, women's nonverbal communication style is dysfunctional because it features the display of nonverbal behaviors that invite the attribution of unflattering image traits. It helps create the impression that women are insincere and dishonest, and it prevents women from effectively utilizing their superior decoding skills.

Many of the dysfunctional features of female–male interaction can be modified. Such modification is not easy, however, because gender-defining cues are reflective of cultural values, which are resistant to change. Dysfunctional nonverbal cues must be raised to the individual communicator's conscious level of awareness before they can be successfully modified. When such modification is attempted, the guidelines presented in this chapter should prove to be useful.

References

Blanck, P. D., Rosenthal, R., Snodgrass, S. E., DePaulo, B. M., & Zuckerman, M. (1981). Sex differences in eavesdropping on nonverbal cues: Developmental changes. *Journal of Personality and Social Psychology, 41*, 391–396.

Cannie, J. K. (1979) *The woman's guide to management success; How to win power in the real organizational world.* Englewood Cliffs, NJ: Prentice-Hall.

Eakins, B. W., & Eakins, R. G. (1978). *Sex differences in human communication.* Boston: Houghton.

Ellyson, S., Dovidio, J. F., Corson, R. L., & Vinicur, D. L. (1980). Visual dominance behavior in female dyads and situational and personality factors. *Social Psychology Quarterly, 43*, 328–336.

Frances, S. J. (1979). Sex differences in nonverbal behavior. *Sex Roles, 5*, 519–535.

Goffman, E. (1979). *Gender advertisements.* Cambridge, MA: Harvard University Press.

Hall, J. A. (1981). Gender effects in decoding nonverbal cues. *Psychological Bulletin, 85*, 845–857.

Heilbrum, A. B., Jr. (1976). Measurement of masculine and feminine sex role identities as independent dimensions. *Journal of Consulting and Clinical Psychology, 44*, 183–190.

Henley, N. M. (1977) *Body politics: Power, sex, and nonverbal communication.* Englewood Cliffs, NJ: Prentice-Hall.

LaFrance M., & Carmen, B. (1980). The nonverbal display of psychological androgyny. *Journal of Personality and Social Psychology, 38*, 36–49.

LaFrance, M., & Mayo, C. (1978). *Moving bodies: Nonverbal communication in social relationships.* Monterey, CA: Brooks/Cole.

LaFrance, M., & Mayo, C. (1979) A review of nonverbal behaviors of women and men. *Western Journal of Speech Communication. 43*, 96–107.

Leathers, D. G., & Emigh, T. H. (1980). Decoding facial expressions: A new test with decoding norms. *Quarterly Journal of Speech, 66*, 418–436.

Mayo, C., & Henley, N. M. (1981). Nonverbal behavior: Barrier or agent for sex role change? In C. Mayo & N. M. Henley (Eds.), *Gender and nonverbal behavior* (3–13). New York: Springer-Verlag.

Porter, N., & Geis, F. (1981). Women and nonverbal leadership cues: When seeing is not believing. In C. Mayo & N. M.Henley (Eds.), *Gender and Nonverbal Behavior* (39–61). New York: Springer-Verlag.

Rosenthal, R., & DePaulo, B. M. Expectancies, discrepancies, and courtesies in nonverbal communication. *Western Journal of Speech Communication, 43*, 76–95.

Thorne, B., & Henley, N. M. (1975). Womanspeak and manspeak: Sex differences and sexism in communication, verbal and nonverbal. In B. Thorne & N. M. Henley (Eds.), *Language and sex: Difference and dominance.* Rowley, MA: Newbury House.

Umiker-Sebeok, J. (1981). The seven ages of woman: A view from American magazine advertisements. In C. Mayo & N. M.Henley (Eds.), *Gender and nonverbal behavior.* New York: Springer-Verlag.

Weitz, S. (1976). Sex differences in nonverbal communication. *Sex Roles, 2,* 175–184.

CHAPTER FOURTEEN

Successful Intercultural Communication

The communication styles characteristic of given cultures are often distinctively different. To communicate successfully with members of another cultural group, we must be able to identify those behaviors that define the unique communication style of the culture. We must identify specific communicative behaviors, both those perceived as positive and those perceived as negative in a particular culture. Then we can adapt our communication to conform to that culture's norms and rules.

A culture's communication style is of course strongly affected by the language of the culture. The potentially powerful impact of language on culture is perhaps most clearly and concisely described in the Sapir-Whorf hypothesis. This hypothesis stipulates that the language of a culture serves not only as a medium of communication but also as a major force in shaping the thought processes and perceptions of members of a culture (Condon & Yousef, 1975). Knowledge of and command of the language of a culture is not apt to be sufficient to assure success in intercultural communication, however. In fact, Almaney and Alway (1982) maintain that "cultural anthropologists consider nonverbal skills as far more important than verbal skills in determining communication success abroad" (p. 18).

Nonverbal messages are particularly important in intercultural communication because they usually contain sets of implicit rules or "commands" (LaFrance & Mayo, 1978a) that specify what is and what is not acceptable behavior in the culture. If outsiders are to become successful communicators in a culture other than their own, they must become thoroughly familiar with the socially learned display rules which make the communication style of the culture distinctive. When the nuances of socially sensitive and appropriate behavior within a given culture remain out-of-awareness to the foreigner, the potential for successful intercultural communication remains limited.

Executives and employees of multinational corporations, exchange students, international travelers, and diplomats all need to communicate effectively in cultural contexts that are unfamiliar to them. This chapter is designed to be helpful to those individuals. To begin, cross-cultural similarities and differences in nonverbal communication are compared and contrasted. In order to demonstrate how a person can become thoroughly familiar with the communication styles of contrasting cultures, the nonverbal communication styles of the Japanese and Arab cultures are examined in detail. Finally, a set of guidelines is included, which can be used to identify with, and adapt to, the nonverbal communication style of the culture where communicative interaction may occur.

Cross-Cultural Similarities in Nonverbal Communication

Darwin (1872) theorized that the "chief" facial expressions will be recognized universally by members of different cultures because the ability to communicate and identify the major classes of facial emotions is innately acquired. Ekman, Friesen, and Ellsworth (1972) have conducted research that supports the view that six basic emotions—happiness, fear, surprise, anger, disgust-contempt, and sadness—are communicated via similar facial displays and are decoded at similar levels of accuracy by members of both literate cultures and by members of a preliterate culture, such as New Guinea.

Eibl-Eibesfeldt (1972) also maintains that members of different cultures use the same facial muscles to communicate emotions such as happiness and anger. For example, he observed the familiar eyebrow flash used in greetings by such diverse cultural groups as Europeans, Balinese, Papuans, Samoans, South American Indians, and Bushmen. He concludes that the "similarities in expressive movements between cultures lie not only in such basic expressions as smiling, laughing, crying, and the facial expressions of anger, but in whole syndromes of behaviour. For example, one of the expressions people of different cultures may produce when angry is characterized by opening the corners of the mouth in a particular way and by frowning, and also by clenching the fists, stamping on the ground and even by hitting at objects" (p. 299).

Eibl-Eibesfeldt maintains, as do Ekman and his associates, that facial communication across cultures is similar in that members of different cultures use the same facial muscles to display basic emotions such as happiness or anger. Although different facial muscles are of course used to display happiness and anger, for example, the look of facial happiness and anger are quite similar in all cultures that have examined. Eibl-Eibesfeldt adds a note of caution, however. He notes that, even though members of all cultures may inherit a facial display that features an eyebrow flash to signal pleasure when greeting someone, the eyebrow flash is not a universal feature of greeting behavior. In Japan the eyebrow flash is suppressed because it is considered indecent.

Izard (1971) has probably done the most detailed examination of the facial communication of emotions in nine national-cultural groups: American, English, German, Swedish, French, Swiss, Greek, African, and Japanese. He concludes that the *ability to encode and decode the basic emotions communicated by facial expressions is innate and universal.*

The different cultural groups studied by Izard were able to identify the basic facial emotions at a level exceeding chance expectation. However, there are some striking differences in the accuracy with which different cultural groups identified given types of facial emotions. For example, the Greeks were much less accurate than the eight other cultural groups in identifying facial interest–excitement; the Africans had difficulty in identifying facial disgust–contempt; and the Japanese were notably inaccurate in their attempts to identify facial shame–humiliation. Because shame is viewed as the most undesirable of emotions in the Japanese culture (Sweeney, Cottle, & Kobayashi, 1980), we might infer that the reluctance to exhibit or acknowledge facial shame in Japan is a socially learned behavior.

In short, there is evidence that a limited number of emotions are communicated by similar facial expressions across cultures. However, La-France and Mayo (1978b) note that the pancultural element in facial communication seems to be limited to four or five basic emotions. They contend emotional expression is subject to both cultural and biological influences. More specifically, "the innate elements link particular emotion with particular facial muscles while cultural elements adapt the facial signal to the environment in which it occurs" (p. 77). Thus, members of some cultures appear to experience and communicate sentiments and emotions that members of other cultures neither know nor recognize. For example, the facial blend that North Americans label "smug" is rarely named or recognized in any other culture. Similarly, the "wry smile" of the English, with one corner of the mouth up and the other corner down, may be unique to England.

Recent research (Leathers & McGuire, 1983) suggests that a person's cultural experiences can have a dramatic *impact on their ability to identify the more subtle kinds of meanings that can be communicated by facial expressions.* A colleague and I, using the Facial Meaning Sensitivity Test described in Chapter 2, compared the decoding performance of samples of American and West German decoders. Consider the results reported in Table 14.1. Germans were significantly less accurate than Americans in identifying 13 of the 30 highly specific facial meanings in Step III of the FMST (page 31). Although Germans were more sensitive than Americans to such specific kinds of facial disgust as repugnance and distaste, they were much less sensitive to specialized kinds of facial sadness, bewilderment, and anger. We attribute the differences in ability to identify subtle nuances of facial meaning not to innately acquired skills but to culturally acquired attitudes about the emotions that are communicated by facial expressions.

The results for the German decoders (see Table 14.1) may be explained at least in part by two forces that may have helped shape the German culture. Leathers and McGuire contend that the German's sense of superiority would seem to encourage the display of and help to develop sensitivity to those emotions that would reinforce, or be consistent with, a feeling of superiority. And the German's national sense of shame would seem to discourage the display of shame and prevent the development of sensitivity to those emotions that might be associated with a sense of shame.

Results in Table 14.1 do suggest that Germans are particularly sensitive to such highly specialized kinds of facial emotions as repugnance, distaste, and disdain. Such emotions traditionally have been associated with a sense of superiority, and with a limited tolerance for individuals and actions that are judged to be inferior.

German decoders exhibited striking insensitivity to subtle differences in specific kinds of emotions that might contradict a feeling of superiority or that might reinforce a sense of shame. Germans were particularly insensitive to different kinds of sadness expressed by facial expressions. Sadness, which is a negative emotional state, may be associated in the German mind with the enormous amount of suffering inflicted on the Jews and others by the Germans, and a sense of shame may have conditioned Germans against the facial display of sadness in public.

Germans were also highly insensitive to such specialized kinds of anger as rage, hate, and annoyance. These emotions also may be linked rather directly in the German mind to a sense of shame, because many of the inhumane acts of Germans during World War II were triggered by emotions such as these. On the other hand, displays of rage would violate the cultural preference for a stoical, controlled, "superior," person.

Finally, the German's insensitivity to specialized kinds of facial bewilderment may be explained by an implicit cultural rule that discourages the public display of bewilderment. Certainly the German's propensity to exercise self-control while cultivating a public image of superiority, or even arrogance, is not consistent with the frequent expression of bewilderment. The most extreme forms of bewilderment suggest uncertainty, and perhaps weakness, which Germans would presumably be reluctant to reveal in public.

In short, the striking differences between German and American decoders in sensitivity to highly specialized kinds of facial emotions seem to be directly related to the impact of different display rules in the two cultures. *Cultural display rules* are a deeply ingrained set of implicit cultural conventions, learned early in life, that specify which emotions should and should not be expressed in public (Ekman & Friesen, 1975). During socialization, an individual learns not only whether the public display of emotions is positively or negatively rewarded, but also "which facial expressions are expected, preferred, or allowed in which circumstances and learns to perform accordingly" (Kilbride & Yarczower, 1980, p. 27).

Because German display rules seem to dictate that sadness, bewilderment, and anger should be infrequently displayed in public, these are emo-

TABLE 14-1. Accuracy of Identification of Specific Facial Expressions by German Decoders Within Each Class of Meaning

Class of Meaning		Photograph Number	Percentage of Correct Identification		Type of Decoding Error Made by German Decoders	Percentage of Decoders Correctly Identifying All Facial Expressions Within a Class	
			American	German		American	German
Happiness	Laughter	9	98.45	94.37	Amusement (5.63) Love (0.00)	90.27	77.33
	Love	26	91.09	82.67	Amusement (10.67) Laughter (6.67)		
	Amusement	2	90.31	83.56	Love (12.33) Laughter (4.11)		
Fear	Terror	10	98.44	91.78	Anxiety (5.48) Apprehension (2.74)	76.74	68.00
	Anxiety	21	77.43	73.97	Apprehension (19.18) Terror (6.85)		
	Apprehension	27	77.82	76.06	Apprehension (23.94) Terror (0.00)		
Disgust	Aversion	30	78.68	77.46	Repugnance (21.13) Distaste (1.41)	42.25	56.00
	Repugnance	12	49.61	62.50	Aversion (19.44) Distaste (18.06)		
	Distaste	8	45.35	80.56	Repugnance (16.67) Aversion (2.78)		

Anger	Rage	28	95.74	61.11	Hate (23.61) Annoyance (15.28)	94.53	56.00
	Hate	1	94.92	67.12	Rage (28.77) Annoyance (4.11)		
	Annoyance	20	98.96	80.56	Hate (11.11) Rage (8.33)		
Interest	Attention	23	89.92	80.28	Excitement (14.08) Anticipation (5.63)	66.15	48.00
	Anticipation	6	67.05	60.27	Excitement (34.25) Attention (5.48)		
	Excitement	15	71.32	52.06	Anticipation (34.25) Attention (13.70)		
Bewilderment	Confusion	18	86.38	50.73	Doubt (34.78) Stupidity (14.49)	85.66	40.00
	Doubt	4	88.72	50.70	Confusion (43.67) Stupidity (5.63)		
	Stupidity	17	93.39	79.45	Doubt (13.70) Confusion (6.85)		
Contempt	Disdain	24	55.25	66.67	Arrogance (29.17) Superiority (4.17)	43.80	36.00
	Arrogance	13	47.47	41.10	Superiority (30.14) Disdain (28.77)		
	Superiority	29	71.98	65.28	Arrogance (30.56) Disdain (4.17)		

Continued

TABLE 14-1. Accuracy of Identification of Specific Facial Expressions by German Decoders Within Each Class of Meaning

Class of Meaning		Photograph Number	Percentage of Correct Identification		Type of Decoding Error Made by German Decoders	Percentage of Decoders Correctly Identifying All Facial Expressions Within a Class	
			American	German		American	German
	Stubborn	11	51.55	38.89	Resolute (36.11) Belligerent (25.00)	37.98	22.67
Determination	Resolute	22	67.05	39.72	Belligerent (31.51) Stubborn (28.77)		
	Belligerent	25	44.19	43.84	Stubborn (31.51) Resolute (24.66)		
	Amazement	16	45.74	54.92	Astonishment (28.17) Flabbergasted (16.90)	20.62	16.00
Surprise	Flabbergasted	19	35.66	32.39	Astonishment (46.48) Amazement (21.13)		
	Astonishment	3	32.17	23.29	Flabbergasted (50.69) Amazement (26.03)		
	Disappointment	14	56.59	4.11	Distress (93.15) Pensiveness (2.74)	53.91	2.67
Sadness	Distress	5	72.48	5.48	Disappointment (39.73) Pensiveness (38.36)		
	Pensiveness	7	68.61	60.27	Disappointment (39.73) Distress (0.00)		

tions that the German decoder presumably sees rarely. Facial expressions one rarely sees but which one does wish to acknowledge, should be the expressions decoded at the lowest levels of accuracy. In West Germany, at least, cultural display rules seem to strongly affect sensitivity to specialized kinds of facial emotions.

Rosenthal, Hall, DiMatteo, Rogers, and Archer (1979) have taken cross-cultural comparisons of nonverbal skills a step further by testing the relative sensitivity of different cultural groups to emotional and attitudinal information transmitted through eleven channels and combinations of channels. The channels are: (a) face alone, no voice; (b) body, from neck to knees, no voice; (c) face and body, down to thighs, face–body, no voice; (d) electronic content-filtered voice, no picture; and (e) randomized spliced voice, no picture. The other six are mixed channels, which use some combination of the first five channels. The PONS Test (Profile of Nonverbal Sensitivity) has been administered by Rosenthal and his colleagues to such diverse cultural groups as Australians, Hawaiians, New Guineans, and Israelis.

Interpreting their results, Rosenthal et al. write that the "cultural universality hypothesis, which suggested that all cultures would do equally well due to the universality of nonverbal behavior, can also be considered disproved by the data. There was a wide variation among cross-cultural groups in their levels of accuracy in decoding the PONS film" (p.211). Interestingly, members of those cultures rated *most similar* to Americans had the highest PONS scores, and those rated *least similar* had the lowest PONS scores. Australian aborigines, Australian psychiatric patients, and Papuan New Guinea Civil Service trainees received the lowest ratings on *similarity* to American culture scales, and three of the four lowest scores on the PONS test.

When considered in their broadest perspective, cross-cultural similarities in nonverbal communication seem to be primarily limited to affect displays. Similar facial expressions are used across cultures to communicate such broadly defined emotions as happiness and anger. The frequency with which such basic emotions are displayed facially varies from one culture to another, however, depending on how the emotion is valued in a given culture. The more specialized the emotional meaning that is being communicated, the greater the cross-cultural differences in encoding and decoding accuracy. These striking differences seem to be related directly to cultural display rules which specify what emotions should and should not be expressed.

As we shall see, cross-cultural differences in nonverbal communication seem to become much more pronounced as we move from a consideration of affect displays to emblems, illustrators, and regulators. Cross-cultural differences are also manifested clearly in the contrasting kinds of proxemic and tactile behaviors exhibited in different cultures. Even with these kinds of nonverbal cues, however, we should recognize that the greater the similarity between two or more cultures the greater the probability that the nonverbal communication styles of these cultures will be similar. As

Rosenthal et al. (1979) have speculated, "similarities among verbal languages in a given language group may be paralleled by similarities among the nonverbal behaviors of speakers of those languages. Nonverbal similarities within a language group could include paralanguage, as well as other nonverbal behaviors like facial expressions, body movements, gestures, etc." (p. 223).

Cross-Cultural Differences in Nonverbal Communication

Members of different cultures all experience the same biological drives that motivate them to satisfy their needs to be relieved of tensions associated with hunger, thirst, sexual desire, inadequate protection from the elements, and fatigue. In their attempt to satisfy these needs, members of different cultures all develop rules tht are used in courtship, in marriage, in family relations, in division of labor, and in developing codes of ethics, for example.

Although our drives and needs are biologically determined, the ways in which we satisfy our needs are socially learned. For example, if you grew up in China, you would probably eat bird's nest soup, well-aged eggs, and rice, among other foods. Members of other cultures eat snakes, grasshoppers, and lizards. From the perspective of intercultural communication, life would be much less complicated if all cultures developed identical behavioral responses to satisfy the same needs. They do not.

If one word best describes the communication that is characteristic of specific culture groups, that word would be *different*. This is particularly true when we consider cultures with dissimilar value and belief systems. In fact one culture is differentiated from another on the basis of difference rather than similarity. A culture is defined as *those values, beliefs, customs, rules, laws, and communicative behaviors that can be used to differentiate one societal group from another.*

Cross-cultural differences in nonverbal communication are so numerous as to defy complete description. Suffice it to say that each "culture has its own distinct nonverbal communication system. Children learn this system before they master verbal skills and rely on it as their major vehicle of communication. As they grow up, nonverbal behavior becomes so deeply rooted in their psyche that they engage in it rather unconsciously" (Almaney & Alwan, 1982, p. 16).

Cross-cultural differences in nonverbal communication are manifested in many ways. Gestural *emblems* are perhaps the most important, and because this is true, gestural emblems are highly susceptible to misinterpretation. Similar gestural emblems have different meanings in different cultures; and different emblems are used in different cultures to communicate the same meaning. For instance, in America, the head nod signals agreement, but in Japan it signals acknowledgment of the message being received. In Italy, "up yours" is communicated by the forearm jerk; Americans use the upraised middle finger.

The diversity that is characteristic of cross-cultural gestural communication is documented in the detailed inventory of European gestures, compiled by Morris, Collett, Marsh, and O'Shaughnessy (1979). They found that not only do the same gestures have different meanings in different European cultures, but that some cultures consistently use different gestures to communicate the same meanings. Furthermore, in some cases gestures used to communicate specialized meaning in one European culture are not used at all, or are not recognized, in another European culture.

Consider the case of the *hand purse* gesture, for example: the fingers and thumb of one hand are straightened and brought together in a point facing upwards; held in this posture, the hand may be kept still, or moved slightly. In Italy this gesture means "please be more precise," or "what are you trying to say?"; in Spain the gesture means "good"; in Tunisia the gesture means "slow down"; in Malta the gesture means "You may seem good, but you are really bad." The *hand purse* gesture, interpreted as "please be more precise," is widely understood throughout the Italian-speaking world, but only 3 percent of the persons surveyed in neighboring southern France knew the meaning of this gesture.

Cross-cultural differences abound, not only with regard to the kinds of gestural emblems, illustrators, adaptors, and regulators that are used, and their culture-specific meanings, but also with regard to cross-cultural proxemic norms and behaviors. We know, for example, that Latin Americans prefer closer interaction distances than do North Americans. We know also that distance preferences vary among Latin Americans. Costa Ricans stand closer to those with whom they interact than do Panamanians or Colombians. Costa Ricans also touch others more frequently than Columbians or Panamanians (Shuter, 1976). When the proxemic behaviors of Italians, Germans, and United States citizens are compared, the finding is that Italians interact with others at the closest distances, Germans communicate at greater distances than Italians, and citizens of the United States are most distant in their interaction with others (Shuter, 1977).

Cross-cultural differences in nonverbal communication are not confined to differences in the visual, proxemic, and tactile behaviors that are exhibited in different cultures, however. Hall (1969) emphasizes that different cultures place greater or lesser emphasis on certain sensory modalities that are used to encode and decode nonverbal messages. He stresses that Americans and Arabs live in different sensory worlds much of the time, and, as a result, attach different priorities to certain kinds of nonverbal communication. Thus, "Arabs make more use of olfaction and touch than Americans. They interpret their sensory data differently and combine them in different ways" (p. 3).

A comprehensive description of all of the major differences in nonverbal communication that help to define the nonverbal communication styles of existing cultures is not possible at this time. Knowledge produced by empirical research is not at this time complete enough to warrant such an undertaking. Many of the more salient differences in the nonverbal communication systems of major cultures have been identified, however (LaFrance & Mayo, 1978a, 1978b).

Cross-cultural studies of nonverbal communication have focused in greatest detail on the functions of nonverbal cues in communicating emotions, greetings, status differences, and intimacy. Each of these functions assumes a central role in defining the distinctive nonverbal communication style of a given culture. In order to understand how knowledge of nonverbal communication styles of specific cultures can be used to facilitate more successful intercultural communication, I will compare and contrast the styles of two cultures of particular importance to Americans: the Japanese culture and the Arab culture.

Communicating Nonverbally With the Japanese and the Arabs

The dominant values of a culture reveal what is important to members of a culture (Shuter, 1983). Cultural values are reflected clearly in the nonverbal communication styles that differentiate one culture from another. Familiarity with a culture's communicative style is absolutely necessary if successful intercultural communication is to occur. This is so because the implicit display rules that suggest how one ought not to behave are an integral part of the nonverbal communication style of a culture.

A comparison and contrast of the nonverbal communication styles of the Japanese and Arab cultures should be useful for at least two reasons. In view of current political and economic realities, American contact with members of these cultures is increasing daily. In addition, we possess more in-depth knowledge of the nonverbal communication that is characteristic of these two cultures than of any other non-Western culture.

Because Japan is geographically isolated, there is a high degree of homogeneity and uniformity in Japanese values. Zen Buddism has exerted a considerable influence on the development of Japanese cultural values. Zen Buddism values introspection more than action. Partially as a result of this value orientation, the Japanese attach great importance to the value of silence. Nonobvious, subtle, and even indirect expression is also viewed as a cultural ideal. The inscrutable (expressionless) face of a Japanese is understandable in view of this value orientation. The importance of maintaining self-control in public requires the conscious inhibition of those emotions that might reveal weakness. For example, to openly express an emotion that is as negatively valued as shame is to lose face in Japan. As Morsbach (1973) puts it, "control of an outward show of pleasant emotions in public is also rarely relaxed in Japan. Women tend to covver their mouth while laughing, and males show true merriment (but also true anger) mainly after hours when their culture allows them greater freedom of behavior while drinking alcohol" (p. 269).

In Japan, it is extremely important that one knows one's place (Lebra, 1976). Commitment and loyalty to the work group and family group are stressed, at the expense of developing the uniqueness of the individual. A person's individual accomplishments are much less important than the organization with which one is affiliated (Ouchi, 1981). Interaction in Japan must conform to carefully prescribed "forms." The importance attached to the values of showing respect for superiors and being polite is manifested in cultural rituals that openly emphasize the importance of these two values (Barnlund, 1975b).

Because the Japanese value subtlety, restraint, indirectness in emotional expression, deference to authority, and politeness, it is not surprising that a rather detailed stereotype of the Japanese communicator has developed. Japanese communicators are viewed by Americans, and by themselves, as *silent, reserved, formal, cautious, serious,* and *evasive.* Because of the strength of the stereotype, these stereotypic qualities have become an important part of the "public" communication style of the Japanese (Barnlund, 1975a).

In contrast, many of the values that are dominant in the Arab culture are quite different from Japanese values. In their insightful book, *Communicating with the Arabs* (1982), Almaney and Alwan expahsize that *hospitality, pride, honor, rivalry,* and *revenge* are particularly important values to the Arabs. Whereas the Japanese value a public presentation of self that is emotionally nondisclosing and unexpressive, polite and withdrawn, Arabs attach great value to the uninhibited expression of emotions that exhibit maximum sensory experience and physical contact.

The expansive hospitality of the Arabs has the effect of promoting social interaction rather than inhibiting it. A real or imagined insult to the Arab's well-developed sense of pride and dignity is apt to be met not with silence but with an immediate, visceral reaction. The Arab's preoccupation with honor, rivalry, and revenge means that the public display of emotions is the rule rather than the exception. Almaney and Alwan (1982) note that the Arabs "are plagued by excessive rivalry, bickering, and backbiting," and that "vengeance murder as a means of settling political disputes is still in evidence throughout the Arab world" (p. 96).

Whereas the Japanese covet privacy, Arabs place no value on privacy in public. Pushing and shoving, crowding, and high noise levels are the norm in Arab states. In fact, Arabs are offended by anything less than intimacy of contact while carrying on a conversation. Such conversations characteristically feature "the piercing look of the eyes, the touch of the hand, and the mutual bathing in the warm moist breath during conversation [which] represent stepped-up sensory inputs which many Europeans find unbearably intense" (Hall, 1969, p. 158).

The obvious question at this point is, how do these contrasting values affect the nonverbal communication styles that are characteristic of the Japanese and Arab cultures? That question can perhaps best be answered by a cross-cultural comparison of the use of nonverbal cues in communicating *emotions, greetings, status differences,* and *intimacy.*

Communicating Emotions

The nonverbal communication style of the Japanese is relatively expressionless. Implicit display rules seem to dictate that the impulse to display felt emotions via facial expressions should be inhibited and suppressed. Thus, Ekman, Friesen, and Ellsworth (1972) found that Japanese subjects who were asked to describe stress-inducing films, which they had just watched, displayed fewer negative expressions and more impassive expressions than their American counterparts.

In fact, the Japanese not only inhibit the expression of emotions but they are known to substitute the display of emotions they do *not* feel for those they *do* feel. They do so in order to avoid displaying such socially unacceptable expressions as shame or anger. The use of these techniques of facial management has undoubtedly reinforced the popular view that the Japanese are evasive. Morsbach (1973) notes that although smiling is viewed universally as an indication of joy, it is used in Japan to hide pleasure, anger, and sorrow.

In the Arab culture, in contrast, the open, direct, and uninhibited display of emotion is positively valued. Arabs slurp their coffee to show that they are enjoying it; and belching after a meal is not uncommon—it indicates that the Arab is full. The emotional richness of conversation with Arabs is also reinforced by their frequent use of gestures. Almaney and Alwan (1982) observe that to "tie an Arab's hands while he is speaking is tantamount to tying his tongue."

The importance that Arabs attach to a sensitive reading of, and response to, the emotions of the person with whom they are communicating is perhaps best revealed in their piercing and unremitting eye contact. Arabs carefully monitor dilation and contraction of the pupils of the eyes, because they believe that pupil dilation accurately reflects the level of interest, as well as information about the emotion(s) being experienced. Japanese communicators, in contrast, do not directly monitor the eyes of the person with whom they are communicating; they look instead at their Adam's apple.

Greetings

For the Japanese, social interaction must begin with the bow. The complex set of rules that govern socially acceptable bowing seem to reflect the importance the Japanese attach to civility, politeness, status, and form in interpersonal communication. In Japan, torso angle is very important. Morsbach (1973) writes that "reciprocal bowing is largely determined by rank: the social inferior bows more deeply and the superior decides when to stop bowing" (p. 268). Bowing is such an integral part of greeting behavior in Japan that animated bowing dolls, with tape recorded voices, have been used to welcome customers to department stores.

When a Japanese business person and a foreigner greet each other, a combination of a bow and a handshake may be in order. Circumspection and restraint, with no mutual touching, is expected. Maximum distance should be maintained after the bow-handshake. Native Japanese prefer greater interaction distances than either Americans or Hawaii Japanese (Engebretson & Fullmer, 1970). Conversation should be kept to a minimum, and business cards should be exchanged.

The nonverbal communication style employed to greet someone in the Arab culture is quite different. Effusive greetings are expected. Pleasantries are encouraged. Considerable verbalization, in the form of "How is the family?," "We pray that you are well," and "We are honored by your presence," is expected. Vigorous handshaking is used in conjunction with the other nonverbal greeting behaviors, to "size up" the person being greeted (Almaney & Alwan, 1982).

The Arab also likes to get close enough to the person being greeted to inhale their body aromas. We know that body scent frequently reveals emotional states, therefore this culture-specific greeting behavior certainly seems to be a useful way of obtaining highly personal information. The intimate and physically involving nature of Arab greeting behavior is reinforced by the lavish hospitality that is typically exhibited if the Arab is the host.

Status Differences

The hierarchical nature of both the Japanese and Arab cultures means that both rank and status must be respected. Although both cultures profess to honor women, they are treated as status inferiors. Business is man's work and the family is woman's work. In Japan, a woman is expected to maintain a proper distance behind her spouse—usually two steps behind. In Arab countries, women are not permitted to drive or to work. They are expected to keep their bodies covered, and when business associates visit the home, they are to be seen but not heard.

In Japan, one's status is perhaps reflected most clearly in the way one bows, and in the artifacts that one exhibits. Badges, costumes, and uniforms assume particular importance in status-conscious Japan because they quite clearly reveal one's status. There are, literally, costumes for hiking, biking, and striking. The uniform and costume serve a central role in establishing and maintaining one's status, and in signaling the appropriate type of interaction between two people.

The business card, or *meishi*, also is used to signal rank. In view of the fact that one's organization is the single most important determinant of status in Japan, one's organization appears first on one's business card, followed by one's position in the organization, academic degree (if one has one), family name, first name, and address (Lebra, 1976; Morsbach, 1973).

Status distinctions are communicated in less formalized and ritualized ways in the Arab culture. In the Arab culture, one's status is determined largely by the nature and magnitude of one's possessions rather than by the rank of the organization with which one is affiliated. Arabs believe that it is better to give than to receive. As a result, the foreign visitor should be careful about expressing admiration of possessions in the home of an Arab. The Arab will feel duty-bound to give the possession to the visitor, as a gift. Although formalized manifestations of status differences are relatively rare in Arab nations, the high status accorded to older people and persons of authority is reflected in a law that forbids smoking in their presence.

Intimacy

The nonverbal communication style of the Japanese clearly prohibits intimacy in public. The characteristic lack of expression, when combined with the Japanese sense of reserve, means that the Japanese expect communication in public to be formal and reserved. Of course, ritualized bowing, costumes that emphasize status differences, and the value placed on silence and subtle expression all militate against the spontaneity which usually promotes intimate interaction in public.

Barnlund (1975a) emphasizes that in Japan, physical intimacy communicated via touch drops off sharply after childhood. Physical inaccessibility because of maximum communicating distances, and lack of touching reveal the negative value the Japanese place on intimate interaction in public. In fact, many "observers have noted the serious composure, lack of facial expression, and gestural restraint of the Japanese. Physical intimacies are avoided and even reinforcing gestures rarely accompany remarks" (p. 109).

In the Arab culture, in contrast, a lack of physical contact and involvement is considered *aberrant*. Arabs frequently communicate with strangers at distances as close as two feet. They encourage reciprocal touching, particularly in greetings, and they like to be breathed on, as well as to breathe on others. The late President Anwar Sadat of Egypt, for example, often placed a hand on the knee of the person with whom he was conversing. And some eyebrows have apparently been raised—at dinners for international diplomats—by the propensity of representatives of Arab states to touch the person with whom they are communicating.

Because Arabs do not value or practice privacy in public, it is not surprising that they are emotionally self-disclosing, physically expressive, and uninhibited. The public presentation of self in the Arab countries places a high value on two types of nonverbal communication that play a central role in the development of intimate relationships: touch and olfaction.

Guidelines for More Successful Intercultural Communication

Successful intercultural communication requires that we become thoroughly familiar with a communication style that may be quite different in important respects from the communication style that is dominant within our own culture. In his illuminating book, *Counseling the Culturally Different* (1981), Sue emphasizes that the culturally skilled counselor is one who moves from being unaware to being aware of and sensitive to his or her "own cultural baggage." This means that we must begin by rejecting the ethnocentric view that the communication style of our own culture is intrinsically superior.

If we are to succeed in our attempts to communicate with members of another culture, we must try to become aware of which communicative behaviors are, and which are not, acceptable in that culture. We can attain this level of awareness by becoming as familiar as possible with the distinctive features of the nonverbal style of the culture in which we seek to communicate.

Successful intercultural communication, requires that we develop skills as impression managers. In a foreign culture, the impression manager should seek to do at least two things. The impression manager should try to associate himself or herself with images that are positively valued, and try to dissociate himself or herself from images that are negatively valued in the culture where communication occurs. Because more weight is usually given to negative than to positive information, it is particularly important that we *avoid* behaving in ways that are considered inappropriate or deviant.

A careful consideration of the information presented in this chapter suggests that there are at least nine guidelines that can be used to facilitate more successful intercultural communication. Each guideline draws attention to a different type of display rule regarding either the appropriateness or inappropriateness of a given type of nonverbal behavior.

Guideline #1: Familiarize yourself with the facial expressions of the culture to determine whether the public display of emotions is encouraged or discouraged; determine which kinds of emotions are positvely and negatively valued; and make the necessary adjustment in your own facial displays of emotion.

Guideline #2: Learn and follow the rules that govern proper form and interaction sequence for greeting behaviors, with an emphasis on the intricacies of cultural rituals.

Guideline #3: Become familiar with the types of status distinctions that must be acknowledged, and use culturally approved nonverbal behaviors for acknowledging such status distinctions.

Guideline #4: Determine the degree of physical contact, involvement, and accessibility that is expected in public, and act accordingly.

Guideline #5: Try to become sensitive to culture-specific touching, proxemic, and eye-behavior norms; in order to avoid the violation of cultural norms and expectations.

Guideline #6:   Become familiar with the nonverbal regulators that should and should not be used in culturally acceptable conversational management.

Guideline #7:   Identify the most important nonverbal behaviors used in cultural ritual so that you may, if necessary, modify your own nonverbal behaviors as a way of identifying with important cultural values.

Guideline #8:   Systematically identify, itemize, and avoid the use of culture-specific emblems that communicate meanings that are apt to be interpreted as an affront or as an insult.

Guideline #9:   Determine the kind of clothing and personal artifacts that are and are not compatible with cultural conventions.

Summary

Successful intercultural communication requires that a visitor to a foreign country acquire an in-depth familiarity with the nonverbal communication style of the culture of that country. This is necessary because the non-verbal communication style of a culture is defined by nonverbal behaviors that contain sets of implicit rules or commands. These implicit display rules, in turn, specify what kinds of communication are and are not appropriate.

Cross-cultural similarities in nonverbal communication are most evident in the use of facial expressions, which communicate a limited number of basic emotions. Cross-cultural differences abound. These differences are strongly reflected in a great variety of gestural emblems that communicate culture-specific meanings and, as a result, are highly susceptible to misinterpretation by the foreigner. Proxemic, tactile, and eye behaviors also tend to be distinctively different in cultures with dissimilar value orientations.

In order to demonstrate how knowledge of the nonverbal communication style of specific cultures can be used to facilitate more successful communication, the Japanese and Arab cultures are compared and contrasted in this chapter. The point is made that important differences in the nonverbal styles of the two cultures are manifested most clearly in the communication of emotions, greetings, status differences, and intimacy.

Finally, a set of nine guidelines is included, which can be used to facilitate more successful intercultural communication. These guidelines can be used to become aware of the specific kinds of communicative behaviors that are and are not acceptable in a foreign culture of importance to us. Such awareness is necessary if we are to engage in intercultural communication that reflects a knowledge of and a desire to adapt to the distinctive communication style of a particular culture.

References

Almaney, A. J., & Alwan, A. J. (1982). *Communicating with the Arabs: A handbook for the business executive.* Prospect Heights, IL: Waveland Press.

Barnlund, D. C. (1975a). *Public and private self in Japan and the United States: Communicative styles of two cultures.* Tokyo, Japan: The Simul Press.

Barnlund, D. C. (1975b). Communicative styles in two cultures: Japan and the United States. In A. Kendon, R. M. Harris & M. R. Keys (Eds.). *Organization of behaviour in face-to-face interaction.* The Hague, The Netherlands: Mouton.

Condon, J. C., & Yousef, F. (1975). *An introduction to intercultural communication.* Indianapolis: Bobbs.

Darwin, C. (1872). *The expression of emotion in man and animals.* London: J. Murray. Reprint, 1965, Chicago: University of Chicago Press.

Eibl-Eibesfeldt, I. (1972). Similarities and differences between cultures in expressive movements. In R. A. Hinde (Ed.). *Non-verbal communication.* Cambridge, MA: Cambridge University Press.

Ekman, P., & Friesen, W. V. (1975) *Unmasking the face.* Englewood Cliffs, NJ: Prentice-Hall.

Ekman, P., Friesen, W. V., & Ellsworth, P. (1972). *Emotion in the human face.* New York: Pergamon.

Engebretson, D. E., & Fullmer, D. (1970). Cross-cultural differences in territoriality: Interaction distances of native Japanese, Hawaii Japanese, and American caucasians. *Journal of Cross-Cultural Psychology, 1,* 261–269.

Hall, E. T. (1969). *The hidden dimension.* Garden City, NY: Anchor.

Izard, C. E. (1971). *The face of emotion.* New York: Appleton.

Kilbride, J. E., & Yarczower, M. (1980). Recognition and imitation of facial expressions: A cross-cultural comparison between Zambia and the United States. *Journal of Cross-Cultural Psychology, 11,* 282.

LaFrance, M., & Mayo, C. (1978a). *Moving bodies: Nonverbal communication in social relationships.* Monterey, CA: Brooks/Cole.

LaFrance, M., & Mayo, C. (1978b) Cultural aspects of nonverbal communication. *International Journal of Intercultural Relations, 2,* 1978b, 71–89.

Leathers, D. G., & McGuire, M. (1983, November). Testing the comparative sensitivity of German and American decoders to specific kinds of facial meaning. Paper presented on program of the Commission on International and Intercultural Communication at annual convention of the Speech Communication Association, Washington, D.C.

Lebra, T. S. (1976). *Japanese patterns of behavior.* Honolulu: The University Press of Hawaii.

Morris, D., Collett, P., Marsh, P., & O'Shaughnessy, M. (1979). *Gestures: Their origins and distribution.* New York: Stein & Day.

Morsbach, H. (1973). Aspects of nonverbal communication in Japan. *The Journal of Nervous and Mental Disease, 157,* 262–277.

Ouchi, W. (1981). *Theory Z: How American business can meet the Japanese challenge.* Reading, MA: Addison-Wesley.

Rosenthal, R., Hall, J. A., DiMatteo, M. R., Rogers, P. L., & Archer, D. (1979). *Sensitivity to nonverbal communication: THE PONS TEST.* Baltimore: The Johns Hopkins University Press.

Shuter, R. (1976) Proxemics and tactility in Latin America. *Journal of Communication, 26,* 46–52.

Shuter, R. (1977). A field study of nonverbal communication in Germany, Italy and the United States. *Communication Monographs, 44,* 298–305.

Shuter, R. (1983).Values and communication: Seeing the forest through the trees. Unpublished paper.

Sue, D. W. (1981). *Counseling the culturally different.* New York: Wiley.

Sweeney, M. A., Cottle, W. C., & Kobayashi, M. J. (1980). Nonverbal communication: A cross-cultural comparison of American and Japanese counseling students. *Journal of Counseling Psychology, 27,* 154.

CHAPTER FIFTEEN

The Communicative Impact of Microenvironmental Variables

In the final section of this book, we have been examining the role of nonverbal behaviors in such important contexts (applied settings) as the job interview the counseling interview, and intercultural communication. This concluding chapter focuses on the impact of microenvironmental variables on communication in the workplace, where we interact with others.

Recently, social scientists have become increasingly interested in the impact of environments, and their distinctive physical features, on our perceptions, attitudes, and behaviors. Macroenvironment and microenvironment both function as powerful mediums of communication. Urban planners have established that the affective tone of our perceptions is strongly influenced by such features of our macroenvironment as the physical dimensions of streets, paths, and districts (Lynch, 1960). Similarly, communication researchers have demonstrated that spatial relationships in the microenvironment may exert a controlling influence on both the quality and the quantity of communicative interaction (Burgoon, 1978).

Sommer (1969) emphasizes the need to know more about the impact of microenvironments on individuals who engage in face-to-face interaction within their confines when he writes that:

> Knowledge about man's immediate environment, the hollows within his shelters that he calls offices, classrooms, corridors, and hospital wards, is as important as knowledge about outer space or undersea life . . . With or without explicit recognition of the fact, designers are shaping people as well as buildings. (p. vii)

267

To the extent that we can exercise control over the physical features of our microenvironments, we may be forced to make a choice between environments that are *arousing* or *pleasant*. Mehrabian (1976) maintains that *high-load environments* are emotionally arousing. They are arousing because their physical features may force individuals who work in these environments to process much information, or cope with many microenvironmental stimuli which are not directly relevant to the work assignment. For example, a business office that features an "open plan," with red wallpaper, no partitions to separate the desks of the occupants, high density, and excessive noise levels, is a high-load environment.

In contrast, a private business office, with walls and a door, subdued wall colors and lighting, and carpeting to control or eliminate disruptive noises, is a *low-load environment*. Although the high-load environment is emotionally arousing and promotes communicative interaction, it may be unpleasant because the collective impact of the microenvironmental stimuli produces fatigue. In contrast, the low-load environment is often perceived as pleasant because one does not have to cope with a multitude of arousing microenvironmental stimuli. Nevertheless, low-load environments may not be sufficiently arousing for individuals who work in them, because they may not facilitate either productivity or effective communicative interaction with one's colleagues.

As we shall see, the physical features of microenvironments, such as the places where we work, *affect not only our own perceptions but the perceptions of individuals we encounter in these environments.* This is particularly true in a workplace such as a private office. To the extent that we can control such variables as the type and placement of furniture we put in our personal office, we can exert a profound influence on the impression we make. In fact, we now know that the decorative items we choose to put in our offices can markedly affect the defining elements of the image that we project to others.

Although we interact with other persons in various work environments, three kinds of workplaces will receive close scrutiny. The classroom, the conference room, and the office seem particularly important for at least two reasons. Most of us will spend a high proportion of our working hours in these types of workplaces. Moreover, our ability to exercise effective conscious control over selected physical features of such environments is greater than in other workplaces, such as a factory or a prison. As we shall see, we can markedly affect the appearance of these three kinds of microenvironments by the decisions we make.

The Classroom Environment

Of the three kinds of workplaces, the classroom represents the microenvironment that is least susceptible to change. This is true in large part because of an apparent conflict between the objectives of administrators on the one hand and students and teachers on the other hand. To a considerable degree, administrators are committed to the development of a distraction-free classroom environment, one that minimizes student interaction and affective response while maximizing the potential to regulate and control students' behaviors. In contrast, students and teachers prefer a classroom environment that minimizes the use of control mechanisms while maximizing opportunities for uninhibited communicative interaction.

Administrators who are committed to the traditional classroom environment prefer fixed, straight-row seating, high density, and drab, institutional colors. Experimental seating arrangements and emotionally arousing colors are thought to produce a level of stimulation for the student which is incompatible with effective discipline. Sommer (1974) describes this environmental perspective graphically when he writes that:

> *The assumption is made that learning can take place best in distraction-free, lockable cells. Human contact in the form of casual conversation ("milling around") is a threat to order and a distraction to the assembly line . . . A humane classroom can represent a refuge in a hard building or a base camp out of which efforts to humanize the environment can gradually radiate through the austere hallways, asphalt yards, workshops, and locked offices. (p. 83).*

The creation of a more humane classroom will not be easily achieved. Administrators typically have almost complete control over such important microenvironmental variables as the size of the classroom, the size of the class, and the type of seating. There are increasing indications, however, that some administrators are beginning to work collaboratively with teachers and students to modify physical features of traditional classrooms that inhibit successful communication and learning. To be successful, such efforts must, at minimum, consider the perceptual and behavioral impact of *room size, class size, seating arrangement and choice, teachers' spatial orientations, and the appearance of the classroom.*

Classroom size is an important variable. Classroom size clearly determines the actual amount of space available for a given student. Students have well-developed preferences as to the amount of usable space that is designated as theirs. Expressed in square feet of space available to each student, ideal personal space for a lecture hall is 19 to 27 feet, for a study hall, 20 to 29 feet, for a library, 24 to 31 feet, and for a discussion group, 31 to 43 feet (Weldon, Loewy, Winer, & Elkin, 1981).

In a classroom, actual space is less important than perceived space, however. Inadequate space usually results in the feeling of being crowded. The result, frequently, is that students have difficulty in maintaining attention, task performance decreases, and aggressive behavior increases. The feeling of being crowded usually occurs when students feel that their personal space and their privacy are being violated by other students. High school students in particular seem increasingly inclined to exhibit aggressive behavior; it therefore seems important that their expectations regarding the "ideal" amount of space available to them in the classroom not be frustrated.

In fact, a number of low-cost steps may be taken in the high-density classroom to moderate the students' perception that they are being crowded. Such steps include the use of room partitions, decreasing the number of entrances, choosing rectangular over square classroom designs, promoting acquaintance and mutual cooperation among students, and maintaining a comfortable room temperature (Weldon et al., 1981).

The question of classroom size seems to be far from simple, however. Bigger is not necessarily better. Indeed, an unlimited amount of classroom space may result in low levels of student arousal. *Moderate density seems to represent a desirable compromise between conditions of either low-density or high-density seating.* Moderate density seems to promote student arousal that results in striking improvement in reading speed and comprehension, with only a slight decrease in the ability to acquire and organize new material. High density is another matter. Under conditions of high density, students find it difficult, if not impossible, to assimilate and organize new material, even though their reading speed and comprehension may increase (Weldon et al., 1981).

Class size has a pronounced impact on the amount of student participation. Sommer (1974) has found that in a small class of 6 to 20, students participate over twice as much as in a class of medium (21 to 50 students) or large (over 50 students) size. Even in small classes, however, students participate only 12 percent of the time during a class hour. If student participation and involvement represent desired educational objectives, the peril of ever-increasing class sizes should be carefully considered.

The impact of varying *seating arrangements* on student-teacher interaction is not so well-documented. In one experiment Sommer (1974) actually had a colleague enter 25 classrooms and change chairs from straight-row seating to a circular arrangement. However, the attachment to the straight-row was so strong that chairs had been rearranged to straight-row seating in 20 of the 25 classrooms before the classes began; in many cases the students themselves returned the chairs to a straight-row arrangement.

Although students have come to expect straight-row seats that are bolted to the floor, they have a negative attitudinal response to this type of seating arrangement. For example, Rubin (1972) found that high-IQ students prefer circular and horseshoe seating arrangements, and low-IQ students prefer a flexible seating arrangement, which allows the teacher to walk about in their midst. Students almost uniformly report a negative reaction to straight-row seating. They believe that this type of seating arrangement inhibits student participation and interaction with the teacher. Moreover, straight-row seating reinforces the unhealthy perception on the part of the students that this seating arrangement is being used primarily to enhance the teacher's ability to regulate and control their behavior.

Although students can rarely exercise control over such variables as room size, class size, or seating arrangement, *they can usually decide where they will sit.* A number of studies have consistently shown that students who sit closest to the teacher, and who have the greatest opportunity for eye contact with the teacher participate most and receive the highest grades. The students who choose the most central seating, closest to the front, consistently perform better (Levine, O'Neal, Garwood, & McDonald, 1980; Sommer, 1974; Wulf, 1977).

Students with low grade-point-averages will not necessarily perform better if they choose front and center seating, however. Also, we should not assume that students with high GPA's will perform more poorly if they are given seats on the periphery or in the back of the classroom. In fact, students who have been arbitrarily assigned to front and center seating have not received better grades than students assigned to seats in the rear. However, arbitrary assignment to seating in front of the classroom does positively affect participation. Whether front and center seating is voluntary or involuntary, *students participate more in this seating zone* (Levine et al., 1980).

A student who is considering the practical implications of seating choice may feel a little like the person who identified himself as an Agnostic Christian. He said he "really did not believe there was a God, but if there was a God he needed some measure of protection." Choosing front and center seating also gives the student some measure of protection. This seating choice may not assure higher grades but it will ensure greater opportunities to participate and to reinforce the impression of high interest.

Aside from the control they exercise over the seating arrangement, teachers can exert a major impact on the classroom environment by the *spatial orientation* they assume vis-à-vis their students. Hesler (1972) examined the perceptual impact of six types of spatial orientations by teachers: (a) *BL*—teacher in front of blackboard or front wall of classroom; (b) *DK*—teacher sitting on, beside, or behind desk; (c) *T*—teacher in front of desk; (d) *S*—teacher positioned along the side seats or along side wall; (e) *BK*—teacher in back of room; and (f) *AM*—teacher among students.

Teachers who sat on, beside, or in back of their desk were seen as *isolated from the students,* and *less warm, friendly,* and *effective* than teachers who stood in front of their desk. So long as their proxemic behavior was deemed appropriate by the students, the teacher was consistently perceived as warmer as he or she moved closer to them. This research supports the conventional wisdom that *the teacher who wishes to cultivate an image of a warm, caring, and emotionally sensitive individual must seek to interact at the closest possible distance with students, but should not violate their personal space or trigger the uncomfortable feeling of being crowded.*

In his provocative essay on an ecological model of classrooms, Doyle (1977) takes a position that seems to be counterintuitive. He maintains that the teacher who is to experience "managerial success" must concentrate not on the stimualtion of affective responses from a limited number of students but must seek to exercise prudent *control* over the activities of all of the students, while including as many students as possible in every classroom activity. These objectives lead him to the novel recommendation that a teacher should actually *increase* the distance between himself or herself and the student with whom he or she is interacting. By increasing interaction distance with the individual student, a greater number of students are supposedly brought within the teacher's conscious level of awareness. The teacher is also advised by Doyle not to maintain direct eye contact with the student who is interacting with the teacher, but to scan wider sections of the classroom, in order to visually involve the greatest number of students possible.

Whether one accepts Doyle's interesting position or not, it highlights a trade-off that teachers must consider. Teachers who give high priority to projecting a favorable image will recognize that the more proximate their interaction with students the better liked they are apt to be. However, as teachers' proximity to individual students increases, their ability to exercise effective control and discipline over the larger number of students is likely to decrease.

Doyle (1977) highlights the difficult choice the teacher must make in choosing a proximate or distant spatial orientation vis-à-vis students. He writes that, with "regard to distance and eye contact, at least, the affective and regulatory uses of nonverbal behavior appear incompatible" (p. 186). To literally maintain one's distance from one's students enhances the teacher's ability to control the students, but at a considerable sacrifice in terms of the type and intensity of students' emotional reponses to the teacher.

The precise effects of *modifying the appearance of classrooms* are not presently known. We have little empirical evidence to bring to bear on this subject because administrators are generally resistant to modifying the appearance of classrooms, which would have to be done if the impact on students' attitudes, communicative behavior, and, ultimately, their learning were to be carefully measured. Uniformity in the appearance of classrooms is justified on two bases: it is democratic (pictures or unusual wall colors might offend some students), and because a uniform and dull appearance enhances the teachers' ability to *control* the behavior of the students.

Sommer (1974), a pioneer in examining the potentially beneficial effects of making the traditional classroom less drab and sterile, identifies the paradoxical nature of the microenvironmental problem when he writes:

> *The arguments against decorations are the precepts of hard architecture. One familiar refrain is that decoration would distract people from whatever they are doing. The fact that this principle never prevails at the higher echelons of the organization is an interesting paradox. (p. 96)*

Sommer goes on to point out that school administrators, such as principals, show no reluctance to decorate the walls of their own offices with pictures and art objects, but they fear the behavioral consequences of similar decorative objects in the classrooms they control.

Sommer actually did modify the appearance of one classroom and found that the impact was highly beneficial. Decorations included three abstract yarn designs on the back wall, two pictures hung on the side wall, and two posters on the front wall. The bulletin board was decorated with flower stickers, a jar of paper flowers was placed on the front table, and a blue fish mobile with three Gods-Eyes was attached to a wall above the windows.

Reactions of students and faculty to the modified classroom was uniformly positive. Those surveyed now *viewed the classroom as pleasant, comfortable, cheerful, and relaxing without being distracting.* In fact, there is reason to believe that students will perform better in such an environment so long as the appearance of the room is not overly arousing, does not reinforce students' perceptions of being crowded, and so long as the students are not working on a highly complex task.

Mehrabian (1976) also maintains that there is a strong need to modify the appearance of the traditional classroom. Because they appear sterile and drab, classrooms typically represent a microenvironment that is both *nonarousing* and *unpleasant* to the student. Aside from cost considerations, Mehrabian contends that school administrators remain committed to the drab classroom because they fear that the introduction of arousing, pleasant stimuli is potentially dangerous. If contrasting wall colors, plants, and paintings were used, these might arouse and stimulate students to such a degree that teachers would no longer be able to exercise the control necessary for effective discipline.

There can be little doubt that the classroom environment can be made more arousing and pleasant for the student by the use of innovative seating arrangements, more brightly colored walls and carpets, and by the use of decorative items, such as those already identified. Because such modifications in classroom appearance are known to positively affect students' attitudes about each other, the teacher, and the school, they would seem well worth experimenting with, in many cases.

Mehrabian (1976) does caution, however, that the appearance of the classroom must be adapted to the type of learning activity being undertaken by the students. He argues that students and teachers who are performing relatively undemanding and unpleasant tasks should be assigned to high-load, arousing classrooms. In contrast, "at times during the day when students and teachers are performing complex, unusual tasks, they should be assigned rooms that are very pleasant but low-load" (p. 158).

The Conference Room Environment

A conference room represents a particularly important type of microenvironment. Many physical features of the conference room can affect the quality and quantity of communicative interaction, the participants's perceptions of each other, and the task performance of a given group. Variables such as room size, room decorations, room color, and even temperature regulation are of course potentially important. Variables such as these are treated elsewhere, therefore they will not be treated separately here. The three microenvironmental variables of greatest importance in the conference room are *seating choice, table configuration,* and *communication networks.*

Seating position at a conference table is of course sometimes determined by status considerations, or by habit. When one has freedom of choice in seating position, the communicative implications should be carefully considered, however. The man who sits at the head of a rectangular table significantly increases his chances of being perceived as the leader. As we saw in Chapter 13, males but not females markedly increase the probability that they will be perceived as a leader simply by virtue of sitting at the head of the table. Because women are stereotyped as followers rather than leaders, they are not afforded this same perceptual advantage. Individuals who choose a seat along the sides of a table not only decrease their chances of being perceived as a leader, but they are apt to be perceived as individuals with lower status and less self-confidence.

Seating position affects not only perceptions of leadership potential but actual leadership emergence in the small group. Strodbeck and Hook (1961) found that a person who chose to sit at the end of a rectangular table was elected jury foreman more often than jury members sitting in the other ten positions. Because the jury foreman is selected before any communicative interaction occurs, the impact of seating choice on leadership emergence is clearly very strong.

Leadership emergence as a result of seating position seems to be jointly determined by the advantages central seating gives a person in controlling communicative interaction and in maintaining direct visual accessibility to the greatest number of discussants. For example, Howells and Becker (1962) conducted an experiment in which five group members sat at a rectangular table, two on one side and three on the other. The leaders who emerged in the five-member groups (by a ratio of more than 2 to 1) were on the two-member side. The greater likelihood that they would emerge as leaders on the two-member side was attributed to the fact that they had visual access to a majority of the group (three), but the people on the three-member side had visual access to only two. Because discussion members seated at the side of rectangular tables have limited visual access to a limited number of group members, it is not surprising that they emerge as leaders much less frequently than discussants seated at the ends of the table.

A field study by Heckel (1973) suggests that individuals who wish to emerge as leaders not only select the central seating position in the conference room but also do so at such nontask functions as meals. And persons who do *not* wish to be chosen as leaders characteristically sit at the side of the table when eating meals. In short, seating choice at a conference table determines to a large degree whether a person will be a dominant figure or a member of the supporting cast in discussions which ensue. *Given the important impression-management and control functions of eye behaviors, it is not surprising that individuals who have limited visual access to other group members are in disproportionate numbers relegated to a supporting role.*

Seating position also has a strong impact on how powerful or influential one is judged to be by other group members. Korda (1975) maintains that in "meetings where people are seated around a table, whatever its shape, the order of power is almost always clockwise, beginning with what would be the number "12" on a clock face, and with power diminishing as it moves around past positions at three o'clock, six o'clock, nine o'clock, etc." (p. 101). If you accept Korda's theory, the most powerful person at a conference table sits at the twelve o'clock position and the least powerful person sits at the eleven o'clock position.

Not everyone agrees of course that power moves clockwise around a conference table by virtue of seating positon. For example, one study (Green, 1975) shows that the amount of the discussants' participation time increases *both* when they choose a seat closer to the leader and when their angle of visual access to the chairperson's line of sight is narrower relative to other discussion members. In Green's study, the important consideration was not whether one sits to the right or left of the centrally seated leader, but how immediate one's visual access to that leader.

Table configuration or *shape* is also an important variable in the conference room. In 1959, for example, the United States, the Soviet Union, France, and Great Britain were meeting in Geneva to discuss the future of Berlin. Before the talks began, a dispute arose over table shape. The three Western powers wanted a square table, which would have given them a three-to-one advantage in negotiating posture, from a perceptual perspective. Not surprisingly, the Soviet Union proposed a round conference table, in an attempt to neutralize the three-to-one-ratio (Sommer, 1969).

Lecuyer (1976) examined the differences between problem-solving groups seated at either round or rectangular tables, and the effect on leadership. He found that a *randomly appointed leader was more successful when a rectangular table was used.* The appointed leader at a circular table had more difficulty controlling the flow of the discussion; discussants seated around the circular table more tenaciously supported their own proposed solutions than those seated at the rectangular table. Because the leader at the circular table loses the potential for control and superiority of status which is associated with central seating at a rectangular table, the negative impact of the circular table seems predictable.

Patterson, Kelly, Kondracki, & Wulf (1979) compared the impact of circular versus L-shaped seating arrangements. Both *quality and amount of communicative interaction deteriorated with the L-shaped seating arrangement.* Discussants were less involved and less comfortable; they exhibited longer pauses in their conversations, displayed more self-manipulative adaptor gestures, and fidgeted more, by way of postural shifts. The negative impact of L-shaped seating on communicative interaction may be attributed in part to the fact that communication was made more difficult because discussants had much more limited visual access to each other than in the circular seating arrangement.

Communication networks consist of the actual paths or channels used by group members to transmit information to one another. In practice, both seating choice and configuration of the conference table are apt to

FIGURE 15.1   COMMUNICATION NETWORKS

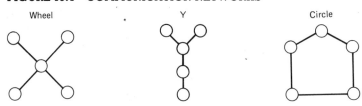

determine the kind of communication network used most frequently. Some discussants may of course choose not to participate, with a consequent impact on the types of communication networks that emerge.

Among the more common communication networks that have been experimentally manipulated in group research are the *wheel* (see Figure 15.1) a *Y*, and a *circle*. The *Y* communication network is used to illustrate a highly centralized type of leadership and the circle is associated with a highly decentralized type of leadership.

In his masterful summary of research on seating arrangements in small groups, and the resultant communication networks that emerge from these seating arrangements, Shaw (1981) provides four generalizations of practical importance: (a) a leader is more likely to emerge in a centralized communication network than in a decenttralized network; (b) group members have higher morale in decentralized than in centralized communication networks; (c) decentralized communication networks are most efficient when groups must solve complex problems, but a centralized network is most efficient when the group must solve simple problems; and (d) centralized communication networks are more likely to result in a work overload for the leader than decentralized communication networks.

From the perspective of communication networks, centralization is desirable for the person who wishes to emerge as leader and retain effective control. Centralization is also desirable when group tasks are relatively simple and when decisions must be made during moments of crisis. When complex tasks are considered and a premium is placed on harmonious interpersonal relationships, the decentralized communication network is preferable.

The Office Environment

With the possible exception of the family home, the office in which we work is the most important microenvironment. The design and physical features of our office are known to strongly affect our attitudes, the quality and quantity of our communication with colleagues, and our productivity. As we shall see, many features of our office have been determined not by us but by our superiors. For example, the size of our office, furniture and carpeting, lighting, and noise control are all important variables which we may not be able to control directly (Cohen & Cohen, 1983).

In the past few years the open-office plan has received much favorable publicity. *Open offices* contain no floor-to-ceiling walls. Panels that do not extend to the ceiling, are used to define the macro-, midi-, and mini-environments in which people interact. Permanent walls and corridors are eliminated. The avowed objective of the open-office plan is to facilitate communication and interaction among employees while increasing employee satisfaction and motivation. Because the open-office plan de-emphasizes depersonalized contacts among employees, proponents of this plan maintain that it also promotes cooperation and friendship formation (Becker, 1981).

In practice, the behavioral impact of the open-office plan seems much less desirable than its supporters would have us believe. In part because employees feel that their privacy is being invaded and that they experience an uncomfortable sensation of crowding, open offices have been found to result in a decrease in employee satisfaction and motivation. In fact, a number of employees who use open offices have been so affected by perceived increases in noise level, visual distractions, and an accompanying loss of privacy, that they report a loss in efficiency (Becker, 1981).

Mehrabian (1976) contends that *a compromise that embodies some of the physical features of the open and the closed office is the most desirable, in terms of its attitudinal and behavioral impact on the occupants of the office.* He maintains that, "since lower-echelon employees who are assigned offices need privacy and low-load settings for occasions when they perform loaded tasks, such offices should have doors. Doorless cubicles do not afford protection from extraneous environmental stimuli—people walking by, a conversation down the hall, and so on—but do on the other hand tend to isolate workers from one another" (p. 145). An employee with a door to his or her office can enjoy privacy when needed, by closing it, and can have stimulation by leaving the door open.

Occupants of open offices have virtually no control over the variables that affect their perceptions of their own office, nor of the perceptions of persons who interact with them in their office. Their inability to exercise conscious control over many variables—which might give a closed or private office a distinctive ambience—may account in large part for employee's negative reaction to the open-office plan. Even those who have their own enclosed office may of course encounter frustrations, because they cannot control such factors as office location, size, and configuration. They may not even have the authority to decide on the colors of the walls. This would be an unfortunate restriction because the colors of walls are known to have a considerable impact on the moods of the occupant of an office (Bellizzi, Crowley, & Hasty, 1983).

Many important intra-office variables are subject to the effective conscious control of the occupant of a private office, however. These intra-office variables serve an important role in shaping the image projected by the office occupant, and in affecting the nature of the communication that occurs in the private office. Of particular importance are *seating* and *spatial arrangements, furniture arrangement,* and *decorative objects.*

Seating and Spatial Arrangements

Where the occupant of an office chooses to sit will probably determine whether the occupant wishes to dominate a conversation or share control of it with other individuals. Where one sits may also indicate whether the office occupant is a superior. You will recall that J. Edgar Hoover sat at a large, elevated desk, and his visitors had to sit below him, at a small table to his right. Nelson Rockefeller went even further to try to assure dominance and perceptions of high power in his office. At times, he ascended a ladder, which folded out of a desk drawer, and addressed office visitors from the top of his desk.

Korda (1975) maintains that it is much more difficult to do business with, and communicate effectively, with an office occupant who sits behind his or her desk. He advocates a variety of stratagems to try to lure a person out from behind a desk. He writes that, if you can not get a person to come out from behind a desk, you can "put your hat or briefcase on the desk if you want to make them nervous. Note that people with old-fashioned desks that serve as barriers almost always leave them to say 'yes,' and sit behind them to say 'no.' Once they have taken refuge behind five-hundredweight of mahogany, you can't argue with them." (p. 177).

If you wish to stimulate communication with others in your office, and to have them perceive themselves as your status equal, you must take pains to sit as close to them as proxemic norms allow. Two studies by Sommer (1961 and 1962) support the conclusion that individuals prefer to sit where they have the greatest visual accessibility to those with whom they interact. Although individuals prefer to be able to face you when interacting with you in a business situation, they will often choose to sit at your side—perhaps on an available sofa—if face-to-face seating would require a separation of over five feet.

Researchers have also established that where an individual sits has a measurable impact on the amount of communication that occurs, and on how individuals perceive someone who selects a certain seat. Siting around a table, as opposed to sitting in chairs along walls, has been found to increase interaction by almost 100 percent (Sommer & Ross, 1958). Finally, Pelligrini (1971) has found that a person who elects to sit at the head of a table, as opposed to other positions, will be perceived as significantly more *talkative, persuasive, dominant, self-confident,* and *intelligent.*

Furniture Arrangement

The business office has been the scene of a number of studies which examine the impact of furniture arrangement on the ways individuals perceive office occupants. Desk placement has been the variable most often manipulated. Results from one study (White, 1953) indicated that patients in a doctor's office were more "at ease" when no desk separated doctor and patient. An extension of this study (Widgery & Stackpole, 1972) found that high-anxiety subjects perceived a counselor to be more credible in the no-desk between condition, and low-anxiety subjects perceived the counselor to be more credible in the desk-between condition. Joiner (1971) found that people in academic offices have their desks touching a wall significantly more often than people in either business or government, and that higher-status office occupants are more likely to place their desks between themselves and the door rather than against a side or back wall.

Whether an office occupant chooses to sit behind a desk or at a table in the office can also have a considerable impact on the impression conveyed. Becker, Gield, and Froggatt (1983) found that a professor who sat at a table in his or her office, as opposed to sitting behind a desk, was perceived as being significantly more *fair, friendly, caring, helpful,* and *open-minded,* and was also viewed as a *better listener.* When seated behind the desk, the professor was perceived as more *authoritative* and *aggressive.*

Occupants of faculty offices, as opposed to occupants of business offices, are less concerned about their ability to *control* communicative interaction in their office than with the *impression* they make. Thus, Preston and Quesda (1974) found that occupants of business offices believe that the primary value of furniture arrangement is control of communicative interaction. Occupants of academic offices, in contrast, are relatively unconcerned about the control potential of objects in their office, but they attach considerable importance to the potential impact of such objects on the image they project.

Aesthetic and Professionally Related Objects

We know that the general appearance of an office can affect the perceptions of those who interact within its confines. In their classic study, Maslow and Mintz (1956) devised three "visually aesthetic" settings: a "beautiful," "average," and an "ugly" room. Subjects were asked to rate a series of ten pictures on two scales, fatigue–energy and displeasure–well-being. Although the same pictures were used in all three settings, subjects who viewed them in the "beautiful" room rated them significantly higher on energy and well-being than subjects in the other two settings.

Subsequent research has established that interviewees are more self-disclosing in a warm, intimate room as opposed to a cold, nonintimate room (Kasmar, Griffin, & Mauritzen, 1976). Hasse and Dimattia (1976) report that counseling interviewees in a large room (13.9 meters square) make significantly more self-reference statements than interviewees in a small room (7.67 meters square). Finally, Bloom, Weigel, and Traut (1977) have established that the appearance of an office can affect the credibility of the office occupant. Female counselors were judged to be more credible in a "traditional" office setting, which featured a desk between the counselor and the client, diplomas on the wall, and file cabinets. By contrast, male counselors were judged to be more credible in a "humanistic" setting, which had no desk between the interactants, modern sculpture, and currently popular wall posters.

This study did indicate that aesthetic objects, such as wall posters, and professionally related objects, such as diplomas, can affect the credibility of an office occupant when they are present in the office. What this study did not do, however, was determine whether these two types of office decor had a different impact on the perceived credibility of the office occupant. Moreover, this study did not attempt to determine whether the individual dimensions of credibility—authoritativeness, trustworthiness, and dynamism—were affected in different ways by the two types of office decor.

Miles and Leathers (1984) recently conducted a study designed to examine these questions. Three photographs were taken of the same faculty office. One photo was taken of the office with aesthetic objects in it; the second was the office with professionally related objects in it; and in the third, there were neither kind of decorative object in it. The aesthetic objects placed in the faculty office were three landscape paintings, two small abstract paintings, one potted fern, one macramé wall hanging, and one calendar with color pictures. The professionally related objects placed in the office were a series of six plaques (suggesting meritorious service by the office occupant; however, the lettering was too small to be read by subjects who viewed photographs of the office), and a professional library consisting of individual scholarly books, another set of books, and six series of professional journals.

Subjects who viewed photographs of the office with and without aesthetic and professionally related objects were asked to use sets of bipolar scales (representing the three dimensions of credibility) to measure the credibility of the office occupant who was not present. Photograph 15.1 shows some of the aesthetic objects in the office; Photograph 15.2 shows some of the professionally related objects.

Results from this study indicate that aesthetic and professionally related objects had a marked impact on the credibility of the office occupant. The presence of aesthetic objects in the faculty office enhanced the perceived trustworthiness of the occupant. The presence of professionally related objects had a positive impact on *both* the occupant's perceived authoritativeness and trustworthiness.

Professionally related objects seem to be a particularly powerful medium of communication, because their presence in a faculty office resulted in a significant increase in both the perceived authoritativeness and trustworthiness of the occupant of the office. Clearly, faculty members—and perhaps occupants of other types of offices as well—who wish to enhance their credibility should consider the potential benefits of displaying professionally related objects in their offices.

Although both professionally related and aesthetic objects in the faculty office had a significant, positive impact on the perceived trustworthiness of the occupant of the faculty office, *aesthetic objects had the strongest impact on perceived trustworthiness.* The finding is particularly provocative because it contradicts the prevailing view that levels of trust are almost exclusively a function of the overt behaviors of interacting individuals.

PHOTOGRAPH 15.1

PHOTOGRAPH 15.2

The finding that trustworthiness can be strongly affected by contextual variables may have important practical implications. Such a finding may provide particular comfort to the individual who inspires little trust, or to one who is widely mistrusted. In one sense, it serves to support the popular belief of image consultants, i.e., that trustworthiness of a distrusted person may be more effectively enhanced by manipulating certain microenvironmental variables than by modifying the individual's communicative behaviors.

Past research has shown that source credibility may be a function of the sources' appearance, reputation, organizational affiliation, and communicative behaviors. This research suggests that source credibility may also be affected by specific decorative objects placed in a person's office. Knowledge such as this should certainly be useful to us as we strive to attain the goal of communicating more successfully in applied settings.

Summary

The physical features of the microenvironments in which we work can exert a profound impact on the nature of our communication with others. Our attitudes, perceptions, and behaviors are strongly affected by how *arousing* and how *pleasant* these environments prove to be. To the extent that we can consciously control the physical features of our microenvironments, we also have the power to shape the image we project.

Microenvironments of particular importance are the *classroom*, the *conference room*, and the *office*. Microenvironmental variables that can play a central role in affecting communicative interaction and student performance in the classroom are *room size, class size, seating arrangement and choice, the teacher's spatial orientations,* and the *appearance of the classroom*. For successful communication to occur in the classroom, space must be used in such a way as to be stimulating and arousing to the student without being distracting. Students react negatively when they perceive that space is being used primarily to regulate and control their behaviors; and also when their personal space and need for privacy are being violated, with the result that they feel crowded. Students and teachers both prefer interacting at the closest possible distances that do not violate proxemic norms.

Microenvironmental variables that have the greatest impact on communication, perceptions, and group performance in the conference room are *seating choice, table configuration,* and *communication networks*. Individuals who choose the end seating position are not only more apt to be perceived as leaders but are more apt to emerge as leaders. Leaders function more effectively at a rectangular, as opposed to a circular, conference table. Both quality and quantity of group interaction are impaired by *L*-shaped seating. Finally, *centralized* communication networks should be used to facilitate effective leadership, to make decisions at moments of crisis, and to solve relatively simple problems. *Decentralized* communication networks are preferable if a high priority is given to group morale and the efficient solution of complex problems.

The office is the work environment where most of us spend most of our working hours. The intra-office variables that are most susceptible to effective conscious control are *seating and spatial arrangement, furniture arrangement,* and *decorative objects.* The impressions we make on office visitors are strongly affected both by where we choose to sit and where we place our office furniture. The decorative objects we choose to place in our office can be particularly important determinants of our own credibility. We know that aesthetic objects can enhance our perceived trustworthiness, and professionally related objects can enhance both our perceived authoritativeness and trustworthiness.

References

Becker, F. D. (1981). *Workspace: Creating environments in organizations.* New York: Praeger.

Becker, F. D., Gield, B., & Froggatt, C. C. (1983). Seating position and impression management in an office setting. *Journal of Environmental Psychology, 3,* 253–261.

Bellizzi, J. A., Crowley, A. E., & Hasty, R. W. (1983) The effects of color in store design. *Journal of Retailing, 59,* 21–45.

Bloom, L. J., Weigel, R. G., & Traut, G. M. (1977). Therapeugenic factors in psychotherapy: Effects of office decor and subject-therapist sex pairing on perception of credibility. *Journal of Consulting and Clinical Psychology, 25,* 867–873.

Burgoon, J. K. (1978). A communication model of personal space violations: Explication and an initial test. *Human Communication Research, 4,* 129–142.

Cohen, E., & Cohen, A. (1983). *Planning the electronic office.* New York: McGraw-Hill.

Doyle, W. (1977). The uses of nonverbal behavior: Toward an ecological model of classrooms. *Merrill-Palmer Quarterly, 23,* 179–192.

Green, C. S. (1975). The ecology of committees. *Environment and Behavior, 7,* 411–425.

Hasse, R. F., & Dimattia, D. J. (1976). Spatial environments and verbal conditioning in quasi-counseling interview. *Journal of Counseling Psychology, 23,* 414–421.

Heckel, R. V. (1973). Leadership and voluntary seating choice. *Psychological Reports, 32,* 141–142.

Hesler, M. W. (1972). An investigation of instructor use of space. (Doctoral dissertation, Purdue University, 1972). *Dissertation Abstracts International, 33,* 3055A.

Howells, L. T., & Becker, S. W. (1962). Seating arrangement and leadership emergence. *Journal of Abnormal and Social Psychology, 64,* 148–149.

Joiner, D. (1971). Office territory. *New Society, 7,* 660–663.

Kasmar, J. V., Griffin, W. F., & Mauritzen, J. H. (1976). The effects of environmental surroundings on outpatient's mood and perception of psychiatrists. *Journal of Consulting and Clinical Psychology, 32,* 223–226.

Korda, M. (1975). *Power! How to get it, how to use it.* New York: Random.

Lecuyer, R. (1976). Social organization and spatial organization. *Human Relations, 29,* 1045–1060.

Levine, D. W., O'Neal, E. C., Garwood, G. S., & McDonald, P. J. (1980). Classroom ecology: The effects of seating position and grades on participation. *Personality and Social Psychology Bulletin, 6,* 409–412.

Lynch, K. (1960). *The image of the city.* Cambridge, MA: Massachusetts Institute of Technology Press.

Maslow, A. H., & Mintz, N. L. (1956). Effects of aesthetic surroundings: I. Initial effects of three aesthetic conditions upon perveiving energy and well-being in faces. *Journal of Psychology, 41,* 247–254.

Mehrabian, A. (1976). *Public places and private spaces.* New York: Basic.

Miles, E. W., & Leathers, D. G. (1984). The impact of aesthetic and professionally related objects on credibility in the office setting. *The Southern Speech Communication Journal, 49,* 361–379.

Patterson, M. L., Kelly, C. E., Kondracki, B. A., & Wulf, L. J. (1979). Effects of seating arrangement on small group behavior. *Social Psychology Quarterly, 42,* 180–185.

Pelligrini, R. J. (1971). Some effects of seating position on social perception. *Psychological Reports, 28,* 887–893.

Preston, P., & Quesda, A. (1974). What does your office say about you? *Supervisory Management, 19,* 28–34.

Rubin, G. N. (1972). A naturalistic study in proxemics: Seating arrangement and its effect on interaction, performance, and behavior. (Doctoral dissertation, Bowling Green State University, 1972). *Dissertation Abstracts International, 33,* 3829A.

Shaw, M. E. (1981). *Group dynamics: The psychology of small group behavior,* 3rd ed. New York: McGraw-Hill.

Sommer, R. (1961). Leadership and group geography. *Sociometry, 24,* 99–110.

Sommer, R. (1962). The distance for comfortable conversation. *Sociometry, 25,* 111–116.

Sommer, R. (1969). *Personal space: The behavioral basis of design.* Englewood Cliffs, NJ: Prentice-Hall.

Sommer, R. (1974). *Tight spaces: Hard architecture and how to humanize it.* Englewood Cliffs, NJ: Prentice-Hall.

Sommer, R., & Ross, H. (1958). Social interaction in a geriatrics ward. *International Journal of Social Psychiatry, 4,* 128–133.

Strodbeck, F. L., & Hook, L. H. (1961). The social dimensions of a twelve-man jury table. *Sociometry, 24,* 397–415.

Weldon, D. E., Loewy, J. H., Winer, J. I., & Elkin, D. J. (1981). Crowding and classroom learning. *Journal of Experimental Education, 49,* 160–176.

White, A. G. (1953). The patient sits down. *Psychosomatic Medicine, 15,* 256–257.

Widgery, R., & Stackpole, C. (1972). Desk position, interviewee anxiety, and interviewer credibility. *Journal of Counseling Psychology, 19,* 173–177.

Wulf, K. M. (1977). Relationship of assigned classroom seating area to achievement variables. *Educational Research Quarterly, 2,* 56–62.

APPENDIX A

Key to the MATCHING TEST in Chapter 5.

A-10

B-12

C-9

D-11

E-15

F-14

G-1

H-13

I-3

J-8

K-6

L-7

M-5

N-4

O-2

INDEX